Puzzle Baron's

LOGIC PUZZLES

ALPHA

A member of Penguin Group (USA) Inc.

ALPHA BOOKS

Published by the Penguin Group

Penguin Group (USA) Inc., 375 Hudson Street, New York, New York 10014, USA

Penguin Group (Canada), 90 Eglinton Avenue East, Suite 700, Toronto, Ontario M4P 2Y3, Canada (a division of Pearson Penguin Canada Inc.)

Penguin Books Ltd., 80 Strand, London WC2R 0RL, England

Penguin Ireland, 25 St. Stephen's Green, Dublin 2, Ireland (a division of Penguin Books Ltd.)

Penguin Group (Australia), 250 Camberwell Road, Camberwell, Victoria 3124, Australia (a division of Pearson Australia Group Pty. Ltd.)

Penguin Books India Pvt. Ltd., 11 Community Centre, Panchsheel Park, New Delhi—110 017, India

Penguin Group (NZ), 67 Apollo Drive, Rosedale, North Shore, Auckland 1311, New Zealand (a division of Pearson New Zealand Ltd.)

Penguin Books (South Africa) (Pty.) Ltd., 24 Sturdee Avenue, Rosebank, Johannesburg 2196, South Africa

Penguin Books Ltd., Registered Offices: 80 Strand, London WC2R 0RL, England

International Standard Book Number: 978-1-61564-032-4

Library of Congress Catalog Card Number: 2010920507

20   23 22

Interpretation of the printing code: The rightmost number of the first series of numbers is the year of the book's printing; the rightmost number of the second series of numbers is the number of the book's printing. For example, a printing code of 10-1 shows that the first printing occurred in 2010.

Printed in the United States of America

Publisher	**Marie Butler-Knight**
Associate Publisher	**Mike Sanders**
Senior Managing Editor	**Billy Fields**
Development Editor	**Ginny Bess Munroe**
Senior Production Editor	**Janette Lynn**
Cover/Book Designer	**Kurt Owens**
Layout	**Brian Massey**
Proofreader	**Laura Caddell**

Introduction

Welcome to the wonderful world of logic puzzles! If you've never solved one before, don't worry—we've got lots of great information in this introduction to help get you started. If you're a life-long logic solver, then feel free to jump right in! Our puzzles vary in difficulty from the very easy to the very difficult, so no matter what your skill level, you'll find hours and hours of solving fun in *Puzzle Baron's Logic Puzzles.*

What Is a Logic Puzzle?

The term "logic puzzle" can apply to a variety of different types of puzzles which require some type of logical deduction, from unique visual and spatial puzzles to the ever-popular Sudoku puzzles. There are literally hundreds, if not thousands, of different kinds of logic puzzles. For the purposes of this book, however, we use the term to describe grid-based logic puzzles, often called "logic grid" puzzles.

There are four major components of a logic grid puzzle: the back-story, the clues, the grid, and the answer key.

The back-story sets up the parameters of the puzzle. It explains the *whats, whens, whos,* and *hows* of the puzzle, and then asks the solver to figure out the relationships between three, four, or five different categories of *objects* (people, places, or things) and *descriptors* (times, locations, orders, colors, and so on).

For example, a back-story might tell you there are three people (Adam, Bob, and Charley), each of whom owns a different pet (cat, dog, or bird), each of which had a different name (Freckles, Kenzie, or Bitsy). Your goal is to use the clues provided to figure out, for instance, that Adam's pet was a dog, and its name was Kenzie—Bob's pet was the bird named Bitsy—and Charley's cat was named Freckles.

The most important thing to remember when solving a logic grid puzzle is that each object and descriptor is used once and only once in each puzzle. So in the previous example, only one person could own the cat, only one pet could be named Kenzie, and so on. Also, each of the three names, owners, and types of pet will be used—no objects or descriptors will ever remain unused in any puzzle. This will be true in each and every logic puzzle in this book!

After the back-story come the clues. Usually this will be a list of between 5 and 10 different statements that will establish relationships between the various objects and descriptors provided in the back-story. A clue in the Adam/Bob/Charley puzzle might read something like: "Charley's pet wasn't named Bitsy" or "Kenzie belonged to Adam." These clues will allow you to mark true and false relationships on the solving grid.

How Do You Solve a Logic Puzzle?

As you begin to establish true and false relationships in a puzzle, you will need to use the grid provided to keep track of them all. To do this most people use Xs to indicate false relationships, and Os to indicate true relationships. So, to continue with our previous example, if we know that Charley's pet wasn't named Bitsy, then we would go to the logic grid, find the box where "Charley" and "Bitsy" intersect, and mark it with an X (false). If another clue tells us that Kenzie belonged to Adam, we'd then find the box where "Adam" and "Kenzie" intersect, and mark it with an O (true).

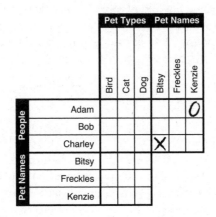

When you mark an O on your logic grid, you can usually also mark a number of additional Xs as a result. Remember: no two individuals in any puzzle will ever share the same object or descriptor. So if we know that Adam's pet is named Kenzie, we also know that Adam's pet isn't named Bitsy or Freckles, and we know that Kenzie isn't owned by Charley or Bob. So we can then go to each corresponding box for each of those false relationships (for instance, Adam and Bitsy, Adam and Freckles, Kenzie and Charley, Kenzie and Bob), and mark them with an X.

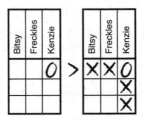

Along the same lines, because we know each and every object and descriptor in any given puzzle will be used once and only once, we can often establish a true relationship when we have previously established false relationships with all but one option in any given row or column. So if we know that Adam's pet wasn't named Bitsy, and that Adam's pet wasn't named Freckles, then by the process of elimination, we would be able to mark an O in the grid for "Adam" and "Kenzie."

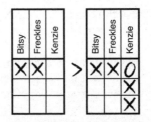

Your goal is to solve the puzzle by filling in the logic grid completely (or at least the top five rows) with Xs and Os. Once that's done, you will know all the true relationships between each individual, object, and descriptor, which you can write into the answer key below the grid and compare your answers to the solution provided in the back of the book.

Hints, Tips, and Tricks

Sounds easy, right? Well, it can be—but on most puzzles you'll be given clues and situations that are a bit more complicated than simple true and false relationships. We'll cover a few of the more common clue types here.

"Neither/Nor" and "Either/Or" Clues

You might occasionally see a clue that reads something like "Neither Adam's pet nor Bitsy was the cat." Most people can see the two obvious false relationships here, and would mark an X for "Adam" and "cat" as well as for "Bitsy" and "cat." But there's another false relationship here that shouldn't be missed! The use of "neither" and "nor" in this clue indicates that Adam's pet and Bitsy were two completely different animals. So you would also mark a third X on the box where "Adam" and "Bitsy" intersect.

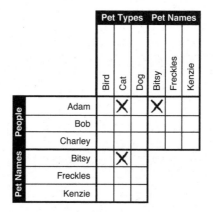

Be careful though! Make sure you don't confuse these "neither/nor" clues with "double-negative" clues! A double-negative clue might read something like "The cat didn't belong to Adam, and wasn't named Bitsy." Here, there is no implied relationship between "Adam" and "Bitsy," apart from the fact that neither of them share a true relationship with the cat. So with a clue like this, we cannot mark an X between "Adam" and "Bitsy."

The same rules apply for "either/or" clues. If a clue reads something like, "Adam's pet was either Bitsy or the dog," the use of "either/or" indicates that "Bitsy" and "dog" are two different entities. Therefore, we would mark an X at the box where "Bitsy" and "dog" intersect.

"The 3/4/5 People Were ..." Clues

Logic solvers often come across a clue that begins "The three/four/five people were ...," and then proceeds to list three, four, or five different objects or descriptors. One such clue in our running example might be, "The three pets were Adam's pet, Bitsy, and the cat." Because we know that each object and descriptor in any puzzle will be used only once, and we know that each of the objects and descriptors listed in the clue belong to different people, we can establish a false relationship between each and every possible pairing of the objects and descriptors mentioned in the clue. Therefore, we would mark Xs for: "Adam" and "Bitsy," "Bitsy" and "cat," and "Adam" and "cat." When a clue like this mentions four or even five different objects and descriptors, you end up with even more negative relationships, and you'll be able to fill many more Xs on your logic grid.

"Of A and B, and C and D" Clues

Another useful clue might read something like "Of Adam and Charley, one owned the dog and the other owned Freckles." In clues of this sort we know that the two objects or descriptors mentioned in each half of the clue belong to different individuals. Therefore, we know that "dog" and "Freckles" share a false relationship, and we can X out the box that connects them. Furthermore, if we already had an X on either "Adam and dog" or "Adam and Freckles," we would be able to establish two true relationships. So for example, if we already had an X on the grid for "Adam" and "Freckles," then just from this one clue we would be able to mark an O (true) for "Adam" and "dog" as well as "Charley" and "Freckles."

Clues of Quantity or Position

Many puzzles contain one or more groups of objects or descriptors that are quantifiable in some way. For example, one group of descriptors may be arrival days, such as "Wednesday," "Thursday," and "Friday." When this is the case, you will often see clues that read something like "Adam arrived one day after the person with the cat."

In a clue like this, you can establish a number of different false relationships right away. First, you know that "Adam" and the "cat" do not belong together (because they arrived on different days), so we can X out that relationship. But we can go even farther than this. Because we know that Adam arrived one day after the person with the cat, we know that Adam couldn't have arrived on the *earliest* day (that is, Wednesday) and that the person who owned the cat couldn't have arrived on the *latest* day (that is, Friday), and we can X out both of those relationships.

Other Clue Types

There are many other types of clues that abound in logic grid puzzles—these are just a small sampling. But knowing how to approach just these few clue types will help you enormously when you're trying to solve your first logic puzzle. Just remember to read every clue carefully to ensure you're extracting all available information from each one!

Logical Deductions

Of course, just reading through each clue and marking the obvious true/false relationships almost never is enough to solve a puzzle. A logic grid solver must also make logical deductions based on these relationships to establish other, more complicated relationships.

So for example, if you know that Adam owns the dog, and that the dog's name is Kenzie, you can mark an O (true) on the box that connects "Adam" and "Kenzie."

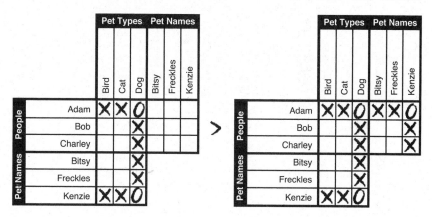

If you know that Charley owns the cat, and the cat's name *isn't* Bitsy, then you can mark an X (false) on the box that connects Charley and Bitsy.

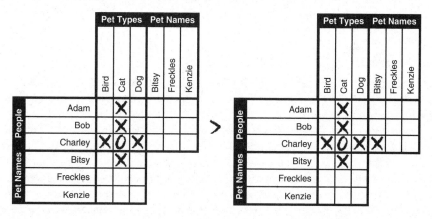

These secondary relationships aren't explicitly mentioned in the clues, but they can be derived from the information you've already gleaned, through the process of logical deduction.

You can also sometimes make more advanced logical deductions. For example, let's say in a given puzzle, there are four people (Adam, Bob, Charley, and Darren), four cars (sedan, coupe, pickup truck, and convertible), and four paint colors (blue, green, orange, and red). If you know that Darren's car is not blue or green, then it must be either orange or red. If you know that the coupe is neither orange nor red (that is, both boxes are marked with X), then you can logically deduce that Darren doesn't own the coupe and mark that relationship with an X of its own.

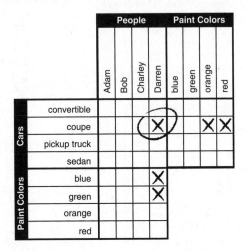

Fill In the Answer Key!

Be sure not to wait until you finish the puzzle completely to start filling in your answer key. After you have one or more true relationships marked on your grid, enter as many of them as you can into the answer grid. Often just seeing the individuals and their associated objects and descriptors come together is enough to help you visualize additional true/false relationships elsewhere in the grid or hidden amongst the clues.

The Puzzles In This Book

Each puzzle in this book comes directly from the Puzzle Baron website, www. Logic-Puzzles.org. We've changed some names and added new back-stories, but the overall structure and solving path for each puzzle has remained the same. This allowed us to include detailed solving statistics for each puzzle, to help you gauge relative difficulty and compare your performance to other logic grid solvers from around the world. Each puzzle includes a completion rate (the percentage of people who were able to successfully complete the puzzle), an average solve time taken from thousands of previously solved online games, and a "best time" that recognizes the current online record holder for that puzzle on www.Logic-Puzzles. org.

Puzzle Baron's Logic Puzzles contains 200 puzzles. Each is numbered and ordered according to its online completion rate. Those that are successfully solved by most of our players appear near the front of the book, and those puzzles that most frequently stump the majority of logic solvers appear near the end. But don't let these numbers intimidate you! A puzzle that may be difficult for one solver may be considered easy by another, and vice versa.

Every puzzle in this book is solvable through logical deduction alone; trial and error and "forward guessing" are never required for a successful solve, though you are welcome to use these methods if you like!

Online Solver's Section

If you're still stuck on a puzzle and want some help, try out our online solver's section at www.Logic-Puzzles.org/book. We've set up a special area of our online forum devoted solely to *Puzzle Baron's Logic Puzzles,* where other solvers and logic puzzle fans can meet and help each other out with some of the more difficult puzzles in this book. (You need to register an account on www.Logic-Puzzles.org in order to post to the solver's section.)

Want More Puzzles?

If you've finished all 200 puzzles in this book and want even more logic solving fun, be sure to check out our website at www.Logic-Puzzles.org! We've got more than 10,000 unique puzzles available to solve online. You can solve them just for fun or you can register for a free account and join more than 15,000 other logic fans to compete head-to-head in our monthly logic puzzle competitions! Trophies are awarded at the end of each month for the most points accumulated and the fastest average solve-time.

Acknowledgments

As with the majority of *Puzzle Baron* projects, I am indebted to my wife, Ally, for her insight and assistance throughout the making of this book. I also have to thank Pearl, on whose dining room table the first lines of code were written that would eventually give rise to www.Logic-Puzzles.org. But a very well-deserved "thank you" also must go out to Laura Christina Warren, who spent countless hours testing and re-testing the puzzles in this book, catching several errors and typos that might otherwise have gone undetected. The finished book is immeasurably better as a direct result of her efforts.

Passport Pandemonium

A normal day at the airport's passport control center quickly devolved into a bureaucratic nightmare when a passenger's dog got loose and ran into the immigration kiosk, knocking over a stack of five passports and their associated paperwork. Each passport belonged to a different person, each with a different nationality, birthday, and career. Using only the clues below, can you sort out the mess before your supervisor returns and discovers the problem?

1. Brodie was born in October and is either American or Swedish.
2. The politician, who is neither Melany nor Ayden, was born on December 6.
3. Of Liliana (who is not Czech) and the person with the Swedish passport, one was born in July and the other is an architect.
4. The lawyer's birthday is earlier in the year than the architect's, which is earlier in the year than the Swede's birthday.
5. The five people are Ayden, the one born in June, the Czech, the engineer (whose birthday is later in the year than the Bulgarian's), and Perla.

		Ayden	Brodie	Liliana	Melany	Perla	Architect	Engineer	Doctor	Lawyer	Politician	American	Bulgarian	Czech	Serbian	Swedish
Birthdays	April 4	X									X					
	June 27	X	X		X						X					
	July 8	X					X				X					
	October 26	X	O	X	X	X					X	X				
	December 6	X					X	X	X	X	O					
Passports	American	X									X					
	Bulgarian										X					
	Czech	X		X		X					X					
	Serbian										X					
	Swedish	X	X				X	X	X	X	O					
Careers	Architect	X	X													
	Engineer	X				X										
	Doctor															
	Lawyer			X												
	Politician	X	X		X											

SOLVE RATE
69%

AVERAGE TIME
12 min, 18 sec

BEST TIME
2 min, 57 sec
by LSupergirl

Birthdays	First Names	Careers	Passports
April 4			
June 27			
July 8			
October 26	Brodie		
December 6		politician	

Conspicuous Consumption

Competitive eating isn't for everyone, but these five friendly competitors make it a point to attend the yearly Pig-Out in Paducah series of contests. This year, they competed separately, each in a different food category, with each contest starting at a different time. Amazingly, all five of them won their competitions, and each was interviewed by a different media outlet after the awards ceremony. Using only the clues below, determine the food, media outlet, and start time associated with each competitor.

1. Of Savanna (who started her contest half an hour after Tristan) and the competitor who started at 2:00 pm, one was interviewed by the local newspaper and the other by a reporter from the competitive-eating television show, "Chow Down."

2. The competitor who scored the radio interview started sometime before the winner of the chicken wing contest.

3. Of Tristan and the person who started at 2:00 pm, one ate chicken wings and the other oysters.

4. The five competitors were the watermelon eater, the one interviewed by the local newspaper, the one who ate a record breaking 92 chicken wings, Zoey (who didn't take part in the blueberry pie contest), and the person whose contest started the latest.

5. Of the oyster eater and the one interviewed by the leading competitive-eating website, one started at 2:00 pm and the other was Carter (who began at 3:00 pm).

		Competitors					Foods					Media Outlets				
		Carter	Micheal	Savanna	Tristan	Zoey	Blueberry Pies	Chicken Wings	Hot Dogs	Oysters	Watermelons	Magazine	Newspaper	Radio	Television	Website
Start Times	2:00 pm															
	2:30 pm															
	3:00 pm															
	3:30 pm															
	4:00 pm															
Media Outlets	Magazine															
	Newspaper															
	Radio															
	Television															
	Website															
Foods	Blueberry Pies															
	Chicken Wings															
	Hot Dogs															
	Oysters															
	Watermelons															

Start Times	Competitors	Foods	Media Outlets
2:00 pm			
2:30 pm			
3:00 pm			
3:30 pm			
4:00 pm			

SOLVE RATE
63.1%

AVERAGE TIME
10 min, 20 sec

BEST TIME
2 min, 24 sec by jade_3031

If You Truly Love a Butterfly

On the day of the big butterfly auction at Liston's Auction House, five wealthy lepidopterists (butterfly enthusiasts) made headlines by each purchasing a different specimen for a record-breaking price. By the end of the auction each bidder realized he had gotten a bit carried away by all the excitement of the auction, and buyer's remorse began to set in—but alas, Liston's doesn't offer refunds! Using only the clues below, determine which bidder bought which specimen, the price the bidder paid, and in what order the specimens were purchased.

1. The *Papilionidae,* which was won by Michael, ended up costing more than the *Nymphalidae,* which sold for more than the third auction.
2. The five auctions were the *Papilionidae,* the lot won by James, the one that ended with the $49,000 bid, the first lot, and the *Nymphalidae.*
3. Harold, who didn't buy the *Hesperiidae,* paid a staggering $188,000 for his specimen.
4. The *Riodinidae* was the fourth butterfly auction, which didn't sell for $91,000.
5. Simon's specimen didn't fetch as high a price as the fifth auction.
6. Of the fifth auction and the *Riodinidae* specimen, one sold for $91,000 and the other went for $179,000.

	First Names					Orders					Butterflies				
	Harold	James	Michael	Pavel	Simon	First	Second	Third	Fourth	Fifth	Hesperiidae	Nymphalidae	Papilionidae	Pieridae	Riodinidae
$49,000	X	X	X	X	O	X	X	O	X	X					X
$91,000	X		X		X	X	X	X	O		X	X	X	X	O
$179,000	X			X	X	X	X	O	X						X
$185,000	X			X	X	O	X	X	X						X
$188,000	O	X	X	X	O	X	X	X	X					X
Hesperiidae	X		X							X					
Nymphalidae			X			X		X	X						
Papilionidae	X	X	O	X	X	X		X	X						
Pieridae			X						X						
Riodinidae			X	X	X	X	X	O	X						
First	O	X	X	X	X										
Second	X				X										
Third	X	X	X	X	O										
Fourth	X				X										
Fifth	X				X										

Winning Bids	First Names	Orders	Butterflies
$49,000			
$91,000			
$179,000			
$185,000			
$188,000			

SOLVE RATE
63%

AVERAGE TIME
11 min, 55 sec

BEST TIME
2 min, 27 sec by Hayden

Burning the Midnight Bean

Caffington University is the preeminent home of serious coffee bean studies, thanks in large part to five research teams made up of one student and one professor, with each team specializing in a different type of coffee. All five teams were awarded sizable grants for their research from the National Institute for Coffee Bean Studies (NICBS), each grant of a different size. Using only the clues below, determine which student worked with which professor, the type of coffee each team researched, and the size of each team's NICBS grant.

1. Dr. Farling's team, which specialized in Columbian coffee, was awarded a smaller NICBS grant than Colin's team.

2. Of Francine and Esther, one worked on the team that got the $203,000 grant and the other worked under Dr. Hunter.

3. The team that studied the brewing characteristics of Harrar coffee won a smaller grant than Francine's team. Dr. Gwynne's team was awarded a larger NICBS grant than the Bugishu study group.

4. The five teams were the one that studied Colombian coffee (which wasn't Donald's team), Francine's group, the one that got the $29,000 NICBS grant, Dr. Gwynne's group, and the one that specialized in Toraja Kalossi coffee (which wasn't Dr. Irving's team).

5. Dr. Hunter's group won the smallest grant offered by NICBS and didn't focus on the Harrar coffee bean.

6. The Columbian coffee study group was awarded either the $109,000 or the $203,000 grant.

		Assistants					Coffees					Scientists				
		Brian	Colin	Donald	Esther	Francine	Bugishu	Colombian	Harrar	Peaberry	Toraja Kalossi	Dr. Earthington	Dr. Farling	Dr. Gwynne	Dr. Hunter	Dr. Irving
Grants	$29,000															
	$47,000															
	$109,000															
	$203,000															
	$244,000															
Scientists	Dr. Earthington															
	Dr. Farling															
	Dr. Gwynne															
	Dr. Hunter															
	Dr. Irving															
Coffees	Bugishu															
	Colombian															
	Harrar															
	Peaberry															
	Toraja Kalossi															

SOLVE RATE
62.5%

AVERAGE TIME
17 min, 22 sec

BEST TIME
3 min, 2 sec by khead

Grants	Assistants	Coffees	Scientists
$29,000			
$47,000			
$109,000			
$203,000			
$244,000			

Recipe Disaster

Thelma's prized recipe notebook was chewed to pieces by her dog just four hours before the family arrives for dinner! Help Thelma save the day by figuring out the proper cooking time and oven temperature for each of the five dishes she'll be preparing and how many people each recipe will feed (so she can adjust to make enough for all 10 dinner guests).

1. The five dishes are the candied yams, the baked ham, the one that needs 35 minutes of baking time, the one that serves eight people, and the one that cooks at 350 degrees.
2. The candied yams require the longest baking time.
3. The roast potatoes shouldn't bake at 340 degrees.
4. Of the roast potatoes and the recipe that serves only two people, one requires 35 minutes of baking time and the other needs to cook at 350 degrees.
5. The recipe that serves eight people requires less baking time than the one that serves 12.
6. The baked ham recipe serves just four people.
7. The recipe that requires the most time to bake doesn't serve the most people and doesn't bake at the lowest temperature.
8. The five recipes are the two that cook at 340 and 365 degrees, the macaroni and cheese, the one that serves six people, and the one that requires the least amount of baking time (which serves only two people).

		Dishes					Temperatures					Servings				
		Baked Ham	Bean Casserole	Candied Yams	Mac & Cheese	Roast Potatoes	325 degrees	340 degrees	350 degrees	365 degrees	375 degrees	Serves 2	Serves 4	Serves 6	Serves 8	Serves 12
Baking Times	25 minutes															
	30 minutes															
	35 minutes															
	40 minutes															
	45 minutes															
Servings	Serves 2															
	Serves 4															
	Serves 6															
	Serves 8															
	Serves 12															
Temperatures	325 degrees															
	340 degrees															
	350 degrees															
	365 degrees															
	375 degrees															

SOLVE RATE
60.9%

AVERAGE TIME
11 min, 56 sec

BEST TIME
2 min, 36 sec by jade_3031

Baking Times	Dishes	Temperatures	Servings
25 minutes			
30 minutes			
35 minutes			
40 minutes			
45 minutes			

Aerial Acrobatics

Five skydivers have decided to perform a notoriously difficult aerial maneuver called the "Spry Fly." For the trick to work, the skydivers (wearing a different color jump suit) must begin their jumps at different heights and then make their way into position while in free-fall. The more difficult positions are given to those with the most experience (meaning those with the most previous jumps under their belts). Using only the clues below, determine the jump height, suit color, and number of previous jumps associated with each skydiver.

1. Between Gregory and the person with the orange suit, one will jump at 7400 feet and the other is the least experienced of the five.
2. The jumper in the black suit (who will not jump at 7800 feet) has done either 3 or 56 previous jumps.
3. The jumper in the purple suit (who isn't Jenya) is not the most experienced of the five.
4. Of Diana and Frank (who will wear the red suit), one has 22 previous jumps and the other has 56.
5. The jumper in the black suit will jump at a height 400 feet lower than the jumper in the purple suit.
6. Of the person who will jump at 9000 feet and Zachary, one has 56 previous jumps and the other has 129.
7. The jumper in the silver suit hasn't done exactly 15 previous jumps.
8. Among the jumper in the red suit and Gregory, one is the least experienced and the other will jump at 9000 feet.

		Skydivers					Previous Jumps					Suit Colors				
		Diana	Frank	Gregory	Jenya	Zachary	3	15	22	56	129	Black	Orange	Purple	Red	Silver
Heights	7400 feet															
	7800 feet															
	8200 feet															
	8600 feet															
	9000 feet															
Suit Colors	Black															
	Orange															
	Purple															
	Red															
	Silver															
Previous Jumps	3															
	15															
	22															
	56															
	129															

Heights	Skydivers	Previous Jumps	Suit Colors
7400 feet			
7800 feet			
8200 feet			
8600 feet			
9000 feet			

SOLVE RATE
60.8%

AVERAGE TIME
14 min, 15 sec

BEST TIME
4 min, 31 sec by Tamar

American Centenarians

Jarvis was putting together a story on some of the oldest living Americans. As part of his research, he interviewed five centenarians (people above the age of 100) from across the country and asked them why they thought they outlived almost everybody else. Not surprisingly, each centenarian had a different explanation! Using only the clues below, determine the age of each centenarian, the state they reside in, and the reason they gave for their longevity.

1. The centenarian who believes her work with children kept her healthy and young-at-heart doesn't live in Kentucky or Oklahoma.
2. Neither Daisy nor the person who swore his or her longevity was a result of three daily cups of tea is 109 years old.
3. Between Max (who is older than the Maryland native) and the centenarian who swears by his or her daily exercise regimen, one is the youngest of the five and the other lives in Virginia.
4. The interviewee who claimed a good dose of daily laughter was the key to a long and happy life doesn't live in Kentucky.
5. Jasmine doesn't live in Nevada; she is one year older than Max.
6. Of Daisy and the 110-year-old person, one lives in Oklahoma and the other lives in Virginia. The Virginian is one year older than Lorenzo.
7. The oldest of the five doesn't live in Oklahoma.
8. The tea-drinking centenarian is one year older than the one who swears by his or her exercise regimen.

		Daisy	Daniella	Jasmine	Lorenzo	Max	Kentucky	Maryland	Nevada	Oklahoma	Virginia	Almonds	Children	Exercise	Laughter	Tea
	109 years															
	110 years															
Ages	111 years															
	112 years															
	113 years															
	Almonds															
Reasons	Children															
	Exercise															
	Laughter															
	Tea															
	Kentucky															
	Maryland															
States	Nevada															
	Oklahoma															
	Virginia															

SOLVE RATE
60.5%

AVERAGE TIME
10 min, 16 sec

BEST TIME
3 min, 36 sec by heathpie

Ages	Names	States	Reasons
109 years			
110 years			
111 years			
112 years			
113 years			

What's Their Sign?

Five friends who share an interest in astrology decided to each get the zodiac symbol of their astrological sign (each has a different one) tattooed on their forearm, each in a different color. Using only the clues below, determine the order in which each person was tattooed, the color each person chose, and each person's astrological sign.

1. Of Brook and the one who got the violet tattoo, one had the first appointment and the other is the Sagittarius.

2. Brook's appointment came sometime after the person who got the cyan-colored tattoo.

3. The Libra was the first to be tattooed.

4. Danny had the fourth appointment.

5. The one who got the crimson-colored tattoo (who wasn't Brook) had a later appointment than the Cancer, who didn't get the gray tattoo.

6. Kevin, whose appointment came sometime after Emily's, got either a gray or a violet-colored tattoo.

7. The five people were the one with the third appointment (who didn't get the blue tattoo), the one with the violet tattoo, the Aquarius, Jason, and the one who was tattooed last.

First Names					Zodiac Signs					Tattoo Colors				
Brook	Danny	Emily	Jason	Kevin	Aquarius	Cancer	Capricorn	Libra	Sagittarius	Blue	Crimson	Cyan	Gray	Violet

Appointments

	Brook	Danny	Emily	Jason	Kevin	Aquarius	Cancer	Capricorn	Libra	Sagittarius	Blue	Crimson	Cyan	Gray	Violet
First															
Second															
Third															
Fourth															
Fifth															

Tattoo Colors

	Brook	Danny	Emily	Jason	Kevin	Aquarius	Cancer	Capricorn	Libra	Sagittarius
Blue										
Crimson										
Cyan										
Gray										
Violet										

Zodiac Signs

	Brook	Danny	Emily	Jason	Kevin
Aquarius					
Cancer					
Capricorn					
Libra					
Sagittarius					

Appointments	First Names	Zodiac Signs	Tattoo Colors
First			
Second			
Third			
Fourth			
Fifth			

SOLVE RATE
59.3%

AVERAGE TIME
11 min, 56 sec

BEST TIME
3 min, 15 sec by kcirderf

Walkie Talkies

The RGA company is best known for its line of children's walkie talkies, each of which goes through a rigorous testing process. In the latest round of tests, five pairs of testers each took a walkie talkie and saw how far away from each other they could get while still being able to hear the other clearly. Each pair used a different channel on the walkie talkies, to see if that would have any effect on the results. Using only the clues below, determine who made up each pair of testers, what channel each pair used, and what the maximum distance was each could reach on the walkie talkies.

1. Of Madison and Santiago, one was paired with David and the other used channel 8 in the test.
2. The five pairs are the one that included Peter (who wasn't paired with Angie), Georgia's pair, Rachael's pair, the one that used channel 8 (which didn't include Wanda), and the one that had a maximum distance of 225 feet (which didn't use channel 11).
3. David's test group reached 25 feet farther than the one that used channel 4.
4. Santiago's group reached a 225 foot maximum distance.
5. Cody's pair didn't have the longest maximum distance.
6. Peter's group, which didn't include Wanda, reached a 200 foot maximum distance.
7. Of Georgia's group and the one that used channel 7, one included Cody and the other had the shortest maximum distance.

		Cody	Madison	Peter	Rachael	Santiago	Angie	David	Georgia	Patsy	Wanda	4	7	8	11	12
Distances	150 feet															
	175 feet															
	200 feet															
	225 feet															
	250 feet															
Channels	4															
	7															
	8															
	11															
	12															
Friends	Angie															
	David															
	Georgia															
	Patsy															
	Wanda															

Friends — **Friends** — **Channels**

Distances	Friends	Friends	Channels
150 feet			
175 feet			
200 feet			
225 feet			
250 feet			

SOLVE RATE
59.1%

AVERAGE TIME
12 min, 24 sec

BEST TIME
3 min, 56 sec by bihlman12

Elemental

It's the year 2156, and five new elements—each brand new to science—have recently been discovered. None of them are believed to exist in nature, but were synthesized artificially in laboratory environments. Using only the clues below, determine the atomic number of each new element, the name of its discoverer, and the country each discoverer is from.

1. Volotomium's atomic number is one more than the one discovered by Dr. Havley, the French scientist (who didn't discover javelonium).
2. Dr. Fabian didn't discover hurdonium.
3. Dr. Jackson isn't Swedish or Russian.
4. Of Dr. Wesley and the Russian scientist, one discovered element #147 and the other #149.
5. Of the English and Russian scientists, one discovered hurdonium and the other synthesized element #147.
6. Element #147 is either poshtunium (which wasn't discovered by the Swedish scientist) or volutomium.
7. Poshtunium doesn't have an atomic number of 146.
8. The Russian discovery had a larger atomic number than the one discovered by the Belgian scientist (which was #148).

	Discoverers					Elements					Countries				
	Dr. Ayden	Dr. Fabian	Dr. Havley	Dr. Jackson	Dr. Wesley	Hurdonium	Javelonium	Poshtunium	Relavisium	Volutomium	Belgium	England	France	Russia	Sweden
146															
147															
148															
149															
150															
Belgium															
England															
France															
Russia															
Sweden															
Hurdonium															
Javelonium															
Poshtunium															
Relavisium															
Volutomium															

Atom. Numbers	Discoverers	Elements	Countries
146			
147			
148			
149			
150			

SOLVE RATE
57.7%

AVERAGE TIME
10 min, 25 sec

BEST TIME
2 min, 20 sec by urielzet

Catching the Wind

Jupiter County is known for having some of the fastest recorded wind speeds in the state. In fact, meteorologists and amateur observers have recorded wind speeds in excess of 155 miles per hour (MPH) in Jupiter County five times in the past century, in five different parts of the county. Using only the clues below, determine the fastest recorded wind speed associated with each location and the month and year in which it was recorded.

1. Mount Vista's record-breaking wind speed was recorded in 1951, but not in March.
2. The wind speed recorded in 1951 was four miles-per-hour slower than the one recorded in November.
3. The record at Parr's Peak wasn't measured in 1988 or 1972.
4. The 160 MPH wind speed was measured in November.
5. The 156 MPH wind speed wasn't recorded in July.
6. Gully Gorge's record wasn't recorded in January.
7. No records were recorded in July of 1988.
8. Of the 1972 record and the one recorded at Rhoden Pass, one was recorded at 160 MPH and the other at 168 MPH.
9. Between the January record and the 160 MPH wind speed, one was recorded in 1944 and the other in 1972.
10. The 1972 record wind speed was faster than the record observed in 1925.

	Cap Canyon	Gully Gorge	Mount Vista	Parr's Peak	Rhoden Pass	January	March	July	September	November	1925	1944	1951	1972	1988
156 MPH															
160 MPH															
164 MPH															
168 MPH															
172 MPH															
1925															
1944															
1951															
1972															
1988															
January															
March															
July															
September															
November															

Wind Speeds	Locations	Months	Years
156 MPH			
160 MPH			
164 MPH			
168 MPH			
172 MPH			

SOLVE RATE
57.5%

AVERAGE TIME
11 min, 37 sec

BEST TIME
3 min, 6 sec by zpalffy33

Higher Education

Five applications came in last week for the newest job opening at Darlington Industries. Although none of the applicants had much applicable experience in this field, all five resumés were impressive enough to call each person in for an interview. Each went to a different school (graduating in different years), and each held a Master's degree in a different field. Using only the clues below, match the school, major, and graduating year to each applicant.

1. The E.S.C. student holds a Master's degree in biology.
2. Kelsey doesn't have an engineering degree.
3. The five applicants are Uriel (who graduated one year after the applicant with a degree in French literature), the one who graduated most recently in 2005 (who wasn't Jack), the one with the engineering degree (who didn't graduate in 2004), Giovanni, and the Linton State graduate.
4. The E.S.C. student graduated sometime after the applicant who went to the University of Wales.
5. Of the 2003 graduate and the one with the engineering degree, one is Kelsey and the other went to Tarleton College.
6. The linguistics student graduated the year before the engineering student.
7. Mackinaw University has never had an anthropology department.

		Students					Schools					Majors				
		Giovanni	Jack	Kelsey	Luna	Uriel	E.S.C.	Linton State	Mackinaw U.	Tarleton Col.	U. of Wales	Anthropology	Biology	French Lit	Engineering	Linguistics
Classes	2001															
	2002															
	2003															
	2004															
	2005															
Majors	Anthropology															
	Biology															
	French Lit															
	Engineering															
	Linguistics															
Schools	E.S.C.															
	Linton State															
	Mackinaw U.															
	Tarleton Col.															
	U. of Wales															

SOLVE RATE
56.9%

AVERAGE TIME
12 min

BEST TIME
3 min, 1 sec by urielzet

Classes	Students	Schools	Majors
2001			
2002			
2003			
2004			
2005			

Supreme Court Precedents

Tabitha spent much of the weekend reviewing five famous Supreme Court cases in preparation for Monday's examination. Using only the clues below, determine each case's plaintiff and defendant, the year it was tried, and the resulting decision. Note: There are nine Supreme Court justices, and a unanimous decision requires a 9–0 ruling.

1. The five cases are the 6–3 decision, the Rosado case, the one that took place in May 1985 (which didn't involve Hubert Hastings), the unanimous decision (which also didn't involve Mr. Hastings), and the Benedict case.
2. Sal Sorenson's case was heard sometime after Edwin Eckert's.
3. Tinsley's case took place three years after Worthington's.
4. Brian Benedict was the plaintiff in the case that was decided 8–1.
5. Edwin Eckert's case took place in 1991 and was decided 6–3.
6. Sorenson wasn't the plaintiff in the Swain case, which wasn't decided 8–1.
7. The most recent case Tabitha studied didn't involve Chester Chamberlain.
8. Of the oldest case and the one that was decided 5–4, one had Tim Tinsley as the plaintiff and the other had Robert Rosado as the defendant.
9. Hubert Hastings wasn't the defendant in the Benedict case.

SOLVE RATE
55.7%

AVERAGE TIME
11 min, 23 sec

BEST TIME
2 min, 18 sec by redsox29

Years	Plaintiffs	Defendants	Decisions
1982			
1985			
1988			
1991			
1994			

Local Papers

Even with the advent of the Internet and online news sites, the folks of Hennisford County still love to read their daily newspaper. The top five newspapers in the county are all weeklies (meaning published once a week, on the same day each week), and each has a circulation between 25,000 and 400,000 total. Using only the clues below, determine the circulation numbers for each newspaper, what day of the week each publishes on, and how much each issue costs.

1. The five papers are the *Silbo Times*, the one with the largest circulation (which isn't the *Daily Record* and doesn't print on Mondays), the one that prints on Thursdays (which isn't the *Norton News*), the *Courier*, and the newspaper that costs 35¢ per issue.
2. The newspaper that charges 40¢ per issue doesn't print on Monday or Tuesday.
3. The paper with the second-highest circulation doesn't print on Thursdays.
4. Of the Thursday paper and the one with 100,000 weekly readers, one is the *Norton News* and the other costs 50¢ per issue.
5. The Thursday paper has twice as many readers as the Friday newspaper.
6. The Tuesday paper costs either 25¢ or 40¢.
7. The *Silbo Times* has twice as many readers as the Wednesday paper.

		Newspapers				Prices					Print Days				
		Courier	Daily Record	Norton News	Observer	Silbo Times	$0.25	$0.35	$0.40	$0.50	$0.75	Monday	Tuesday	Wednesday	Thursday	Friday
Circulations	25,000															
	50,000															
	100,000															
	200,000															
	400,000															
Print Days	Monday															
	Tuesday															
	Wednesday															
	Thursday															
	Friday															
Prices	$0.25															
	$0.35															
	$0.40															
	$0.50															
	$0.75															

SOLVE RATE
55.6%

AVERAGE TIME
12 min, 32 sec

BEST TIME
3 min, 6 sec by khead

Circulations	Newspapers	Prices	Print Days
25,000			
50,000			
100,000			
200,000			
400,000			

Speed Trap

Most Perryville natives know that Frasier Street is what's known as a speed trap—a place where police often sit and wait to catch people driving over the 35 MPH speed limit. Of course, that doesn't mean everyone's learned this lesson! Five locals were pulled over on Frasier Street this week. Using only the clues below, figure out the day each driver was pulled over, how fast each was driving, and the name of the officer who wrote the ticket.

1. The five drivers are Owen, the one Officer Kipco pulled over, Cynthia (who wasn't ticketed for driving 49 MPH), the one that was pulled over on Thursday morning (who wasn't ticketed at 51 MPH), and the one who was caught driving 21 MPH over the speed limit.
2. Owen was pulled over by Officer Lipton.
3. Neither Owen nor Savannah was ticketed for driving 49 MPH.
4. Lesly (who got a ticket for going 51 MPH) was pulled over earlier in the week than Cynthia.
5. Officer Payton wasn't at Frasier Street on Thursday.
6. The driver ticketed by Officer Kipco was pulled over the day after the one who was pulled over by Officer Vilray.
7. The driver who was ticketed for driving less than 10 MPH over the speed limit was pulled over earlier in the week than Cynthia.
8. Either the driver who was pulled over on Monday or the one who was caught driving 11 MPH over the speed limit was Owen.

		Drivers					Officers					Speeds				
		Cynthia	Graham	Lesly	Owen	Savannah	Off. Freeh	Off. Kipco	Off. Lipton	Off. Payton	Off. Vilray	44 MPH	46 MPH	49 MPH	51 MPH	56 MPH
Days	Monday															
	Tuesday															
	Wednesday															
	Thursday															
	Friday															
Speeds	44 MPH															
	46 MPH															
	49 MPH															
	51 MPH															
	56 MPH															
Officers	Off. Freeh															
	Off. Kipco															
	Off. Lipton															
	Off. Payton															
	Off. Vilray															

SOLVE RATE
55.6%

AVERAGE TIME
13 min, 47 sec

BEST TIME
4 min, 18 sec by jemazi

Days	Drivers	Officers	Speeds
Monday			
Tuesday			
Wednesday			
Thursday			
Friday			

Favorite Sons

As part of a plan to revitalize interest in Gunther County, some of the higher-ups have suggested renaming five of its lesser-known cities in honor of their favorite sons—men who were born there and went on to do great and memorable things. The councils for each of the five cities under consideration will have a vote this week to determine whether the renaming will take place. Using only the clues below, determine the new names suggested for each city, the person the city will be renamed after, and what day the change will be voted upon.

1. The five cities are the one that will hold its vote on Monday, Lafayette, Cortez (which wasn't the birthplace of the astronaut), the one that might be renamed Carroll, and the one that might be renamed after a famous botanist.
2. Lawrence wasn't the new name suggested for the city of Cortez.
3. Between Evans and the city whose favorite son was a jazz singer, one will hold its vote on Monday and the other is considering renaming itself Randolph.
4. The astronaut's name isn't Lawrence or Howard.
5. The town of Evans will hold its vote the day after Cortez.
6. Lafayette will hold its vote the day before the town that wants to rename itself after a famous Olympic athlete that grew up there.
7. Of the town of Evans and the one that was home to the Olympic athlete, one is considering the new name Randolph and the other will hold its vote last of all five cities.
8. The people of Parker will vote on their name change sometime after the city that's considering Randolph as its new name.

	Cortez	Evans	Lafayette	Northglenn	Parker	Carroll	Desha	Howard	Lawrence	Randolph	Astronaut	Botanist	Jazz Singer	Olympian	Philanthropist
Old Names						**New Names**					**Honorees**				
Monday															
Tuesday															
Wednesday															
Thursday															
Friday															
Astronaut															
Botanist															
Jazz Singer															
Olympian															
Philanthropist															
Carroll															
Desha															
Howard															
Lawrence															
Randolph															

Days	Old Names	New Names	Honorees
Monday			
Tuesday			
Wednesday			
Thursday			
Friday			

The Film Festival

Briarton's annual film festival is known for bringing together lesser-known film directors and getting them noticed by Hollywood. This year, five films were chosen to be showcased, each by a different director and each in a different genre. None of the films was the same length, which made scheduling a bit difficult, but it all worked out in the end. Using only the clues below, determine the genre, director, and length of each film, and determine the order in which the films were screened at the festival.

1. The five directors were Bill, the one whose film was screened second (who wasn't Linus), the one who directed the musical, Miley (whose film was screened fourth), and the one whose film took 2 hours and 20 minutes to screen (which wasn't aired third).
2. Bill's film, which wasn't screened last, was 10 minutes shorter than the drama (which wasn't directed by Aaron).
3. The comedy wasn't the longest film at the festival.
4. Neither Bill nor the director with the longest film was screened third.
5. Between Aaron and the person whose film was screened second, one directed the documentary (which was 10 minutes longer than the musical) and the other directed the drama.

		Directors					Genres					Orders			
		Aaron	Bill	Clara	Linus	Miley	Action	Comedy	Documentary	Drama	Musical	First	Second	Third	Fourth	Fifth
Lengths	1:50															
	2:00															
	2:10															
	2:20															
	2:30															
Orders	First															
	Second															
	Third															
	Fourth															
	Fifth															
Genres	Action															
	Comedy															
	Documentary															
	Drama															
	Musical															

SOLVE RATE
55.2%

AVERAGE TIME
12 min, 53 sec

BEST TIME
5 min, 13 sec by bihlman12

Lengths	Directors	Genres	Orders
1:50			
2:00			
2:10			
2:20			
2:30			

Shipwreck Diving

A team of underwater archaeologists has split up to investigate five different mid-nineteenth century shipwrecks in five different locations around the world. Using only the clues below, determine which archaeologist is studying which shipwreck, and the year and location in which each ship was sunk.

1. The five shipwrecks are the ones that sunk in 1846 and 1847, the *Hermione* (which sunk one year before the *Juvenal*), the one Madeline is studying (which didn't sink on the Peruvian coastline), and the ship that wrecked in the treacherous waters off the coast of South Africa.
2. The ship that wrecked off the coast of Vietnam wasn't the *Hermione* and isn't being studied by Madeline.
3. Of the 1846 shipwreck and the one Philip is studying, one is the *Guerrero* and the other is the *Hermione*.
4. The *Ibineza* sank one year after the *Guerrero*.
5. Mya (who's working in Indonesia right now) isn't studying the *Guerrero*.
6. The South Africa shipwreck isn't the *Juvenal* and isn't the ship Matthew is currently working on.

		Divers					Shipwrecks					Locations				
		Jonathan	Madeline	Matthew	Mya	Philip	Fortitude	Guerrero	Hermione	Ibineza	Juvenal	Georgia	Indonesia	Peru	South Africa	Vietnam
Years	1845															
	1846															
	1847															
	1848															
	1849															
Locations	Georgia															
	Indonesia															
	Peru															
	South Africa															
	Vietnam															
Shipwrecks	Fortitude															
	Guerrero															
	Hermione															
	Ibineza															
	Juvenal															

SOLVE RATE
55.0%

AVERAGE TIME
11 min, 16 sec

BEST TIME
2 min, 3 sec by Vaughns

Years	Divers	Shipwrecks	Locations
1845			
1846			
1847			
1848			
1849			

Moving Men

The Happy Helpers moving company has a full schedule today, with each of its five regular timeslots filled by a different family. Each move is handled by two different Happy Helper employees. Using only the clues below, determine which movers are working together and figure out which family they will move and at what time.

1. Michael's move is scheduled two and a half hours earlier than the Templeton family's appointment.
2. Paul won't be working on the Roger family move.
3. Landon will work with Bill today.
4. Of Paul's move (which isn't scheduled for 3:30 pm) and the 1:00 pm appointment, one is for the Roger family and the other has George assigned to it.
5. The five appointments are Paul's, Carlos's, the Braxton family's move, the Templeton family's move, and the latest one on the schedule (which isn't for the Frasier family and doesn't have Jackson assigned to it).
6. Jackson and Frank aren't scheduled for the same move today.
7. Steve's job today is scheduled two and a half hours earlier than Paul's.

		Families					Movers					Movers			
		Braxton	Frasier	Roger	Smith	Templeton	Bill	Carlos	Frank	George	Herb	Jackson	Landon	Michael	Paul	Steve
Times	8:00 am															
	10:30 am															
	1:00 pm															
	3:30 pm															
	6:00 pm															
Movers	Jackson															
	Landon															
	Michael															
	Paul															
	Steve															
Movers	Bill															
	Carlos															
	Frank															
	George															
	Herb															

Times	Families	Movers	Movers
8:00 am			
10:30 am			
1:00 pm			
3:30 pm			
6:00 pm			

SOLVE RATE
54.9%

AVERAGE TIME
11 min, 24 sec

BEST TIME
2 min, 48 sec by kcirderf

Solar Eclipses

The next five solar eclipses that will pass over Wakamunga, Idaho will occur in different months between 2012 and 2016. Each will have a different magnitude, or percentage of the sun that is obscured; anything below 1.0 is a partial eclipse, and anything 1.0 or above is a total eclipse. Using only the clues below, determine the month and year of each eclipse, its magnitude, and its central duration.

1. The five eclipses are the one in 2014, the one that will occur in January (which won't have a 0.97 magnitude), the eclipse with the longest duration, the one that will reach a magnitude of 0.92, and the 2016 eclipse (which won't last 4 minutes and 52 seconds).
2. The December eclipse will happen before the May eclipse.
3. The eclipse with the 5 minutes and 26 seconds duration is not scheduled for May.
4. Neither the eclipse of the smallest magnitude nor the one of the longest duration will take place in August.
5. The 0.92 magnitude eclipse will occur before the one that will last 4 minutes and 52 seconds.
6. The shortest eclipse will not happen in August.
7. The December eclipse will occur precisely 23 months after the January eclipse (which will last 2 minutes and 10 seconds).
8. The only total eclipse won't occur in December and won't be in 2013.
9. Of the August eclipse and the one with the second-smallest magnitude, one will be the longest of all five and the other will take place in 2012.

	Months					Magnitudes					Durations				
	January	May	July	August	December	0.78	0.85	0.92	0.97	1.01	1 min 45 sec	2 min 10 sec	2 min 33 sec	4 min 52 sec	5 min 26 sec
2012															
2013															
2014															
2015															
2016															
1 min 45 sec															
2 min 10 sec															
2 min 33 sec															
4 min 52 sec															
5 min 26 sec															
0.78															
0.85															
0.92															
0.97															
1.01															

SOLVE RATE 54.6%

AVERAGE TIME 12 min, 15 sec

BEST TIME 2 min, 56 sec by urielzet

Years	Months	Magnitudes	Durations
2012			
2013			
2014			
2015			
2016			

Broken Bones

You name the extreme sport—from base jumping to rock climbing, skiing to skydiving—Andre's done it all. He's also broken quite a few bones along the way! Using only the clues below, figure out the year Andre broke each bone or body part, what he was doing when he broke it, and how many weeks it took him to heal from each injury.

1. The five injuries Andre sustained are the ones from 1996 and 1999, the broken collarbone, the rock climbing injury (which didn't require the most healing time), and the one that took eight weeks to heal.
2. Of the broken wrist and the injury that occurred in 1996, one was sustained while Andre was cycling in the Appalachians and the other happened during a rock climbing expedition in Utah.
3. Andre's broken rib (which wasn't sustained during his cycling trip) took five weeks to heal properly.
4. The broken femur didn't take exactly eight weeks to heal.
5. The cycling injury occurred just before the skiing accident.
6. Andre's broken collarbone didn't take exactly 6 or 10 weeks to heal.
7. Andre's rock climbing accident occurred just before his skydiving injury (which didn't require eight weeks to heal).

SOLVE RATE
54.5%

AVERAGE TIME
10 min

BEST TIME
2 min, 33 sec by redsox29

Years	Bones	Activities	Lengths
1992			
1996			
1999			
2000			
2004			

Roller Coasters

Five roller coaster enthusiasts share all their latest rides together online with photos and blog entries describing their experiences. Each of the five rode a different roller coaster last week, each of which had a different, unique feature. Using only the clues below, determine which rider rode which coaster, what unique feature each coaster had, and how tall each coaster is.

1. The five riders are the one who rode the coaster with the dark tunnel in the middle, the rider who went on the 345-foot tall coaster, the rider who rode the one with the huge vertical drop, Delilah (who didn't ride The Maniac), and the one who rode The Chiller.

2. The five roller coasters are the one that goes entirely in reverse (which isn't the one Jessie rode), the 345-foot tall coaster, the tallest coaster, the one Melany rode (which is 370 feet tall), and The Monster.

3. Of Delilah's latest roller coaster and the one that is 329 feet tall, one has an enormous vertical drop and the other has a stomach-twisting double loop.

4. The Gremlin (which isn't the coaster Jessie rode last week) is not as tall as the coaster with the dark tunnel.

5. Lola didn't ride the shortest of the five roller coasters.

		Daniel	Delilah	Jessie	Lola	Melany	Dark Tunnel	Double Loop	Inverted Seats	Reverse Ride	Vertical Drop	The Chiller	The Gremlin	The Maniac	The Monster	The Thriller
Heights	312 feet															
	329 feet															
	345 feet															
	370 feet															
	391 feet															
Coasters	The Chiller															
	The Gremlin															
	The Maniac															
	The Monster															
	The Thriller															
Features	Dark Tunnel															
	Double Loop															
	Inverted Seats															
	Reverse Ride															
	Vertical Drop															

SOLVE RATE
54.1%

AVERAGE TIME
10 min, 48 sec

BEST TIME
3 min, 5 sec by khead

Heights	Riders	Features	Coasters
312 feet			
329 feet			
345 feet			
370 feet			
391 feet			

And the Award Goes To ...

Juniper Hills Academy is one of the most prestigious private schools in the country, and its professors (all Ph.D.s) are frequently recognized in the yearly National Excellence in Education Awards (NEEA). This year, five Juniper Hills professors were recognized, each in a different field. Using only the clues below, determine the first and last name of each professor, each professor's field of expertise, and the order in which the awards were presented.

1. Between the professor who received the first NEEA award (who wasn't Talia or Victor) and Dr. Ackerman, one specialized in theology and the other in engineering.
2. Katherine was the biology professor.
3. Hector received his award just before Dr. McGuire.
4. Dr. Clarke didn't specialize in biology.
5. The five professors were Talia (who received her award just before Hector did), Dr. Ackerman (who specialized in theology), Dr. Thompson, the one who received the second NEEA award, and the philosophy professor.

	Camille	Hector	Katherine	Talia	Victor	Ackerman	Clarke	Marks	McGuire	Thompson	Biology	Engineering	Mathematics	Philosophy	Theology
First															
Second															
Third															
Fourth															
Fifth															
Biology															
Engineering															
Mathematics															
Philosophy															
Theology															
Ackerman															
Clarke															
Marks															
McGuire															
Thompson															

SOLVE RATE 53.6%

AVERAGE TIME 12 min, 24 sec

BEST TIME 2 min, 54 sec by khead

Orders	First Names	Last Names	Fields
First			
Second			
Third			
Fourth			
Fifth			

Relocation Time

When the one and only tech company in Bascalusa shut down, its highly skilled employees had little choice but to relocate somewhere else to find work. So far, five workers have had the good fortune to find tech jobs elsewhere. Each left Bascalusa in a different month, for a different job in a different city. Using only the clues below, determine which month each person left, the city the person went to, and the company the person is now working for.

1. The person who went to Seattle didn't leave in May and didn't get a new job working for Selera Inc.
2. Between Sara (who didn't leave in June) and Vanessa, one went to work for Selera Inc. and the other went to San Francisco.
3. The five people are the one who went to San Francisco, Alina, the Compuweb employee, the person who left in May, and the one who left in August.
4. Vanessa left one month before the Nanoware employee.
5. Jason didn't go to Chicago and didn't get a job with Compuweb.
6. The Selera employee left sometime after the person who went to San Francisco.
7. Vanessa went to work for either Nanoware or Selera.
8. Betabytes isn't located anywhere near San Francisco.
9. The person who went to New York City left sometime after Vanessa.

	Alina	Hector	Jason	Sara	Vanessa	Betabytes	Compuweb	Interslice	Nanoware	Selera	Chicago	Miami	New York City	San Francisco	Seattle
May															
June															
July															
August															
September															
Chicago															
Miami															
New York City															
San Francisco															
Seattle															
Betabytes															
Compuweb															
Interslice															
Nanoware															
Selera															

SOLVE RATE
53.6%

AVERAGE TIME
12 min

BEST TIME
3 min, 24 sec by The James

Months	Names	Companies	Cities
May			
June			
July			
August			
September			

Gas Guzzlers

Mrs. Dickinson's class has been learning about environmental issues lately, and part of the students' homework has been to measure the average fuel efficiency in miles per gallon (MPG) of their parents' everyday car. So far, five students have come back with mileage estimates after several days of driving with their parents. Using only the clues below, determine each car's gas mileage, its model year, and the student to whose family it belongs.

1. The five students are the one who found their car got 25 MPG, the one with the hatchback, the one who found the second-highest mileage out of the family's automobile, Patrick (whose family doesn't drive a minivan), and the student whose family drives the oldest car.

2. The least fuel-efficient car was Caiden's 2007-model car.

3. Grayson had a blast testing the mileage for his family's cherry-red convertible sports car (which isn't a 2004 model).

4. The sedan is less fuel efficient than the 2006 model car.

5. The person whose car got 28 MPG is not Andrea or Patrick.

6. The student who tested the 2005 model car got three more miles per gallon than Andrea's car.

		Andrea	Brody	Caiden	Grayson	Patrick	2004	2005	2006	2007	2008	Convertible	Coupe	Hatchback	Minivan	Sedan
Gas Mileages	22 MPG															
	25 MPG															
	28 MPG															
	31 MPG															
	34 MPG															
Cars	Convertible															
	Coupe															
	Hatchback															
	Minivan															
	Sedan															
Years	2004															
	2005															
	2006															
	2007															
	2008															

SOLVE RATE
52.8%

AVERAGE TIME
12 min, 23 sec

BEST TIME
2 min, 35 sec by jade_3031

Gas Mileages	Students	Years	Cars
22 MPG			
25 MPG			
28 MPG			
31 MPG			
34 MPG			

Merit Badges

There was a big celebration at this evening's merit badge ceremony, when five different scouts were each awarded a new merit badge in a different area of expertise. Each of the scouts is from a different camp and is of a different age. Using only the clues below, determine the age of each scout, the camp the scout is in, and the activity for which he won his merit badge.

1. Paul earned either his lifesaving or climbing merit badge.
2. Either the 11-year-old scout (who wasn't from Camp Bravo) or Andre was awarded the orienteering merit badge.
3. The oldest of the five scouts isn't from either Camp Boulder or Camp Bravo.
4. Of the scout from Camp Cedar and Brian, one is the oldest of the five and the other was awarded the climbing merit badge.
5. The five scouts were the one from Camp Grizzly, Andre, Brian (who hadn't yet earned his sailing merit badge), the 13 year old, and the one who earned his orienteering merit badge.
6. Either Gregory or Brian was awarded the climbing merit badge.
7. The scout from Camp Cedar is one year older than Andre.

	Scouts					Camps					Merit Badges				
	Andre	Brian	Cartman	Gregory	Paul	Camp Boulder	Camp Bravo	Camp Cedar	Camp Grizzly	Camp Tinder	Canoeing	Climbing	Lifesaving	Orienteering	Sailing
Ages 10															
11															
12															
13															
14															
Merit Badges Canoeing															
Climbing															
Lifesaving															
Orienteering															
Sailing															
Camps Camp Boulder															
Camp Bravo															
Camp Cedar															
Camp Grizzly															
Camp Tinder															

SOLVE RATE
52.8%

AVERAGE TIME
11 min, 4 sec

BEST TIME
2 min, 31 sec by caliphonte

Ages	Scouts	Camps	Merit Badges
10			
11			
12			
13			
14			

Breakfast Rituals

The Stop & Sip is a local institution, where dozens of people come every morning for a quick pastry and coffee. Five customers in particular are there every weekday, without fail. Each comes in at a specific time and orders a different coffee and a different pastry. Using only the clues below, match the coffee and pastry to each customer and determine what time the customer comes in to the Stop & Sip.

1. The five patrons are the one who gets a Boston cream doughnut (who arrives 15 minutes after the one who gets the mocha latte), the one who always orders a cappuccino (who isn't Zander), the one who loves pink-frosted doughnuts, Tatum, and the person who arrives each day at precisely 6:15 am.
2. Griffin never orders decaffeinated coffee and isn't the latest one to arrive at the Stop & Sip.
3. Between Tatum and the customer who always arrives at 6:45 am, one orders a jelly doughnut and the other always gets a café latte.
4. The customer who always gets an apple fritter isn't Tatum and doesn't ever pair it with black coffee.
5. Alana doesn't order black coffee and gets either the pink-frosted doughnut or the Boston cream doughnut.
6. The person who orders the jelly-filled doughnut always comes in 15 minutes after Tatum.

		Customers					Coffees					Pastries				
		Alana	Griffin	James	Tatum	Zander	Black Coffee	Café Latte	Cappuccino	Decaf Coffee	Mocha Latte	Apple Fritter	Bear Claw	Boston Cream	Jelly Filled	Pink Frosted
Times	5:45 am															
	6:00 am															
	6:15 am															
	6:30 am															
	6:45 am															
Pastries	Apple Fritter															
	Bear Claw															
	Boston Cream															
	Jelly Filled															
	Pink Frosted															
Coffees	Black Coffee															
	Café Latte															
	Cappuccino															
	Decaf Coffee															
	Mocha Latte															

Times	Customers	Coffees	Pastries
5:45 am			
6:00 am			
6:15 am			
6:30 am			
6:45 am			

SOLVE RATE
52.3%

AVERAGE TIME
13 min, 56 sec

BEST TIME
2 min, 35 sec by jade_3031

Classes and Classmates

Richard's school schedule this year suits him just fine; he ended up sharing five of his seven scheduled classes with close friends of his. A different friend shares each class with him, and each class is in a different room of the school. Using only the clues below, determine which friend shares each class with Richard and the subject and room number of each class.

1. Morgan shares his sixth period class with Richard.
2. The class Richard has in room 415 (which he doesn't share with Savannah) comes immediately after the class he has in room 145.
3. Richard's English class is scheduled right after his drama class.
4. Of the class taught in room 415 and the one Richard shares with Andrew, one is scheduled for fourth period and the other is woodshop.
5. The class Richard shares with Allison is scheduled right after the class he has in room 221.
6. Of home economics (which isn't taught in room 102) and Richard's third period class, one is shared with Morgan and the other is held in room 415.

| | | Students | | | | | Subjects | | | | | Room Numbers | | | | |
		Allison	Andrew	Leilani	Morgan	Savannah	Drama	English	History	Home Ec.	Woodshop	102	145	221	406	415
Periods	Second															
	Third															
	Fourth															
	Fifth															
	Sixth															
Room Numbers	102															
	145															
	221															
	406															
	415															
Subjects	Drama															
	English															
	History															
	Home Ec.															
	Woodshop															

SOLVE RATE
52.1%

AVERAGE TIME
11 min

BEST TIME
1 min, 41 sec by Vaughns

Periods	Students	Subjects	Room Numbers
Second			
Third			
Fourth			
Fifth			
Sixth			

Robot Warriors

Five students signed up for this year's Robot Warrior challenge. Each had to build a battery-powered robot from scratch and then pit the robots against each other in robot-to-robot battle. Points were awarded for the victor, but also for other criteria, such as originality of design and most efficient use of energy. Using only the clues below, match each robot to each builder, and determine what kind of batteries each used and how many batteries each required. Note: Batteries sizes (in order) are AAAA (the smallest), AAA, AA, C, and D (the largest).

1. The five robots are Trasher (which isn't Jackie's robot), the one Aden built, the one that ran on the smallest batteries, Destroyer, and the one that required five batteries.

2. Giselle's robot didn't require the largest battery type.

3. One robot ran on three AA batteries.

4. Of Wrecker and Jackie's robot, one ran on D batteries and the other used three batteries.

5. The five builders are Zachary, the one who built Mangler, the one whose robot required five batteries, and the ones who built robots that used AA and C batteries.

6. Trasher didn't run on four batteries.

7. Giselle's robot used larger batteries than Jackie's.

8. The robot that required the fewest batteries didn't use C batteries.

9. The robot that required AAA batteries didn't use four of them.

		Builders					Batteries					Robots				
		Aden	Giselle	Jackie	Stephen	Zachary	Two	Three	Four	Five	Six	Crusher	Destroyer	Mangler	Trasher	Wrecker
Battery Types	AAAA															
	AAA															
	AA															
	C															
	D															
Robots	Crusher															
	Destroyer															
	Mangler															
	Trasher															
	Wrecker															
Batteries	Two															
	Three															
	Four															
	Five															
	Six															

SOLVE RATE
52.0%

AVERAGE TIME
11 min, 31 sec

BEST TIME
2 min, 49 sec by urielzet

Battery Types	Builders	Batteries	Robots
AAAA			
AAA			
AA			
C			
D			

Fudge Sale

Five amateur confectioners make fudge in their spare time and sell it at the local candy shop. Each makes a specific type of fudge that has one special ingredient inside. Using only the clues below, determine what type of fudge is made by each confectioner, what special ingredient is inside, and how much (per pound) each charges for the fudge.

1. The five confectioners are the one who makes vanilla fudge, the one who charges the least, the one who charges $2.50/lb, Bradford (who makes chocolate fudge), and the one who puts pecans in the fudge.
2. Of Amari and the confectioner who uses raisins, one sells the fudge for $2.20/lb and the other makes maple fudge.
3. Either Bradford or Devon charge $2.20/lb.
4. The fudge with cranberries in it costs 15¢ more than the macadamia fudge.
5. The peanut butter fudge doesn't have pecans in it.
6. Mitchell doesn't make the most expensive fudge.
7. Of the macadamia fudge and the one that costs $2.50/lb, one is made by Moses and the other by Amari.

	Confectioners					Fudge Types					Ingredients				
	Amari	Bradford	Devon	Mitchell	Moses	Chocolate	Maple	Marbled	Peanut Butter	Vanilla	Cranberries	Macadamias	Pecans	Raisins	Walnuts
$2.05															
$2.20															
$2.35															
$2.50															
$2.65															
Cranberries															
Macadamias															
Pecans															
Raisins															
Walnuts															
Chocolate															
Maple															
Marbled															
Peanut Butter															
Vanilla															

Prices	Confectioners	Fudge Types	Ingredients
$2.05			
$2.20			
$2.35			
$2.50			
$2.65			

SOLVE RATE
51.7%

AVERAGE TIME
12 min

BEST TIME
3 min, 6 sec by moodymom

The Piano Quintet

Walter and four of his musician friends recently formed a piano quintet, and they're already planning their first performance. Each musician plays one of four instruments (there are two violinists—first violin and second violin), and each selects a piano quintet, written by each musician's favorite composer, to include in the first concert. Using only the clues below, determine the composer whose work was chosen by each musician, which instrument each musician plays in the group, and the order in which each piece will be performed.

1. The five musicians are Walter, the one who plays second violin (whose selection won't be first on the program), the cellist, the one who selected a Goldmark piano quintet, and the violinist whose selection will be played second.

2. Neither Michael nor Noe plays first violin.

3. Amari's selection will be played fourth in the upcoming performance.

4. Neither the person who selected a Shostakovich quintet (which won't be played third in the program) nor the one whose selection will be played last is Noe.

5. Michael didn't select his quintet from the works of Edward Elgar.

6. The five pieces selected are the ones that will be performed first and last, the Boccherini piano quintet, Walter's selection, and the one chosen by the cellist.

7. The piano quintet chosen by the violist will be performed immediately before the one selected by the cellist.

		Musicians					Instruments					Composers				
		Amari	Michael	Noe	Philip	Walter	Cello	First Violin	Piano	Second Violin	Viola	Boccherini	Elgar	Goldmark	Saint Saëns	Shostakovich
Orders	First															
	Second															
	Third															
	Fourth															
	Fifth															
Composers	Boccherini															
	Elgar															
	Goldmark															
	Saint Saëns															
	Shostakovich															
Instruments	Cello															
	First Violin															
	Piano															
	Second Violin															
	Viola															

SOLVE RATE
51.6%

AVERAGE TIME
13 min, 59 sec

BEST TIME
3 min, 7 sec by khead

Orders	Musicians	Instruments	Composers
First			
Second			
Third			
Fourth			
Fifth			

Purposeful Puzzlers

Puzzle Baron's next book will include contributions from five separate puzzle editors, each of whom specializes in only one type of puzzle. Each of the five contributors has been with the company for a different length of time, and each had a different number of puzzles accepted for the final manuscript. Using only the clues below, determine how long each puzzler has been employed by Puzzle Baron, the type of puzzle each person specializes in, and how many of each person's puzzles made it into the book.

1. Of the person who specializes in drop quotes and the one who's been with Puzzle Baron for six months, one is Amir and the other had the fewest puzzles make it into the book.

2. The five individuals are Emilia (who doesn't work on acrostic puzzles), the person who specializes in drop quotes, Jonah, the person who's been with the company for just one year (who doesn't create Sudoku puzzles), and the one who has nine of his or her puzzles included in the next book (who hasn't been with Puzzle Baron for exactly two years).

3. Among Kaiden (who has nine puzzles included in the next book) and Cynthia, one specializes in cryptograms and the other has been with Puzzle Baron for exactly a year.

4. The puzzler who specializes in cryptograms has two more puzzles make it into the next book compared to the person who's been with Puzzle Baron for the shortest period of time. Emilia had exactly seven non-Sudoku puzzles included in the next book. Either Cynthia or the one who creates logic puzzles has the most puzzles included in the forthcoming publication.

SOLVE RATE
51.2%

AVERAGE TIME
11 min

BEST TIME
2 min, 35 sec by urielzet

Puzzles	Authors	Types	Seniorities
3			
5			
7			
9			
11			

The Best-Sellers List

Last week's best-selling fiction list was a surprise to everyone, because five different first-time novelists rounded out the top five spots for the first time in decades. Using only the clues below, match each author's first and last name to the title of the book each wrote, and determine the author's ranking on last week's best-sellers list. Note: The lower the number, the higher the ranking, which means more books were sold.

1. Neither Lyla nor the author ranked #5 wrote *Palimpsests*.
2. The author of *How We Walk* doesn't have the surname England.
3. Lyla sold more books last week than the author of *Palimpsests* (who isn't Dr. Booker).
4. Of Lyla and Rodney, one was the #2 top-selling author and the other wrote *How We Walk*.
5. The author whose last name is Foster was next highest on the best-sellers list last week than the one named Fuller (who didn't write *A Man Like Him*).
6. Of the #1 top-selling author and the one who wrote *Westward Winds*, one is Lyla and the other has the surname Fuller.
7. The #4 ranked author isn't named Mcclure and didn't write *Palimpsests*.
8. The five authors are the one who wrote *Westward Winds*, Dr. Booker, the author of *How We Walk*, Denise (who was thrilled to be the #1 ranked author), and Jenna.

		First Names					Last Names					Titles				
		Denise	Jenna	Kelly	Lyla	Rodney	Booker	England	Foster	Fuller	Mcclure	A Man Like Him	How We Walk	Palimpsests	Valley of Hurt	Westwd. Winds
Ranks	#1															
	#2															
	#3															
	#4															
	#5															
Titles	A Man Like Him															
	How We Walk															
	Palimpsests															
	Valley of Hurt															
	Westwd. Winds															
Last Names	Booker															
	England															
	Foster															
	Fuller															
	Mcclure															

SOLVE RATE
51.2%

AVERAGE TIME
14 min, 6 sec

BEST TIME
3 min, 20 sec by Kazemizu

Ranks	First Names	Last Names	Titles
#1			
#2			
#3			
#4			
#5			

The Model U.N.

As part of Gryllis High School's Model U.N. project, students were encouraged to correspond with a pen pal of the same age in a different country, chosen by their teacher. Five students have begun the project so far; each of them is a different age and has a different teacher who has assigned them a pen pal from a different country. Using only the clues below, determine the age of each student, the name of the student's teacher, and the nationality of the student's pen pal.

1. Of Christopher (who isn't Mr. Dykstra's student) and the 12 year old, one has the Nepalese pen pal and the other has the Chinese pen pal.
2. Of Mrs. Baer's student and the 15 year old, one has the Chinese pen pal and the other has the Libyan pen pal.
3. John is not the youngest student in the project.
4. The five individuals are the person with the Libyan pen pal (who isn't Emily), the 13 year old, the 15 year old, Kaden (who is 14 years old), and Mr. Manzella's student.
5. Mrs. D'Amico's student (who isn't Emily) is younger than the student with the Belgian pen pal.

	Amaya	Christopher	Emily	John	Kaden	Belgian	Chinese	Dominican	Libyan	Nepalese	Mrs. Baer	Mrs. D'Amico	Mr. Dykstra	Mr. Manzella	Mrs. Schwartz
11															
12															
13															
14															
15															
Mrs. Baer															
Mrs. D'Amico															
Mr. Dykstra															
Mr. Manzella															
Mrs. Schwartz															
Belgian															
Chinese															
Dominican															
Libyan															
Nepalese															

SOLVE RATE
51%

AVERAGE TIME
12 min, 9 sec

BEST TIME
3 min, 30 sec by heathpie

Ages	Students	Pen Pals	Teachers
11			
12			
13			
14			
15			

Domino Day

In celebration of World Domino Day, five teams met in Brussels to compete for the most elaborate and interesting domino displays. Each team, headed by a captain or team leader, set up a different number of dominoes. Using only the clues below, determine how many dominoes each team set up, who each team's captain was, and the place in which each finished.

1. Of the team that came in fourth place and the one led by Ivan, one set up 4,450,000 dominoes and the other set up 4,750,000.
2. Grady (whose team finished third) wasn't captain of the Fall Guys.
3. The team that won the competition actually set up fewer dominoes than the team that finished fourth (which wasn't led by Hope).
4. The display set up by the Kinetics (who didn't finish fifth) didn't have the fewest dominoes of all five teams.
5. Chance wasn't the team leader of the Dominotes.
6. Of the Dominotes and the Topplers (who set up 4,450,000 dominoes), one finished second and the other finished fourth.
7. The Topplers set up 150,000 more dominoes than the team that finished in third place.
8. Hope's team didn't finish in fifth place.

		Captains					Teams					Places				
		Ayden	Chance	Grady	Hope	Ivan	Dominotes	Fall Guys	Kinetics	Setters	Topplers	First	Second	Third	Fourth	Fifth
Dominoes	4,300,000															
	4,450,000															
	4,600,000															
	4,750,000															
	4,900,000															
Places	First															
	Second															
	Third															
	Fourth															
	Fifth															
Teams	Dominotes															
	Fall Guys															
	Kinetics															
	Setters															
	Topplers															

Dominoes	Captains	Teams	Places
4,300,000			
4,450,000			
4,600,000			
4,750,000			
4,900,000			

SOLVE RATE
50.4%

AVERAGE TIME
12 min, 59 sec

BEST TIME
3 min, 36 sec by jevin2008

Shades of White

Adriana just moved into a beautiful new house in a great neighborhood, but there is just one problem: Every room in the house is painted in bright, gaudy colors. Hot pink, forest green, lipstick red … it is just too much for her to bear! So Adriana visits the paint store and buys five different neutral, off-white colors, a different one for each of the five rooms she needs to repaint. Of course, she can't do all this painting alone, so she enlists four of her friends to help her. Each friend (plus Adriana) takes a different room, and each takes a different amount of time to finish the room. Using only the clues below, determine who painted each room, in what color, and how long it took the painter to complete the room.

1. Nelson didn't use the antique white paint.
2. Of Antonio and the painter who finished the quickest, one painted the living room and the other painted the bedroom.
3. Adriana finished painting in exactly four hours.
4. The five painters are the one who used the wicker paint, the one who painted the bedroom, the one who painted a room in ivory, Nelson, and the painter who took the longest to complete the job.
5. Of Lillie and the fastest painter, one used the ivory paint and the other used seashell.
6. The kitchen painter finished faster than the one who used the ivory paint.
7. Between the office painter and the one who used seashell, one finished in just three hours and the other was Adriana.

	Painters					Colors					Rooms				
	Adriana	Amaya	Antonio	Lillie	Nelson	Antique White	Ivory	Linen	Seashell	Wicker	Bathroom	Bedroom	Kitchen	Living Room	Office
Times 3 hours															
3.5 hours															
4 hours															
4.5 hours															
5 hours															
Rooms Bathroom															
Bedroom															
Kitchen															
Living Room															
Office															
Colors Antique White															
Ivory															
Linen															
Seashell															
Wicker															

Times	Painters	Colors	Rooms
3 hours			
3.5 hours			
4 hours			
4.5 hours			
5 hours			

SOLVE RATE
50.2%

AVERAGE TIME
11 min, 52 sec

BEST TIME
3 min, 21 sec by riffraff

Plate Problems

Bill's used car shop saw a lot of new business last week, with five big sales coming in all at once. Unfortunately, with all the rushing around, Bill's filing system went a little haywire, and now he can't quite remember which cars belong to which buyers! Each buyer is supposed to come in to pick up a new car and new license plate on a different day this week. Using only the clues below, help Bill determine the car and license plate belonging to each buyer, as well as the day the buyer will be coming in to pick up the new set of wheels.

1. Brad is scheduled to come in sometime before the person who bought the pickup.
2. The buyer who gets the MRM-019 license plate will come in the day after the one with the JTR-500 license plate (who isn't Lacey).
3. The station wagon doesn't get the MNU-665 license plate.
4. Of Landon and the person who's scheduled to arrive on Tuesday, one has the JTR-500 license plate and the other has the MNU-665 license plate.
5. The five buyers are the one scheduled to come in on Wednesday, the one who gets the MNU-665 license plate, Josephine (who didn't buy either the station wagon or the sedan), the one who chose the sports car (who isn't Karina), and the person who comes in on Tuesday.
6. The buyer with the SUV-332 license plate will come in the day after the one with the MNU-665 license plate.
7. Lacey bought the minivan.

		Buyers					License Plates					Vehicles			
		Brad	Josephine	Karina	Lacey	Landon	DIV-996	JTR-500	MNU-665	MRM-019	SUV-332	Pickup	Minivan	Sedan	Sports Car	Station Wagon
Days	Monday															
	Tuesday															
	Wednesday															
	Thursday															
	Friday															
Vehicles	Pickup															
	Minivan															
	Sedan															
	Sports Car															
	Station Wagon															
License Plates	DIV-996															
	JTR-500															
	MNU-665															
	MRM-019															
	SUV-332															

Days	Buyers	License Plates	Vehicles
Monday			
Tuesday			
Wednesday			
Thursday			
Friday			

SOLVE RATE
50.1%

AVERAGE TIME
12 min, 56 sec

BEST TIME
3 min, 28 sec by The James

A Spoonful of Sugar Helps the Medicine Go Down

Dr. Lowenstein's pediatric practice was completely booked this morning with sick children and worried parents looking for a diagnosis. Each of her first five appointments ended up having a different ailment, some more serious than others. Although none of the children felt particularly well, each perked up a little bit when she was given the opportunity to pick a lollipop from Dr. Lowenstein's desk drawer. (Each chose a different flavor.) Using only the clues below, determine the order in which each patient was seen by Dr. Lowenstein, the diagnosis she gave to each, and the lollipop flavor each patient selected on her way out.

1. The five patients were Meghan (who chose the lime-flavored candy), the girl who had the mumps, the one who chose the grape-flavored lollipop, the patient with the fourth appointment (who didn't choose the orange lollipop), and Alice (who also didn't have the flu).
2. Neither Meghan nor Naomi had the flu.
3. The first patient Dr. Lowenstein saw this morning didn't have the mumps.
4. The girls who had the chicken pox and the measles both had their appointments sometime before Alice.
5. Jennifer had a bad case of the measles.
6. The patient who left with the grape lollipop had their appointment immediately after the one who chose the pineapple lollipop.
7. The girl who had the fourth appointment didn't have the measles.

	Patients					Lollipops					Diagnoses				
	Alice	Brittany	Jennifer	Meghan	Naomi	Cherry	Grape	Lime	Orange	Pineapple	Chicken Pox	Common Cold	Flu	Measles	Mumps
First															
Second															
Third															
Fourth															
Fifth															
Chicken Pox															
Common Cold															
Flu															
Measles															
Mumps															
Cherry															
Grape															
Lime															
Orange															
Pineapple															

SOLVE RATE
49.9%

AVERAGE TIME
16 min, 38 sec

BEST TIME
2 min, 48 sec by urielzet

Appointments	Patients	Lollipops	Diagnoses
First			
Second			
Third			
Fourth			
Fifth			

Better Than Birdies ...

The annual Orchard Hills Women's Invitational golf tournament was held today, and some top-notch play was on display. The top five players all finished under par, each with a different score, and each scored an amazing eagle (2 under par) on a different hole! Using only the clues below, find the final score for each player, determine on which hole each scored an eagle, and find the total distance in yards for each of those holes.

1. Neither Jasmine nor the golfer who eagled hole #12 finished with the lowest score.

2. Of Heidi and the player with the highest score, one eagled the first hole and the other eagled the tenth (which wasn't 520 yards long).

3. Of the first hole and the sixteenth hole, one was 132 yards long and the other was eagled by the player who shot an impressive 67.

4. The golfer who finished the round in 66 strokes didn't eagle the hole that was 411 yards long.

5. The golfer who eagled the fifth hole finished one stroke higher than Tracy, but with a lower score than Allison (who didn't shoot a 69).

6. The player who eagled the tenth hole scored lower than the one who eagled hole #12.

7. Whoever eagled the hole that was 342 yards long finished one stroke higher than the player who eagled the fifth hole (which wasn't 520 yards long).

		Players				Eagle Holes					Distances				
	Allison	Heidi	Jasmine	Sarah	Tracy	#1	#5	#10	#12	#16	132 yards	342 yards	411 yards	497 yards	520 yards
Final Scores 66															
67															
68															
69															
70															
Distances 132 yards															
342 yards															
411 yards															
497 yards															
520 yards															
Eagle Holes #1															
#5															
#10															
#12															
#16															

SOLVE RATE
50.2%

AVERAGE TIME
12 min, 17 sec

BEST TIME
3 min, 10 sec by jade_3031

Final Scores	Players	Eagle Holes	Distances
66			
67			
68			
69			
70			

Record Lows

Although Beecham County wasn't particularly known for its cold winters, the weather dipped below zero degrees Fahrenheit several times over the past century. Five towns in particular hold negative low temperatures. Using only the clues below, determine each town's lowest recorded temperature and the month and year in which it was recorded.

1. Jasper's record low (which wasn't -2 degrees) wasn't in November.
2. The five record lows are -2 degrees (taken back in 1889), the one recorded in December, the coldest of the five, the one recorded in Audubon, and the 1960 record low.
3. Crawford's record low wasn't recorded in 1908.
4. Of the low temperature recorded in January and the one that was -6 degrees, one was recorded in Audubon and the other in 1908.
5. Of the 1933 record low and Jasper's, one was recorded in November and the other in February.
6. Guthrie's record low wasn't -6 degrees and wasn't recorded in March.
7. The 1908 record low was four degrees warmer than the one recorded in January.

		Towns					Months					Years				
		Audubon	Crawford	Guthrie	Jasper	Kossuth	November	December	January	February	March	1889	1908	1933	1960	1978
Record Lows	-2															
	-6															
	-10															
	-14															
	-18															
Years	1889															
	1908															
	1933															
	1960															
	1978															
Months	November															
	December															
	January															
	February															
	March															

Record Lows	Towns	Months	Years
-2			
-6			
-10			
-14			
-18			

Pickle People

Sales were strong at this year's pickle festival, which showcased some of the best local pickle makers from the state. Five separate booths were set up, each with a different seller offering a different type of homemade pickle. Using only the clues below, determine which seller was in which booth, what type of pickles each was selling, and how many jars each sold during the festival.

1. Hector didn't set up shop in booth #5.
2. The best-selling pickle was neither the dill nor the bread and butter variety.
3. Either Camila (who sold six fewer jars of pickles than the gherkin-seller) or the person who sold precisely 30 jars of pickles was in booth #4.
4. Victor sold his pickles out of booth #3.
5. The person who sold dill pickles didn't sell exactly 30 jars.
6. Of Hector and the person who sold gherkins, one sold the most of all five vendors and the other was in booth #2.
7. The five sellers are Camila, Hector, the one who sold half-sour pickles, the one in booth #4, and the one who sold exactly 42 jars.
8. Either Talia or Hector was in booth #2.

SOLVE RATE
53.1%

AVERAGE TIME
11 min, 54 sec

BEST TIME
3 min, 2 sec by pallyfour

Diamonds Are a Girl's Best Friend

Valentine's Day is just around the corner, and ARS Jewelry is flooded with men looking to buy gifts for their sweethearts. Five in particular are shopping for diamonds in the 2–3 carat range, to be set in titanium rings. Using only the clues below, determine the size (in carats) of the diamond each man purchased, the country it originated from, and the total price of each. Note: Larger diamonds don't always mean larger prices—clarity, color, and cut also help determine a diamond's price!

1. The five customers are Jay (who bought the Canadian diamond), the one who bought the most expensive diamond, the one who bought the diamond from Botswana, Abe, and the man who bought the 3.1 carat diamond.
2. Either the person who bought the smallest diamond or the one who paid $2,950 for their diamond is Jay.
3. The $2,950 diamond is larger than the one that cost $4,090.
4. The South African diamond is 0.3 carats smaller than the one from Botswana.
5. Ian bought his diamond for $4,090. Grayson spent only $3,675 for his.
6. Abe's diamond is larger than the one that sold for the least amount of money.
7. The second-largest diamond didn't sell for $4,090 and isn't Russian in origin.

		Customers					Countries					Prices				
		Abe	Grayson	Ian	Jay	Walt	Australia	Botswana	Canada	Russia	South Africa	$2,400	$2,950	$3,675	$4,090	$5,250
Carats	2.2 carats															
	2.5 carats															
	2.8 carats															
	3.1 carats															
	3.4 carats															
Prices	$2,400															
	$2,950															
	$3,675															
	$4,090															
	$5,250															
Countries	Australia															
	Botswana															
	Canada															
	Russia															
	South Africa															

	SOLVE RATE
	49.1%

AVERAGE TIME
10 min, 45 sec

BEST TIME
3 min, 20 sec by moodymom

Carats	Customers	Countries	Prices
2.2 carats			
2.5 carats			
2.8 carats			
3.1 carats			
3.4 carats			

Catch of the Day ...

Five friends decided to meet for dinner at the famous ocean-side restaurant, Crabby Pete's. Because it was a weekday, everyone decided to arrive separately, straight from work. Each friend ordered a different seafood entrée, and each had a different white wine paired with the meal. Though some wine purists might scoff at their choices, everyone thoroughly enjoyed the meals. Using only the clues below, determine the order in which each diner arrived at the restaurant and the wine and entrée each ordered.

1. The five friends were Sarah, the one who drank the Chardonnay, the one who ordered swordfish, the person who arrived first, and Bruce (who didn't arrive second and didn't order mussels).

2. The Chardonnay drinker arrived just before the one who had a Riesling with the meal.

3. Either Valeria or Katelyn enjoyed clams for dinner.

4. The one who ordered clams arrived just before the one who drank the Pinot Grigio (who didn't order mussels).

5. The five friends were Valeria, the one who drank the Viognier, the person who arrived second, the one who ordered clams, and Mariana (who didn't order the swordfish and arrived sometime after Bruce).

6. Neither the one who ordered tuna nor the person who arrived third was Valeria.

		Friends					Wines					Seafood				
		Bruce	Katelyn	Mariana	Sarah	Valeria	Chardonnay	Chenin Blanc	Pinot Grigio	Riesling	Viognier	Clams	Mussels	Oysters	Swordfish	Tuna
Arrivals	First															
	Second															
	Third															
	Fourth															
	Fifth															
Seafood	Clams															
	Mussels															
	Oysters															
	Swordfish															
	Tuna															
Wines	Chardonnay															
	Chenin Blanc															
	Pinot Grigio															
	Riesling															
	Viognier															

SOLVE RATE
48.9%

AVERAGE TIME
16 min, 19 sec

BEST TIME
3 min, 34 sec by myerslite

Arrivals	Friends	Wines	Seafood
First			
Second			
Third			
Fourth			
Fifth			

Change of Diet

Five friends, each between the ages of 35 and 47 (and each a different age), have decided to each make a small change in their diet in order to improve their health and well-being. The five women have started taking a different vitamin supplement each morning and have swapped out their usual, junk food snacks with a different healthy alternative. Using only the clues below, match each woman to her age, vitamin supplement, and choice of healthy snack.

1. The five friends are the one who takes vitamin E, Briana, Julianna (who would never agree to drink wheat grass juice, regardless of the benefits), the 44-year-old, and the one who swapped soda for soy milk.
2. The woman who now takes vitamin D supplements each morning is three years older than Briana.
3. Leila now snacks on either broccoli or apple slices when she gets an attack of the munchies.
4. The 47-year-old isn't taking vitamin A or C.
5. Either Lauryn or Julianna has substituted apple slices for potato chips.
6. Kayden isn't 35 years old.
7. The 38-year-old isn't taking vitamin C supplements.
8. Of Julianna and the friend who now takes vitamin D each morning, one is 47 years old and the other snacks on apple slices.

	Health Nuts					Vitamins					Healthy Snacks				
	Briana	Julianna	Kayden	Lauryn	Leila	Vitamin A	Vitamin C	Vitamin D	Vitamin E	Vitamin K	Almonds	Apples	Broccoli	Soy Milk	Wheat Grass
35															
38															
41															
44															
47															
Almonds											
Apples											
Broccoli											
Soy Milk											
Wheat Grass											
Vitamin A						
Vitamin C						
Vitamin D						
Vitamin E						
Vitamin K						

SOLVE RATE 56.1%

AVERAGE TIME 11 min, 9 sec

BEST TIME 3 min, 2 sec by gullypad12

Ages	Health Nuts	Vitamins	Healthy Snacks
35			
38			
41			
44			
47			

Unsafe Safes

The main event at this year's locksmith convention was a safe-cracking exhibition by five of the industry's top locksmiths. Each safe cracker was given 10 minutes to open a locked safe (each of which contained a different "treasure") using only the combination wheel and a listening device. Using only the clues below, determine how long it took each person to open the safe, what the combination was, and what type of treasure each found within.

1. The safe cracker who took the longest to open his or her safe didn't find a diamond inside. The one who opened his or her safe in six minutes and nine seconds had a 14 in their final combination.

2. The five safe crackers were Khalil, the ones with the 33-44-41 and 25-11-55 combinations, the one who took the longest, and the one who found a necklace in the safe.

3. Either the person who opened the safe the quickest (who didn't have a 55 in the combination) or the one who found a gold bar was Nancy.

4. Lauryn took longer to open her safe than Cameron, who didn't have a 25 in his final combination.

5. Between the one who took six minutes and nine seconds and the one who found the paintings, one had the 14-52-35 combination and the other had 45-50-19.

6. Neither Nancy nor the person who had the combination with a 50 in it took the longest to open the safe.

7. The one who found the gold bar took 4 minutes and 54 seconds to open the safe (but wasn't Nancy).

	Allison	Cameron	Khalil	Lauryn	Nancy	12-22-14	14-52-35	25-11-55	33-44-41	45-50-19	Diamond	Gold Bar	Necklace	Old Books	Paintings
Times 3:15															
4:54															
6:01															
6:09															
8:26															
Contents Diamond															
Gold Bar															
Necklace															
Old Books															
Paintings															
Combinations 12-22-14															
14-52-35															
25-11-55															
33-44-41															
45-50-19															

SOLVE RATE
48.9%

AVERAGE TIME
9 min, 36 sec

BEST TIME
4 min, 13 sec by steph612

Times	Safe Crackers	Combinations	Contents
3:15			
4:54			
6:01			
6:09			
8:26			

Concert Night

The Cumberland Public Schools Administration put on a concert night last week. There were five acts, each focusing on the works of a different composer. Each act was performed by a different class orchestra, which was led by the orchestra's own unique teacher. Using only the clues below, determine the order in which each class appeared, the name of the teacher of each class, and the composer whose works each class performed.

1. Mrs. Asia's 6th grade orchestra didn't perform the works of Mozart.
2. Mr. Aden doesn't teach the 9th grade orchestra.
3. Mrs. Irving led the 10th grade orchestra, but didn't perform first or second.
4. Between the 7th grade orchestra and the one that performed second, one performed pieces by Beethoven and the other focused on the works of Franz Lizst.
5. Mr. Aden's orchestra (which appeared first) performed Edvard Grieg's *Symphonic Dances*.
6. Of the orchestra that showcased works by Franz Lizst and the one that performed fourth, one was led by Mrs. Irving and the other by Mr. Marvins.
7. The 7th grade orchestra (which didn't perform third) didn't perform anything by Lizst.

	Instructors					Grades					Orders				
	Mr. Aden	Mrs. Asia	Mrs. Celeste	Mrs. Irving	Mr. Marvins	6th grade	7th grade	8th grade	9th grade	10th grade	First	Second	Third	Fourth	Fifth
Beethoven															
Grieg															
Lizst															
Mozart															
Schubert															
First															
Second															
Third															
Fourth															
Fifth															
6th grade															
7th grade															
8th grade															
9th grade															
10th grade															

Composers	Instructors	Grades	Orders
Beethoven			
Grieg			
Lizst			
Mozart			
Schubert			

SOLVE RATE
48.8%

AVERAGE TIME
13 min, 33 sec

BEST TIME
3 min, 7 sec by khead

Chess Champions

Five different players won the last five regional chess championships. Each of these championship games was thrilling to watch, because each displayed a textbook example of a different well-known opening chess move. All the games are timed, but some lasted longer than others. Using only the clues below, determine the opening and length of each championship game, the name of the winner, and the year in which it took place.

1. The game that began with the Evans Gambit, which wasn't played by Avery, wasn't the shortest of the five. Either Cesar or Avery won in 2004.

2. The championship game that lasted 15 minutes and 22 seconds took place sometime after the game that began with the infamous Caro-Kann opening (which wasn't the 2006 game).

3. Between the 2008 winner and Victor, one used the English Opening in his or her championship game and the other played the shortest game.

4. Ruben, who won his championship sometime after Avery, has never played in a game in which the Dutch Defense was used.

5. The game that lasted 9 minutes and 44 seconds was played the year before the championship that featured the English Opening.

6. Between Victor (who didn't win the 2006 championship) and the 2007 winner, one played the second-longest game and the other played the game that lasted 13 minutes and 19 seconds.

7. Between Avery and the person who played the English Opening, one played the second-longest game and the other won in 2005.

		Openings					Winners					Game Lengths				
		Caro-Kann	Dutch Defense	English Opening	Evans Gambit	French Defense	Avery	Cesar	Dallas	Ruben	Victor	8:23	9:44	13:19	15:22	20:09
Years	2004															
	2005															
	2006															
	2007															
	2008															
Game Lengths	8:23															
	9:44															
	13:19															
	15:22															
	20:09															
Winners	Avery															
	Cesar															
	Dallas															
	Ruben															
	Victor															

SOLVE RATE
48.6%

AVERAGE TIME
14 min, 49 sec

BEST TIME
2 min, 31 sec by jade_3031

Years	Openings	Winners	Game Lengths
2004			
2005			
2006			
2007			
2008			

Power Plants

As part of her schoolwork on environmental issues, Wilma had to write a brief paper on the inner workings of five different types of power plants currently operating within 250 miles of her hometown. In her paper, she discussed the history of each plant (each of which was founded in a different year) and the total output in mega-watts (MW) each plant produces. Using only the clues below, determine the output, founding year, and fuel source for each power plant.

1. The five plants are the oldest and newest ones, the Kentfield plant (which, like Larkspur, doesn't generate 575 MW), the hydroelectric (water-powered) plant, and the one that generates 650 MW.
2. The coal plant wasn't founded in 1979.
3. Gustine is a coal power plant.
4. The Kentfield nuclear plant generates more power than the plant that runs on natural gas.
5. Kentfield generates 75 MW less than Escalon, which generates 75 MW less than the plant founded in 1983.
6. Of the natural gas and wind-powered plants, one generates the least power output and the other was founded earliest.

SOLVE RATE
48.5%

AVERAGE TIME
13 min, 40 sec

BEST TIME
3 min, 45 sec by e-klectric

Output	Plants	Years	Types
575 MW			
650 MW			
725 MW			
800 MW			
875 MW			

Buyer's Market

Loretta's real estate business brought in five big sales last week, all in the same neighborhood. Each house had a different, unique selling point (such as high ceilings), and each sold for a different price. Using only the clues below, match each family to the house each bought and determine what street it was on, how much each paid, and what unique feature convinced each family to buy it.

1. The five houses are the one on Eustis Way, the cheapest home (which had high ceilings), the most expensive home, the one with the sunroom, and the one that was bought by the Carson family.

2. The house on Minter Boulevard sold for more money than the one that boasted hardwood floors.

3. Of the Felton Drive house and the one that sold for $199,000 (which wasn't bought by the King family), one had a Jacuzzi and the other was purchased by the Carsons.

4. The Kemps didn't buy the house on Baker Court, and the Kings didn't buy the home on Wesley Road.

5. The house with the hardwood floors sold for more than the house with the Jacuzzi (which wasn't bought by the Jardens).

6. Of the house with the skylights and the one bought by the Kemp family, one was on Minter Boulevard and the other was on Baker Court.

		Carsons	Jardens	Kings	Kemps	Martinsons	Baker Ct.	Eustis Way	Felton Dr.	Minter Blvd.	Wesley Rd.	High Ceilings	Jacuzzi	Skylights	Sunroom	Wood Floors
Sales Prices	$145,000															
	$199,000															
	$239,000															
	$255,000															
	$285,000															
Features	High Ceilings															
	Jacuzzi															
	Skylights															
	Sunroom															
	Wood Floors															
Streets	Baker Ct.															
	Eustis Way															
	Felton Dr.															
	Minter Blvd.															
	Wesley Rd.															

Sales Prices	Families	Streets	Features
$145,000			
$199,000			
$239,000			
$255,000			
$285,000			

SOLVE RATE
48.4%

AVERAGE TIME
10 min, 20 sec

BEST TIME
2 min, 35 sec by urielzet

The Only Thing We Have to Fear ...

Dr. Masterson, an expert in diagnosing and treating severe phobias, had a full appointment schedule last week. Five different patients had appointments with him, each on a different day, and each went in to discuss a different phobia. Although none of them were cured just yet, the patients made good progress during their last session. Using only the clues below, determine the phobia each patient came in to discuss, the day of the patient's appointment, and the number of total sessions each had with Dr. Masterson.

1. One patient had a third session with Dr. Masterson on Monday.
2. The person who had a ninth session had an appointment sometime earlier in the week than the patient suffering from coulrophobia (a fear of clowns).
3. Kristopher isn't the agoraphobe (someone who fears open spaces).
4. The claustrophobic patient had an appointment the day after the person who had the fourth session with the doctor last week.
5. The five patients were the arachnophobe, the one with the Monday appointment, the one with the Friday appointment, Dean, and the one who had an eighth session with Dr. Masterson last week.
6. Holly didn't have her fourth session last week.
7. Of the person who had a sixth session last week and Kristopher, one is coulrophobic and the other is agoraphobic.
8. Julio, who isn't the glossophobe, didn't have his appointment on Tuesday.

		Patients					Phobias					Sessions				
		Dean	Holly	Julio	Kristopher	Morgan	Agoraphobic	Arachnophobic	Claustrophic	Coulrophobic	Glossophobic	Third	Fourth	Sixth	Eighth	Ninth
Days	Monday															
	Tuesday															
	Wednesday															
	Thursday															
	Friday															
Sessions	Third															
	Fourth															
	Sixth															
	Eighth															
	Ninth															
Phobias	Agoraphobic															
	Arachnophobic															
	Claustrophic															
	Coulrophobic															
	Glossophobic															

Days	Patients	Phobias	Sessions
Monday			
Tuesday			
Wednesday			
Thursday			
Friday			

SOLVE RATE
48.3%

AVERAGE TIME
13 min, 32 sec

BEST TIME
2 min, 56 sec by kcirderf

It's All About Thyme!

It was Rosemary's turn this year to host the annual neighborhood holiday party, but she just realized her prized herb garden had been destroyed by rabbits the night before! Fortunately, several of her guests had arrived early, and purely by chance, five of them each had at home one of the five herbs Rosemary needed to complete her recipes. They each went to their respective homes to retrieve the ingredients and, within half an hour, the holiday dinner was saved. Using only the clues below, determine the herb retrieved by each guest, as well as the street each lived on, and how long it took each of them to get back to Rosemary's house.

1. The five guests were the one from Deadwood Drive, Sidney (who took 15 minutes to get home and back), the one from Pavel Place, the one who had some fresh basil growing at home, and the one who took only 10 minutes to retrieve the herb.

2. The guest who brought back the basil took five minutes longer to get home and back than the one who miraculously had some fresh cilantro in the fridge.

3. The guest who took the longest to return didn't live at Pavel Place.

4. Of the person who had the thyme and the one from Winsome Way, one was Georgia and the other took 20 minutes to complete the trip home and back.

5. Beau took five minutes longer to grab his herbs than the person who lived at Lorry Lane. Mallory wasn't the quickest to return.

6. The guest who returned in exactly 10 minutes saved the day by bringing back either thyme or cilantro. The one who grabbed some cilantro from home returned to Rosemary's house quicker than the one who had to procure the parsley.

		Guests					Herbs					Streets				
		Addison	Beau	Georgia	Mallory	Sidney	Basil	Cilantro	Mint	Parsley	Thyme	Cedar Court	Deadwood Dr.	Lorry Lane	Pavel Place	Winsome Way
Travel Time	5 minutes															
	10 minutes															
	15 minutes															
	20 minutes															
	25 minutes															
Streets	Cedar Court															
	Deadwood Dr.															
	Lorry Lane															
	Pavel Place															
	Winsome Way															
Herbs	Basil															
	Cilantro															
	Mint															
	Parsley															
	Thyme															

SOLVE RATE
48.3%

AVERAGE TIME
11 min, 24 sec

BEST TIME
2 min by Kazemizu

Travel Time	Guests	Herbs	Streets
5 minutes			
10 minutes			
15 minutes			
20 minutes			
25 minutes			

Near-Earth Asteroids

Although the chances of an impact are incredibly small, a group of dedicated researchers devote their lives to discovering and tracking all near-Earth asteroids in the solar system to ensure none of them are on a collision course with us. In fact, five new near-Earth asteroids were discovered just this year. Using only the clues below, determine the name and size of each asteroid, the month it was discovered, and the name of the astronomer who discovered it.

1. The five asteroids are SS51MWE, 8DOQ01P, the largest one (which isn't IB80PLZ and wasn't discovered in March), the one discovered by Dr. Millicent, and the one first recorded in November.
2. Wallingford's asteroid is smaller than the one discovered by Dr. Halberstrom.
3. Dr. Rogers didn't make her discovery in March or April.
4. The asteroid discovered in November (which isn't LP4G9MO, and isn't 12 miles across) is twice the size of the one discovered a month later.
5. Asteroid SS51MWE is twice the size of the asteroid discovered in August.
6. Of the asteroid discovered in November and the one that is 6 miles across, one is designated LP4G9MO and the other was discovered by Denise Tibbits.

	8DOQ01P	IB80PLZ	LP4G9MO	MQUYT3Z	SS51MWE	Halberstrom	Millicent	Rogers	Tibbits	Wallingford	March	April	August	November	December
1.5 miles															
3 miles															
6 miles															
12 miles															
24 miles															
March															
April															
August															
November															
December															
Halberstrom															
Millicent															
Rogers															
Tibbits															
Wallingford															

Sizes	Asteroids	Astronomers	Months
1.5 miles			
3 miles			
6 miles			
12 miles			
24 miles			

SOLVE RATE
48.2%

AVERAGE TIME
9 min, 56 sec

BEST TIME
2 min, 9 sec by Vaughns

For the Birds ...

The Belleville Bird-Watching Society meets once a month at the state nature preserve to observe the local bird population. The previous meeting involved fewer people than usual, with only five members attending, each of a different age. What's worse, each member managed to see only one bird during the entire three-hour excursion, and none of the birds were seen by more than one person! Afterward, to get their minds off their nearly empty bird logs, each member stopped by the nature preserve's cafeteria and ordered a different snack. Using only the clues below, determine the age of each member, the bird each saw, and the snack each ordered at the cafeteria.

1. Of Phoenix and Hailey, one is 21 years old and the other ordered potato skins.
2. Cadence is older than the person who ordered chili fries.
3. The 18 year old ordered potato skins but never did see a heron.
4. The bird watcher who ordered the soup of the day didn't see a vulture.
5. The one who saw the blue jay is younger than the person who ate an entire plate full of onion rings.
6. The five people are the bird watcher who saw the condor, Phoenix (who is older than the person who saw the heron), the 18 year old, the one who ordered onion rings, and the one who caught a glimpse of the vulture.
7. The bird watcher who ordered chili fries (who is not Felipe) saw the condor and is either 20 or 21 years old.

		Alesandra	Cadence	Felipe	Hailey	Phoenix	Blue Jay	Condor	Heron	Oriole	Vulture	Buffalo Wings	Chili Fries	Onion Rings	Potato Skins	Soup of the Day
		First Names					**Birds**					**Appetizers**				
Ages	18															
	19															
	20															
	21															
	22															
Appetizers	Buffalo Wings															
	Chili Fries															
	Onion Rings															
	Potato Skins															
	Soup of the Day															
Birds	Blue Jay															
	Condor															
	Heron															
	Oriole															
	Vulture															

SOLVE RATE
48.1%

AVERAGE TIME
12 min, 22 sec

BEST TIME
5 min, 54 sec by smartypants

Ages	First Names	Birds	Appetizers
18			
19			
20			
21			
22			

Pool Heaters

Five pool owners got together at the latest neighborhood barbecue to talk about their pool heaters. Each owned a different pool heater and a different-size pool, and each liked to keep the pool at a different, specific temperature. Using only the clues below, determine the size of each person's pool, the temperature each likes to keep it at, and the brand name of the heater each uses.

1. The homeowner with the largest pool (who isn't Grant) doesn't use the Buford X62.

2. The person with the 18,000 gallon pool (who isn't Levi) doesn't have a Cozy Comfort heater.

3. Between Sawyer and the owner who keeps his or her pool at 81 degrees, one uses an Aquatron heater and the other swears by his Buford X62.

4. The five homeowners are the ones who keep their pools at 81 and 83 degrees, the one with the Buford X62 heater, Grant, and the one with the 18,000 gallon pool.

5. The pool that's heated with the Chlorfree II is kept two degrees warmer than the one heated by the Aquatron.

6. Pablo's 13,000 gallon pool doesn't use an Aquatron heating system.

7. Grant's pool isn't exactly 15,000 gallons.

8. The pool heated by the Cozy Comfort heating system is kept two degrees warmer than the one that uses the Buford X62.

		Homeowners					Heaters					Pool Sizes				
		Cyrus	Grant	Levi	Pablo	Sawyer	Amanus 250	Aquatron	Buford X62	Chlorfree II	Cozy Comfort	10,000 gal.	13,000 gal.	15,000 gal.	18,000 gal.	25,000 gal.
Temperatures	79°F															
	81°F															
	83°F															
	85°F															
	87°F															
Pool Sizes	10,000 gal.															
	13,000 gal.															
	15,000 gal.															
	18,000 gal.															
	25,000 gal.															
Heaters	Amanus 250															
	Aquatron															
	Buford X62															
	Chlorfree II															
	Cozy Comfort															

SOLVE RATE
48.1%

AVERAGE TIME
12 min

BEST TIME
2 min, 25 sec by urielzet

Temperatures	Homeowners	Heaters	Pool Sizes
79°F			
81°F			
83°F			
85°F			
87°F			

Dress Shoes

Dennis was the only sales associate available when five separate customers came in to the Darlington Dress Shoe store, but he did a fine job finding the customers exactly what they needed. Using only the clues below, match each customer to the type of dress shoe he was shopping for and to the size and color each chose.

1. Of the customer who needed a pair of wingtip shoes and the one that ended up buying black shoes, one needed a size 11 and the other was Daven.
2. The person who needed a pair of derby shoes has smaller-size feet than the one who bought the oxfords.
3. The dark brown shoes Dennis sold were one size larger than the loafers Albert purchased.
4. Everett didn't buy white shoes and had no interest in looking at oxfords.
5. The customer with size 9 feet ended up buying a pair of monks.
6. The derbies Dennis sold weren't chestnut in color.
7. Of Philip and the customer who bought the oxfords, one has the largest-size feet and the other chose the chestnut shoes.
8. The customer with the smallest shoe-size wasn't shopping for derbies. The customer who bought the derbies needed a smaller shoe-size than Albert (who didn't buy a pair of monks).

		Customers					Shoe Types					Colors				
		Albert	Daven	Everett	Gustavo	Philip	Derby	Loafer	Monk	Oxford	Wingtip	Black	Burgundy	Chestnut	Dark Brown	White
Shoe Sizes	8															
	9															
	10															
	11															
	12															
Colors	Black															
	Burgundy															
	Chestnut															
	Dark Brown															
	White															
Shoe Types	Derby															
	Loafer															
	Monk															
	Oxford															
	Wingtip															

SOLVE RATE
48.0%

AVERAGE TIME
13 min, 47 sec

BEST TIME
3 min, 10 sec by tormenz

Shoe Sizes	Customers	Shoe Types	Colors
8			
9			
10			
11			
12			

Poker Hands

Five friends (each of whom carried a different good luck charm) each played poker well into the early morning hours. By 2:30 am though, everyone was pretty tired, so the friends decided that this would be their final hand. Using only the clues below, determine each player's final poker hand, each player's good luck charm, and how many chips (in dollars) each had at the end of the final round. Hint: King high is the worst hand and four aces is the best.

1. The five friends were the one who finished with the most chips, the one who had only two eights in the last hand (who didn't finish with $24 or wear sunglasses), Kelsey, the one with the lucky gold coin, and the one who ended with just $39 in chips.
2. The player who wore a lucky ring didn't finish with the fewest chips.
3. Either Uriel or Jack had the worst final hand.
4. Of Jack and the one with the rabbit's foot, one finished with $46 in chips and the other had the best final hand.
5. The player who finished with the most chips had the hand immediately better than the hand held by the player who finished with just $24 in chips.
6. Of Luna and the player who finished with $24 in chips, one wore a lucky hat and the other wore lucky sunglasses.
7. Uriel's final hand was better than the player who finished with the most chips.

		Players					Chips					Luck Charms			
		Giovanni	Jack	Kelsey	Luna	Uriel	$15	$24	$39	$46	$178	Coin	Hat	Rabbit's Foot	Ring	Sunglasses
Final Hands	King High															
	Two Eights															
	Pair Of Nines															
	Three Fours															
	Four Aces															
Luck Charms	Coin															
	Hat															
	Rabbit's Foot															
	Ring															
	Sunglasses															
Chips	$15															
	$24															
	$39															
	$46															
	$178															

SOLVE RATE
47.9%

AVERAGE TIME
14 min, 6 sec

BEST TIME
2 min, 51 sec by kcirderf

Final Hands	Players	Chips	Luck Charms
King High			
Two Eights			
Pair Of Nines			
Three Fours			
Four Aces			

Balancing the Checkbook

Mathilde and Jeremy Newson returned from their whirlwind honeymoon to find a huge pile of wedding-related bills waiting for them in the mailbox. Jeremy wrote and mailed checks for each (using sequentially numbered checks, in order from lowest to highest) but forgot to let Mathilde make a note of them so that they could keep their checkbook balanced. Using only the clues below, help Mathilde make sense of it all by matching each check number to the appropriate amount and payee (and the payee's profession).

1. Check #408 wasn't the $250.00 check, which wasn't made out to Carol Rowe. Jeremy made out Carol's check sometime before the landscaper's check.

2. Of check #408 and the one made out to Bill Johnson, one was for the baker and the other was for $105.56.

3. Jeremy wrote out the check for the wedding singer right before he made out the check for the landscaper (who did a wonderful job setting up the backyard for the outdoor ceremony).

4. Everyone loved the fabulous seven-layer cake the Newsons ordered from Fanny Taylor's bakery (which didn't cost $72.98).

5. Ernest Cowell's check was made out right before Bill Johnson's.

6. The five payees were the plumber, Ernest Cowell, Fanny Taylor, the one who charged the least of all five, and the one who received check #409.

	Bill Johnson	Carol Rowe	Derrick Pile	Ernest Cowell	Fanny Taylor	$56.40	$62.16	$72.98	$105.56	$250.00	Baker	Decorator	Landscaper	Plumber	Singer
406															
407															
408															
409															
410															
Baker															
Decorator															
Landscaper															
Plumber															
Singer															
$56.40															
$62.16															
$72.98															
$105.56															
$250.00															

Check Numbers	Payees	Amounts	Professions
406			
407			
408			
409			
410			

SOLVE RATE
47.7%

AVERAGE TIME
12 min, 18 sec

BEST TIME
3 min, 18 sec by russellduagn

Mountaineers

The local mountaineering club invited five famous women climbers to speak at its latest meeting. Each was the first woman to climb a different mountain, and each was from a different state. Using only the clues below, determine which mountain each woman was the first to climb, how tall it was, and what state each speaker is from.

1. Of Cali and the one who first climbed the 21,750 foot mountain, one is from New Hampshire and the other is from Wyoming.
2. Neither Mount Timsickle (which is 500 feet taller than Mount Dharma) nor the mountain that Cali first climbed is the shortest of the five.
3. The New Hampshire native wasn't the first woman to scale the tallest of the five mountains.
4. Neither the New Hampshire climber nor the Alabama climber has ever ascended Mount Coffin.
5. The mountain Daynara climbed is 500 feet taller than the one Lilly was first to scale. Daynara isn't from Michigan.
6. The mountaineer from Alabama has never climbed Mount Miniver (though it's next on her list).
7. Lilly's mountain is taller than the one scaled by the California climber, who isn't Cory.
8. Of the climber who scaled the shortest of the five mountains and the one from Wyoming, one was Lilly and the other climbed Mount Dharma.

		Cali	Cory	Daynara	Katherine	Lilly	Alabama	California	Michigan	New Hampshire	Wyoming	Mt Alaska	Mt Coffin	Mt Dharma	Mt Miniver	Mt Timsickle
Heights	21,250 feet															
	21,750 feet															
	22,250 feet															
	22,750 feet															
	23,250 feet															
Mountains	Mt Alaska															
	Mt Coffin															
	Mt Dharma															
	Mt Miniver															
	Mt Timsickle															
States	Alabama															
	California															
	Michigan															
	New Hampshire															
	Wyoming															

SOLVE RATE
47.7%

AVERAGE TIME
11 min, 56 sec

BEST TIME
3 min, 39 sec by maxcat1220

Heights	Climbers	States	Mountains
21,250 feet			
21,750 feet			
22,250 feet			
22,750 feet			
23,250 feet			

Comic Books

Esther and four of her friends visited The Little Shop of Comics, where each bought a rare first edition of a different old comic book. Using only the clues below, figure out which comic each person bought, how much each paid for it, and what year each first edition was published.

1. Neither Esther nor Jamie bought the comic book published in 1963.
2. The five comic books are *Dinodramas* (which wasn't published in 1978), the one Ralph bought, *Terror Eyes,* the least-expensive one, and the oldest one.
3. *Li'l Legends* wasn't the most expensive comic book.
4. The five people are Ralph, the one who paid $65 for the comic (which was published in 1972), the one who bought *Lia Luxor* (which was published in 1963), and the two whose comic books were published in 1945 and 1978.
5. Esther didn't spend $49 for her comic book.
6. Catherine bought her favorite comic book *Magnet Man.*
7. Neither *Terror Eyes* nor the most expensive comic book was bought by Jamie.

		Customers					Years					Prices				
		Catherine	Esther	Jamie	Kendra	Ralph	1945	1963	1972	1978	1983	$25	$49	$65	$79	$99
Comic Books	Dinodramas															
	Lia Luxor															
	Li'l Legends															
	Magnet Man															
	Terror Eyes															
Prices	$25															
	$49															
	$65															
	$79															
	$99															
Years	1945															
	1963															
	1972															
	1978															
	1983															

SOLVE RATE
47.7%
AVERAGE TIME
12 min, 30 sec
BEST TIME
2 min, 12 sec by khead

Comic Books	Customers	Years	Prices
Dinodramas			
Lia Luxor			
Li'l Legends			
Magnet Man			
Terror Eyes			

Bowling Night

Felipe and four of his friends went bowling last weekend. Unfortunately, an emergency came up at his friend Wendy's house, and they could only get in one game before they had to leave. Using only the clues below, figure out the final score each of the five players earned during the game and the color and weight of the bowling ball each player used.

1. The five bowlers are Wendy (who didn't use the 14-pound ball), Mariana, the one who used the black ball, the one who got the lowest score (and whose ball weighed 13 pounds), and the one who used the lightest ball.
2. Wendy's score was higher than the person who used the black ball.
3. The player who used the blue ball scored 105.
4. The pink bowling ball wasn't the heaviest of the five.
5. Between the person who bowled the best game and Mitchell (who didn't get the lowest score), one used the heaviest ball and the other person used the green ball (but didn't score 124 points).
6. Gary's ball didn't weigh 13 pounds.
7. The 12-pound ball was blue.

Scores	Bowlers	Weights	Colors
92			
105			
124			
163			
202			

Tallest Trees

The Forestry Department just released an updated list of the five tallest trees in Oregon—each of which has its own individual name and is a different species of tree. Using only the clues below, figure out the height and name of each tree, what kind of tree it is, and where it is located.

1. The five trees are the two that are 279 and 285 feet tall, the Douglas fir, Hannah (which isn't in Monessen or Exeter), and the one in Kulpsville (which isn't named Lillith).
2. Mellifont (which isn't a coast redwood) grows deep in the woods in Donora.
3. The coast redwood is six feet shorter than the sequoia.
4. The record-holding tree in Monessen isn't a Douglas fir.
5. The Douglas fir is six feet shorter than the Sitka Spruce.
6. The tree in Catasauqua is taller than Aldrich.
7. Between San Pejedro and the tree that's 279 feet tall, one is a coast redwood, and the other is a Douglas fir.

	Tree Names					Tree Types					Locations				
	Aldrich	Hannah	Lillith	Mellifont	San Pejedro	Bald Cypress	Coast Redwood	Douglas Fir	Sequoia	Sitka Spruce	Catasauqua	Donora	Exeter	Kulpsville	Monessen
273 feet															
279 feet															
285 feet															
291 feet															
297 feet															
Catasauqua															
Donora															
Exeter															
Kulpsville															
Monessen															
Bald Cypress															
Coast Redwood															
Douglas Fir															
Sequoia															
Sitka Spruce															

SOLVE RATE 47.4%

AVERAGE TIME 12 min, 50 sec

BEST TIME 3 min, 44 sec by Vaughns

Heights	Tree Names	Tree Types	Locations
273 feet			
279 feet			
285 feet			
291 feet			
297 feet			

Comedy Night

The Giggle Room holds open-mic comedy nights every first Thursday of the month, with five open time-slots of 30 minutes apiece. Tonight every slot was taken up by a different comedian, each of whom hailed from a different city. Each routine covered a specific topic, all of them different. Using only the clues below, determine the time slot for each comedian, the theme of each performance, and the city where each comedian lives.

1. The five comedians were the ones who had the 8:30 pm and 9:00 pm time slots, the one who did a routine about the food and restaurant business, Harmony, and the comedian from St. Louis.
2. Of Nolan and the comedian who cracked jokes about food and restaurants (who wasn't from Omaha), one went up at 8:30 pm and the other had the last time slot of the night.
3. The Chicago native had the 9:30 pm time slot.
4. Harmony performed sometime before Daniel (who wasn't from New York).
5. Juan did a hilarious routine about life in an office cubicle right after the comedian who joked about the ups and downs of parenting.
6. Nolan isn't from New York.
7. The first comedian to perform didn't have a routine about relationships.

SOLVE RATE
47.3%

AVERAGE TIME
14 min, 36 sec

BEST TIME
2 min, 16 sec by khead

Eco-Friendly Employees

Earthcore Industries prides itself on being a green company, and its employees have recently been encouraged to use alternative forms of transportation to get to work each morning. On the first morning after the announcement, five employees accepted the challenge. Each of the five employees works on a different floor of the building, and each used a different form of green conveyance to get to the office. None of them arrived at the same time (although none of them were late for the 9 am opening). Using only the clues below, determine the conveyance used by each employee, the floor the employee works on, and the time each employee arrived at the office.

1. The employee who works on the 1st floor arrived sometime after the commuter who rode the mountain bike (who wasn't Joe).

2. The five individuals are the employee who works on the 4th floor (who isn't Joe), the person who arrived at 8:46 am, the person who arrived at 8:58 am, Sasha (who arrived at 8:52 am), and the commuter who rode the Segway.

3. Nathaniel didn't arrive at 8:34 am.

4. Between Dulce (who didn't ride the scooter to work) and the person who arrived at 8:40 am, one works on the 2nd floor and the other works on the 5th floor of Earthcore Industries.

5. Between the commuter who rode the 10-speed bike and the person who arrived on 8:58 am, one works on the 2nd floor and the other works on the 4th floor.

		Employees					Floors					Conveyances				
		Ariel	Dulce	Joe	Nathanael	Sasha	1st floor	2nd floor	3rd floor	4th floor	5th floor	10-Speed Bike	Mountain Bike	Scooter	Segway	Skateboard
Arrival Times	8:34 am															
	8:40 am															
	8:46 am															
	8:52 am															
	8:58 am															
Conveyances	10-Speed Bike															
	Mountain Bike															
	Scooter															
	Segway															
	Skateboard															
Floors	1st floor															
	2nd floor															
	3rd floor															
	4th floor															
	5th floor															

SOLVE RATE
47.2%

AVERAGE TIME
12 min, 15 sec

BEST TIME
1 min, 48 sec by Kazemizu

Arrival Times	Employees	Floors	Conveyances
8:34 am			
8:40 am			
8:46 am			
8:52 am			
8:58 am			

For the Dogs ...

Tabitha's dog training service was going well, but there were five "students" this year who were having difficulty learning certain commands. Each of these five puppies is of a different breed, and each had trouble learning a different command. Of course, they all eventually learned their commands, thanks to Tabitha's team of training professionals, though it took some longer than others. As a result, each of the five puppies earned its doggie diploma on a different day. Using only the clues below, determine the breed and graduation day of each puppy and the command with which each had the most difficulty.

1. Of Diva and the border collie, one graduated on September 5 and the other had the hardest time learning the "Speak" command.

2. The Pomeranian had no trouble whatsoever learning how to roll over.

3. The border collie graduated sometime before Theo, who graduated sometime before the Maltese.

4. The Pomeranian graduated sometime after the puppy who, for the longest time, couldn't learn the command "Sit."

5. The five puppies were Sadie (whose most difficult command was "Roll Over"), the one who graduated on November 17, Marmot, the dachshund, and the one who had difficulty mastering the "Stay" command.

6. Diva was either the Chihuahua (who graduated on September 5) or the dachshund.

		Diva	Kenzie	Marmot	Sadie	Theo	Border Collie	Chihuahua	Dachshund	Maltese	Pomeranian	Come	Roll Over	Speak	Sit	Stay
		Names					**Breeds**					**Commands**				
Birthdays	May 17															
	August 7															
	September 5															
	September 22															
	November 17															
Commands	Come															
	Roll Over															
	Speak															
	Sit															
	Stay															
Breeds	Border Collie															
	Chihuahua															
	Dachshund															
	Maltese															
	Pomeranian															

SOLVE RATE
44.8%

AVERAGE TIME
13 min, 12 sec

BEST TIME
3 min, 35 sec by The James

Birthdays	Names	Breeds	Commands
May 17			
August 7			
September 5			
September 22			
November 17			

Some Heavy Lifting ...

The final round of the Nordic weight-lifting championships proved to be an exciting competition, with five contestants, each representing a different country, each performing admirably. Using only the clues below, determine the coach and country associated with each weight lifter and the amount of weight each was able to lift in the final round.

1. Pavel didn't finish with a lift of 166 pounds.
2. Of Titus and the one who lifted 164 pounds, one had Coach Kinski as a trainer and the other represented Finland.
3. Lee wasn't the Danish competitor, who didn't lift exactly 162 pounds in the final round.
4. The one who lifted the most didn't have Grigory Padoll as his coach.
5. The Swedish competitor had either Coach Mitka or Coach Padoll.
6. The five contestants are Magnus, the person who lifted 162 pounds, Pavel, the one from Iceland (who lifted two pounds more than Pavel), and the one who had Coach Ervatz.
7. Coach Herzog's weight lifter was able to lift two pounds more than Coach Ervatz's.
8. Of the person who lifted the least amount of weight in the final round and Jakku, one was from Iceland and the other had Coach Kinski.

	Competitors					Countries					Coaches				
	Jakku	Lee	Magnus	Pavel	Titus	Denmark	Finland	Iceland	Norway	Sweden	Coach Ervatz	Coach Kinski	Coach Herzog	Coach Mitka	Coach Padoll
162 lb.															
164 lb.															
166 lb.															
168 lb.															
170 lb.															
Coach Ervatz															
Coach Kinski															
Coach Herzog															
Coach Mitka															
Coach Padoll															
Denmark															
Finland															
Iceland															
Norway															
Sweden															

SOLVE RATE
47.1%

AVERAGE TIME
16 min, 23 sec

BEST TIME
3 min, 19 sec by redsox29

Weights	Competitors	Countries	Coaches
162 lb.			
164 lb.			
166 lb.			
168 lb.			
170 lb.			

At the Salon

There must be a big event going on in town tonight, because there was a line extending right around the corner at Sally's Salon this morning, full of customers waiting to get their hair styled. Using only the clues below, determine the order in which the first five customers were seated, the hair color of each, and the stylists who served each customer.

1. Tiffany's client, who wasn't Callie, wasn't served fourth.
2. The black-haired woman was seated sometime after the one with long, silver hair.
3. Of Tiffany's customer and the one who was served third, one was Callie and the other has red, curly hair.
4. Helga's customer doesn't have brown hair and wasn't served fifth.
5. Vonda's customer was seated just before Tiffany's.
6. The customer who had Sharon as a stylist was seated right before Patty.
7. The five customers are Patty, the person who was seated fifth (who wasn't Brianna), Tiffany's client, the blonde, and Anna.
8. Jackie's client doesn't have brown hair.

		Customers					Hair Colors					Stylists				
		Anna	Brianna	Callie	Gloria	Patty	Black	Blonde	Brown	Red	Silver	Helga	Jackie	Sharon	Tiffany	Vonda
Orders	First															
	Second															
	Third															
	Fourth															
	Fifth															
Stylists	Helga															
	Jackie															
	Sharon															
	Tiffany															
	Vonda															
Hair Colors	Black															
	Blonde															
	Brown															
	Red															
	Silver															

SOLVE RATE
46.9%

AVERAGE TIME
14 min, 47 sec

BEST TIME
2 min, 30 sec by khead

Orders	Customers	Hair Colors	Stylists
First			
Second			
Third			
Fourth			
Fifth			

High IQs

Quinca, a national high-IQ society, regularly holds IQ exams for potential members looking to join the club. Today, it held a small exam for five people in Gladwin. Using only the clues below, determine the name and age of each test taker, each person's profession, and each person's final IQ score.

1. The five test takers are the ones who scored 160 and 168, Bryan, the 31 year old, and the artist.
2. Of the artist and the oldest of the five, one is Skyler and the other scored 164 on the IQ exam.
3. Esther isn't the writer (who isn't 31 years old).
4. Neither the writer nor the person who scored 164 (who isn't the artist) is 45 years old.
5. The person who scored highest on the IQ test is younger than 35.
6. The 38 year old scored four points higher on the exam than the professor.
7. The youngest of the five scored lower than Ramon.
8. The physicist also scored lower on the IQ exam than Ramon.
9. The writer didn't get the second-highest score.

		Test Takers					Ages					Professions				
		Andy	Bryan	Esther	Ramon	Skyler	23	31	38	45	57	Artist	Astronomer	Physicist	Professor	Writer
IQ Results	156															
	160															
	164															
	168															
	172															
Professions	Artist															
	Astronomer															
	Physicist															
	Professor															
	Writer															
Ages	23															
	31															
	38															
	45															
	57															

IQ Results	Test Takers	Ages	Professions
156			
160			
164			
168			
172			

SOLVE RATE
46.8%

AVERAGE TIME
13 min, 57 sec

BEST TIME
4 min, 9 sec by khead

Driest Deserts

Meteorologists recently released an updated list of the 50 driest places on Earth (the places with the smallest amount of average yearly rainfall). Five little-known deserts were added to this list for the first time, thanks to some groundbreaking fieldwork in recent years. Using only the clues below, figure out the area (in square miles) of each desert, the average yearly rainfall (in inches) of each desert, and the country in which it is located.

1. The five new deserts are the one with the least average yearly rainfall (which doesn't cover exactly 609,000 square miles), the one in Mexico, Darukapa Desert, the second-largest desert (which isn't the Li-Licapite Desert, and isn't in Mali), and the second-smallest desert.
2. The Li-Licapite Desert receives less average rainfall than the Fumarote Desert.
3. The desert in Mali doesn't receive only 1.2 inches of rain each year.
4. Of the Eritrean desert and the one that receives the most rainfall (which isn't Fumarote Desert), one is Li-Licapite Desert and the other is the largest of the five.
5. The five new deserts are the Mexican Desert, the one that spans 609,000 square miles, the Tenexalub Desert, the one that receives 1.7 inches of rain each year (which isn't in China), and the one that gets only 1.5 inches of average yearly rainfall.

	Deserts					Countries					Areas				
	Darukapa	Fumarote	Li-Licapite	Pocamo	Tenexalub	China	Eritrea	Mali	Mexico	Peru	300,000 sq mi	445,000 sq mi	609,000 sq mi	756,000 sq mi	883,000 sq mi
Av. Rainfalls 1.1 inches															
1.2 inches															
1.5 inches															
1.7 inches															
2.3 inches															
Areas 300,000 sq mi															
445,000 sq mi															
609,000 sq mi															
756,000 sq mi															
883,000 sq mi															
Countries China															
Eritrea															
Mali															
Mexico															
Peru															

SOLVE RATE
46.7%

AVERAGE TIME
11 min, 41 sec

BEST TIME
2 min, 7 sec by Kazemizu

Av. Rainfalls	Deserts	Countries	Areas
1.1 inches			
1.2 inches			
1.5 inches			
1.7 inches			
2.3 inches			

Light Testers

The research and development department of Illumination Nation, a lightbulb manufacturer, constantly subjects its own products to rigorous testing. This month, five testers each examined a different wattage bulb in a different type of light fixture to see how long each bulb remained illuminated before it burned out. Using only the clues below, match each bulb to the light fixture it was tested on, who ran the test, and how long each bulb ultimately lasted.

1. The five bulbs are the one that lasted 192 hours (which wasn't in Priscilla's test), a 60-watt and a 100-watt bulb, the one Russell tested (which was 75 watts), and the one that was tested in the track light.
2. The bulb in the desk lamp (which wasn't tested by Priscilla) was of a lower wattage than the one that burned out the quickest.
3. Of the bulb Nicholas tested and the 40-watt bulb, one lasted the longest and the other lasted 139 hours.
4. Of the highest-wattage bulb and the one tested in the ceiling fan, one lasted 139 hours and the other lasted 192 hours.
5. Nicholas didn't perform his test with an outdoor lamp.
6. Roman didn't test the 25-watt bulb.

SOLVE RATE
46.6%

AVERAGE TIME
11 min, 58 sec

BEST TIME
2 min, 16 sec by khead

Bulb Wattage	Tester	Hours	Fixtures
25 W			
40 W			
60 W			
75 W			
100 W			

Rainy Days

Williwaw County is recognized as the rainiest county in the United States, with five of its towns holding daily rainfall records of 18 or more inches! Using only the clues below, determine the daily rainfall record for each town and the day and year it was recorded.

1. The five towns are Astera, the towns with the 19- and 20-inch rainfall records, the one that set its record in 1972, and the one that had the most daily rainfall in February.
2. Either Haylow's record or the one set in 1972 was the largest of the five.
3. The record set in Blue Hills was 20 inches of rain in a single day.
4. The 1933 record (which wasn't set in July) was one inch higher than the one set in 1914 (which wasn't set in March).
5. Quillayute's record was one inch higher than the one recorded in 1988.
6. The biggest daily rainfall record wasn't set in March.
7. Neither the 1933 record nor the one set in Tallyhon (which wasn't 19 inches) was the smallest of the five.
8. Of Quillayute's record and the one set in July, one was 20 inches of rain in a single day and the other was set in 1972 (but not in November).

SOLVE RATE 46.4%

AVERAGE TIME 12 min, 37 sec

BEST TIME 3 min, 2 sec by Derek

Two Tickets to Paradise

The Fraylington Women's Book Club recently read the best-selling travel book *Finding Paradise in Islands* as its March selection, and as a result, five members decided to take their husbands on spur-of-the-moment holidays, each to a different island destination. Each couple left on a different day. Using only the clues below, match each wife to her husband and determine the couple's destination and departure date.

1. The couple that left for Grenada left the day before the couple that went to Saint Kitts.
2. Mia and her husband Emeril didn't go to Barbuda.
3. The book club member who decided to whisk her husband off to Barbuda (who wasn't Mia) left the day before the couple who went to Martinique.
4. Bryanna isn't married to Franklin or Hubert.
5. Dexter and his wife left for their island paradise sometime after Bethany and her husband.
6. The five couples were the one that left on March 21, the one that went to the island of Grenada, Bryanna and her husband, George and his wife (who wasn't Johanna), and the couple who left on March 20.
7. Hubert and his wife didn't go to Grenada.
8. Between Nayeli and the woman who left on March 20, one went to Barbuda and the other to Grenada.

		Wives					Islands					Husbands			
		Bethany	Bryanna	Johanna	Mia	Nayeli	Aruba	Barbuda	Grenada	Martinique	Saint Kitts	Dexter	Emeril	Franklin	George	Hubert
Days	March 19															
	March 20															
	March 21															
	March 22															
	March 23															
Husbands	Dexter															
	Emeril															
	Franklin															
	George															
	Hubert															
Islands	Aruba															
	Barbuda															
	Grenada															
	Martinique															
	Saint Kitts															

Days	Wives	Islands	Husbands
March 19			
March 20			
March 21			
March 22			
March 23			

SOLVE RATE
46.3%

AVERAGE TIME
10 min, 20 sec

BEST TIME
3 min by haley

Dance Lessons

The Tappy Toes dance studio offers a different type of dance class each weeknight. Each class is scheduled to start at a different time, and each has its own unique instructor. Using only the clues below, try to piece together the weekly class schedule.

1. The five classes are Thursday's class, Friday's class, the waltz class, the one that starts at 7:30 pm, and Taylor's class.
2. Kelvin (who doesn't teach Friday's class) doesn't know the rumba.
3. The cha-cha class is held earlier in the week than the one that starts at 8:00 pm.
4. The class with the latest start time (which isn't taught by Janiya) is held earlier in the week than the class with the earliest start time (which isn't the rumba class).
5. Of Kaitlyn's class and the one that begins at 7:00 pm, one class teaches the mambo and the other is held on Wednesday.
6. Of Monday's class and the waltz class, one is held at 7:00 pm and the other at 8:00 pm.

		Instructors					Dances					Class Times				
		Janiya	Kaitlyn	Kelvin	Ricky	Taylor	Cha-Cha	Foxtrot	Mambo	Rumba	Waltz	6:30 pm	7:00 pm	7:30 pm	8:00 pm	8:30 pm
Days	Monday															
	Tuesday															
	Wednesday															
	Thursday															
	Friday															
Class Times	6:30 pm															
	7:00 pm															
	7:30 pm															
	8:00 pm															
	8:30 pm															
Dances	Cha-Cha															
	Foxtrot															
	Mambo															
	Rumba															
	Waltz															

SOLVE RATE
46.3%

AVERAGE TIME
15 min, 27 sec

BEST TIME
2 min, 58 sec by Vaughns

Days	Instructors	Dances	Class Times
Monday			
Tuesday			
Wednesday			
Thursday			
Friday			

New Species

Malcolm Meniford was a world-renowned biologist and explorer who discovered dozens of new animal species in South America during his career. He was known to have named each new species he discovered after someone he knew and respected—friends, family, co-workers, and so on. Using only the clues below, determine the name of each of his last five discoveries, what type of animal it was, the year it was discovered, and the country in which it was discovered.

1. The five new species are the monkey (which was Malcolm's final discovery), the one discovered in 1970, the frog, *drewsilia* (which wasn't the turtle), and the one discovered in Paraguay.
2. Malcolm's new bee discovery wasn't made in 1969.
3. Neither the rodent nor the animal discovered in Uruguay was named *elijahphicus*.
4. *Randolphia* was discovered the year before *elijahphicus*.
5. Malcolm's new monkey species wasn't found in Suriname.
6. The earliest of the five discoveries wasn't made in Uruguay.
7. Of the turtle species and *horacinia*, one was discovered in 1969 and the other was found in Guyana.
8. Malcolm discovered his turtle the year before he found the new frog species.
9. *Randolphia* wasn't discovered in 1970.

	Species Names					Animals					Countries				
	Calvinicus	Drewsilia	Elijahphicus	Horacinia	Randolphia	Bee	Frog	Monkey	Rodent	Turtle	Bolivia	Guyana	Paraguay	Suriname	Uruguay
Years 1968															
1969															
1970															
1971															
1972															
Countries Bolivia															
Guyana															
Paraguay															
Suriname															
Uruguay															
Animals Bee															
Frog															
Monkey															
Rodent															
Turtle															

SOLVE RATE
46.3%

AVERAGE TIME
17 min, 54 sec

BEST TIME
2 min, 59 sec by khead

Years	Species Names	Animals	Countries
1968			
1969			
1970			
1971			
1972			

Lumberjack Games

The twenty-second annual Lumberjack Games were a great success. More than 175 people competed across five different contests, but only the top five total scorers were awarded trophies. Each of the top-five winners was assigned a different competition number, and each came in first place in a different contest. Using only the clues below, determine the names and numbers of each of the top-five competitors and which contests each won.

1. The top-five winners are the ones who finished third and fourth overall, the one who won the single buck competition, Kyle (who wasn't assigned the lowest number), and #98.

2. Of Sydney and the competitor who finished fifth, one emerged victorious in the block chop and the other won the hot saw competition.

3. Victor didn't win the logroll.

4. When all the points were tallied, the speed climb winner finished just before the competitor who won the hot saw contest.

5. The block chop winner finished in a lower place than #90 (who wasn't Victor and didn't win the hot saw contest).

6. Neither the person who finished fifth nor #90 was Cameron.

7. #154 (who didn't come in third place) finished just after #98 at the end of the games.

	Cameron	Howard	Kyle	Sydney	Victor	Block Chop	Hot Saw	Logroll	Single Buck	Speed Climb	#36	#90	#98	#121	#154
First															
Second															
Third															
Fourth															
Fifth															
#36															
#90															
#98															
#121															
#154															
Block Chop															
Hot Saw															
Logroll															
Single Buck															
Speed Climb															

SOLVE RATE
46.2%

AVERAGE TIME
17 min, 58 sec

BEST TIME
3 min, 29 sec by Kazemizu

Finishes	Competitors	Competitions	Numbers
First			
Second			
Third			
Fourth			
Fifth			

Musical Tryouts

The state symphony orchestra held open tryouts this week for dozens of musicians around the world, but it was the Eastern Europeans in particular who most wowed the audience. Five were selected as new members; each musician is from a different country and each played a different instrument. Using only the clues below, match the instrument and country to each musician, and determine the order in which each performed.

1. The five musicians were Sebastian (who wasn't Polish), the Ukrainian, the one who played the French horn, Brennan, and the musician who played fourth.
2. Taylor isn't from Poland.
3. Either the musician who performed first or the one from Moldova was Sebastian, who played the guitar.
4. Brennan, who isn't Polish, performed sometime after the Romanian (who didn't perform fourth) and sometime after the Bulgarian.
5. The pianist didn't perform fourth.
6. The musician who played the viola performed right before the one who played the French horn.
7. Kayleigh is the Romanian musician.

		Musicians					Instruments					Countries				
		Brennan	Giovanni	Kayleigh	Sebastian	Taylor	Cello	French Horn	Guitar	Piano	Viola	Bulgaria	Moldova	Poland	Romania	Ukraine
Orders	First															
	Second															
	Third															
	Fourth															
	Fifth															
Countries	Bulgaria															
	Moldova															
	Poland															
	Romania															
	Ukraine															
Instruments	Cello															
	French Horn															
	Guitar															
	Piano															
	Viola															

SOLVE RATE
46%

AVERAGE TIME
13 min, 26 sec

BEST TIME
4 min, 23 sec by CherylRwfm

Orders	Musicians	Instruments	Countries
First			
Second			
Third			
Fourth			
Fifth			

Skyscraper Dreams

The allure of designing the tallest skyscraper in the world has driven five cutting-edge architects to develop plans for their own 3,000+ foot buildings. Each building is a different height and has a different number of stories, and each design has been purchased by developers in a different country. Using only the clues below, determine the height and number of stories in each architect's design and the country in which it will eventually be developed.

1. The 3,105-foot tall building will have 124 stories.
2. Of the design purchased for development in the United States and the building that will have 122 stories, one was designed by Delilah DeSouza and the other by Boris Bellachoz.
3. Neither Einrich Eisenberg's design nor the design with the fewest number of stories will be built in Japan. Allen Ainsworth's design won't be built in India.
4. Eisenberg's building is going to be 45 feet taller than Celine Cuniford's design.
5. The design that will be developed in Malaysia won't be 3,150 feet tall and won't have exactly 122 stories.
6. The tallest building won't have the fewest number of stories.
7. The design purchased for development in Japan will be 45 feet shorter than Eisenberg's building.
8. Of DeSouza's skyscraper and the one with the most stories, one will be the shortest of the five and the other will be built in India.
9. The 3,060 foot building will have either 114 or 119 stories.
10. The DeSouza building will not be constructed in the United States.

		Architects					Stories					Countries				
		Ainsworth	Bellachoz	Cuniford	DeSouza	Eisenberg	114 stories	116 stories	119 stories	122 stories	124 stories	China	India	Japan	Malaysia	United States
Heights	3,015 feet															
	3,060 feet															
	3,105 feet															
	3,150 feet															
	3,195 feet															
Countries	China															
	India															
	Japan															
	Malaysia															
	United States															
Stories	114 stories															
	116 stories															
	119 stories															
	122 stories															
	124 stories															

Heights	Architects	Stories	Countries
3,015 feet			
3,060 feet			
3,105 feet			
3,150 feet			
3,195 feet			

Bike-a-Thon

Jason and four friends volunteered in the annual Save the Kelp bike-a-thon. Each raised a certain amount of money pledged by sponsors and supporters, and each biked a different distance during the event. Using only the clues below, figure out how much each biker raised, how far each went, and what type of bicycle each rode in the event.

1. The five bicyclists are Layla, Dana (who didn't raise $295 for the event), the one who rode the Zelok 5, the one who bicycled 28 miles, and the one who raised $250 in pledges (and rode the Trak T450).

2. Either Isaiah or the one who rode the Rollins II bicycle went a total of 28 miles.

3. The bicyclist who rode the Rollins II (who didn't raise $295 in pledges) rode three miles farther than the bicyclist on the Actron ZX.

4. The bicyclist who raised $250 in pledges rode three miles farther than Layla.

5. The one who rode for 31 miles wasn't Dana and didn't raise $375. The bicyclist who did raise $375 didn't ride as far as Dana.

6. The bicyclist on the Cobra X50 didn't ride for as many miles as the one who rode the Zelok 5.

7. Of Bailey and the cyclist who rode the Actron ZX, one racked up a total of 28 miles and the other raised $250 in pledges.

8. Dana didn't raise the most money in pledges.

		Bailey	Dana	Isaiah	Jason	Layla	$250	$295	$320	$375	$425	Actron ZX	Cobra X50	Rollins II	Trak T450	Zelok 5
Distances	28 miles															
	31 miles															
	34 miles															
	37 miles															
	40 miles															
Bicycles	Actron ZX															
	Cobra X50															
	Rollins II															
	Trak T450															
	Zelok 5															
Pledges	$250															
	$295															
	$320															
	$375															
	$425															

SOLVE RATE
46.0%

AVERAGE TIME
12 min, 3 sec

BEST TIME
3 min, 36 sec by jade_3031

Distances	Bikers	Pledges	Bicycles
28 miles			
31 miles			
34 miles			
37 miles			
40 miles			

Lost in Translation

Five celebrated linguists have converged on an archaeological excavation in Manakea, eager to decipher an inscription on a pottery shard that had recently been unearthed. Unfortunately, none of the experts can agree! Each believes the inscription came from a different extinct language, and each is absolutely certain it means something different. Using only the clues below, determine the order in which each linguist examined the artifact, and the linguist's interpretation of the meaning and language of the inscription.

1. The linguist who believes the inscription means "spear" examined the artifact sometime before Riley (who doesn't believe the inscription refers to someone's "mother").

2. Of the linguist who translated the inscription as "spear" (who wasn't Collin) and the one who examined the artifact third, one is Seth and the other believes it to be in the Siclamian language.

3. Of Riley and the one who suggested it was a Siclamian inscription, one examined the artifact fourth and the other concluded it refers to a "spear."

4. The Gestapian proponent (who wasn't the last to see the pottery shard) examined the artifact immediately after the one who is pushing the Liburnian theory. Jordan translated the inscription to mean either "sun" or "horse."

5. The linguist who was the first to examine the pottery shard believes the inscription means "mountain."

6. The first linguist to examine the artifact didn't push the Raythean theory.

7. The linguist who insists the inscription referred to a "horse" does not believe it was written in the Raythean language.

		Linguists					Languages					Translations				
		Alyssa	Collin	Jordan	Riley	Seth	Liburnian	Gestapian	Oskian	Raythean	Siclamian	Horse	Mother	Mountain	Spear	Sun
Orders	First															
	Second															
	Third															
	Fourth															
	Fifth															
Translations	Horse															
	Mother															
	Mountain															
	Spear															
	Sun															
Languages	Liburnian															
	Gestapian															
	Oskian															
	Raythean															
	Siclamian															

SOLVE RATE
45.9%

AVERAGE TIME
12 min, 55 sec

BEST TIME
3 min, 43 sec by urielzet

Orders	Linguists	Languages	Translations
First			
Second			
Third			
Fourth			
Fifth			

One Romantic Night

It was a busy evening at Chez Pierre, which allows only five reservations a night in order to ensure that each table gets top-notch service. On this particular night, purely by chance, each of the five available reservation slots was booked months in advance by five different men, each of whom planned to use this romantic occasion to offer a ring to his sweetheart. Each man bought a ring made of a different precious metal, and each ring had a different type of gemstone set inside. Using only the clues below, determine the reservation time, precious metal, and gemstone associated with each of the five men.

1. Dirk made an earlier reservation than the man who bought the amethyst ring, who had an earlier reservation than Eli.

2. Brad made the earliest reservation so he could make it back home in time for the football game.

3. The person who bought the white gold ring had an earlier reservation than the person with the silver ring.

4. The five people were Chet (who didn't buy the sapphire), the person with the titanium ring, the one who bought the ruby stone, the man with the 6:30 pm reservation, and Adam.

5. The man who bought the yellow gold ring (which didn't have a ruby set in it) made an 8:00 pm reservation. Adam didn't make a reservation for 8:30 pm.

6. The man with the emerald ring made an early reservation before 6:45 pm.

7. Of Dirk and the one with the white gold ring, one bought the diamond and the other bought the amethyst.

	First Names					Metals					Stones				
	Adam	Brad	Chet	Dirk	Eli	Platinum	Silver	Titanium	White Gold	Yellow Gold	Sapphire	Diamond	Amethyst	Ruby	Emerald
6:00 pm															
6:30 pm															
7:00 pm															
8:00 pm															
8:30 pm															
Sapphire															
Diamond															
Amethyst															
Ruby															
Emerald															
Platinum															
Silver															
Titanium															
White Gold															
Yellow Gold															

SOLVE RATE
45.7%

AVERAGE TIME
8 min, 47 sec

BEST TIME
3 min, 6 sec by LSupergirl

Reservations	First Names	Metals	Stones
6:00 pm			
6:30 pm			
7:00 pm			
8:00 pm			
8:30 pm			

The Numismatist

Nate's been a numismatist (or coin collector) for most of his life, and this week he had the opportunity to showcase five of his rarest coins at a New York trade show. He chose five coins for his exhibit, each minted in different years and different countries. Using only the clues below, determine the year and country of origin of each coin, the condition (poor is the worst condition, very fine is the best), and the price tag Nate affixed to each.

1. Nate's five coins are the two in the best and worst condition, the coin minted in 1836, the English coin (which isn't priced at $125), and the one he's selling for the lowest price.

2. The coin in poor condition was minted sometime after the coin that's priced at $90 (which isn't French).

3. The five coins on display are the one in fine condition (which isn't French), the two minted in 1836 and 1862, the Spanish coin (minted in 1858), and the one priced at $160.

4. Of the English coin and the 1815 coin, one is in fair condition and the other one is graded very fine.

5. The oldest coin isn't Italian.

	Dutch	English	French	Italian	Spanish	Poor	Fair	Good	Fine	Very Fine	$85	$90	$125	$160	$239
1789															
1815															
1836															
1858															
1862															
$85															
$90															
$125															
$160															
$239															
Poor															
Fair															
Good															
Fine															
Very Fine															

Years	Origins	Conditions	Prices
1789			
1815			
1836			
1858			
1862			

SOLVE RATE
45.6%

AVERAGE TIME
10 min, 25 sec

BEST TIME
3 min, 3 sec by Vaughns

Mesa Peoples

There are five distinct peoples currently known to have inhabited Mesa Corlando between roughly 240 and 840 AD. An exhibition was held at the mesa last week, at which five experts (each an expert in one of the five peoples of Mesa Corlando) gave short presentations on what they believe life was like for the people of these civilizations. Using only the clues below, match each expert to the people each studies, the time period during which the studied people inhabited the mesa, and the rough estimate of the maximum population size of each civilization.

1. The five experts are Cassandra, the one who studies the Pachape, Christopher, the one who studies the civilization that peaked at a population of 50,000, and the expert on the people who inhabited the mesa from 600 to 720 AD.

2. The Cochupta weren't the last civilization to inhabit Mesa Corlando.

3. The civilization that numbered 15,000 at its peak is studied by either Lionel or Christopher. The people Kevin studies numbered 25,000 at their zenith.

4. Of the Minapiato and the people Christopher studies (who didn't have a maximum population higher than 60,000), one had a maximum population of 15,000 and the other was the last civilization to inhabit the mesa.

5. The people Cassandra studies inhabited the mesa immediately before the Minapiato civilization moved in.

6. The Kipaquatl people didn't live on Mesa Corlando from 360 to 480 AD, and they weren't the last people to inhabit the mesa.

7. The earliest known civilization at the mesa isn't studied by Jason.

		Experts					Peoples					Populations				
		Cassandra	Christopher	Jason	Lionel	Kevin	Cochupta	Kipaquatl	Minapiato	Pachape	Tucakopi	5,000	15,000	25,000	50,000	75,000
Periods	240–360 AD															
	360–480 AD															
	480–600 AD															
	600–720 AD															
	720–840 AD															
Populations	5,000															
	15,000															
	25,000															
	50,000															
	75,000															
Peoples	Cochupta															
	Kipaquatl															
	Minapiato															
	Pachape															
	Tucakopi															

SOLVE RATE
45.5%

AVERAGE TIME
10 min, 49 sec

BEST TIME
2 min, 47 sec by kathy_c

Periods	Experts	Peoples	Populations
240–360 AD			
360–480 AD			
480–600 AD			
600–720 AD			
720–840 AD			

Early Flights

Five co-workers at Hermes Enterprises each had to take an early morning flight to a different part of the country as part of the company's new sales and marketing effort for its latest product launch. Each traveler took a different flight, at a different time, to a different destination. Using only the clues below, determine the flight number, departure time, and destination of each passenger.

1. Flight 555 left at 6:25 am.
2. Of Tarlton and the passenger on Flight 555, one went to Boise and the other left at 6:25 am.
3. Collin didn't leave on Flight 392 (which left at either 6:25 am or 6:05 am).
4. Flight 345 didn't leave at 6:45 am.
5. The Cranston-bound flight didn't leave at 6:15 am.
6. Neither Collin nor the passenger headed to Boise left on Flight 102.
7. The five travelers were the one headed to Baltimore (which left at 6:35 am), the one on Flight 102, the Boise-bound passenger (who didn't leave at 6:15 am), Iris, and the person who left on 6:05 am.
8. Johnny left sometime after the passenger headed to Cedar Rapids.

		Travelers				Destinations					Flight Numbers				
		Collin	Iris	Johnny	Sydney	Tarlton	Baltimore	Boise	Cedar Rapids	Cranston	Lincoln	102	229	345	392	555
Times	6:05 am															
	6:15 am															
	6:25 am															
	6:35 am															
	6:45 am															
Flight Numbers	102															
	229															
	345															
	392															
	555															
Destinations	Baltimore															
	Boise															
	Cedar Rapids															
	Cranston															
	Lincoln															

SOLVE RATE
45.4%

AVERAGE TIME
11 min, 58 sec

BEST TIME
5 min, 24 sec by Laura

Times	Travelers	Destinations	Flight Numbers
6:05 am			
6:15 am			
6:25 am			
6:35 am			
6:45 am			

Mythology Papers

The students in Mrs. Halberstram's Ancient Mythology class each had to submit a paper on the subject of a mythological figure. Although more than 30 were submitted, Mrs. Halberstram only had time last night to grade five of them. Using only the clues below, determine the order in which she graded each paper, the subject of each paper, and the final score she awarded it.

1. Mrs. Halberstram graded the paper on Eurydice sometime after Noah's paper.
2. Of the Antigone paper (which wasn't graded second) and the one she graded first (which scored either an 86 or an 89), one was Hannah's and the other was Noah's.
3. The paper on Agamemnon was graded sometime after the paper on Eurydice.
4. The Endymion paper didn't get the 92.
5. Josiah didn't get the highest score or the 86.
6. Johnny's paper was graded immediately before the one that got the 98.
7. Between the Lycurgus paper and the one that got the lowest score, one was graded first and the other was Noah's.

		George	Hannah	Johnny	Josiah	Noah	98	92	89	86	83	Agamemnon	Antigone	Endymion	Eurydice	Lycurgus
Orders	First															
	Second															
	Third															
	Fourth															
	Fifth															
Subjects	Agamemnon															
	Antigone															
	Endymion															
	Eurydice															
	Lycurgus															
Scores	98															
	92															
	89															
	86															
	83															

SOLVE RATE
45.3%

AVERAGE TIME
16 min, 33 sec

BEST TIME
3 min, 41 sec by khead

Orders	Students	Scores	Subjects
First			
Second			
Third			
Fourth			
Fifth			

Put That on a Record and Sell It ...

These days, everyone thinks they've got what it takes to make it in the music world, and so business is booming at Ricardo's local recording studio. In fact, every single day last week was booked by a different artist, each of whom recorded a different song for a different label. Using only the clues below, determine the song, day, and label associated with each artist.

1. The five singers are the one who recorded *Sad to See You,* Angela, Gary (who isn't represented by Titustown), the one who was scheduled to record on Thursday, and the one from the Streetwise label.

2. Leonite represented either Ian or Gary.

3. Either Angela or the singer who booked the studio for Tuesday was signed to the Streetwise label.

4. The artist who recorded on Friday didn't sing *A Single Kiss* or *Happy Times.*

5. *Happy Times* wasn't recorded on Tuesday.

6. The singer who co-wrote his or her own hit song, *One More Time,* was scheduled to record the day after Angela.

7. Of Gary and the singer known for *One More Time,* one recorded his or her song on Friday and the other is represented by Leonite.

8. Jorge is represented by either Leonite or Panoply.

	Angela	Gary	Hayden	Ian	Jorge	A Single Kiss	Happy Times	One More Time	Sad to See You	Summer Blues	Ballyhoo	Leonite	Panoply	Streetwise	Titustown
Monday															
Tuesday															
Wednesday															
Thursday															
Friday															
Ballyhoo															
Leonite															
Panoply															
Streetwise															
Titustown															
A Single Kiss															
Happy Times															
One More Time															
Sad to See You															
Summer Blues															

SOLVE RATE
45.2%

AVERAGE TIME
11 min, 38 sec

BEST TIME
3 min by riffraff

Days	Artists	Songs	Labels
Monday			
Tuesday			
Wednesday			
Thursday			
Friday			

Chili Peppers

Chili lovers, rejoice! Scientists discovered five brand new kinds of naturally growing peppers this year, each in a different month and each in a different country. The spiciness of each pepper—measured in Scoville heat units, or SHUs—varies widely, with higher values indicating a spicier pepper. Using only the clues below, figure out when and where each new pepper was discovered and how many SHUs each pepper packs!

1. The pepper discovered in India (which isn't the Tarawa pepper) was found to be twice as spicy as the Riki-kuku pepper.
2. Of the Riki-kuku pepper and the one discovered in February, one is the least spicy of all five (but isn't from Panama) and the other was discovered in the jungles outside of Chiang Mai, Thailand.
3. The pepper discovered in July was found to be quite hot, at 100,000 SHUs.
4. The new Thai pepper was discovered in either July or September.
5. The Devil's Hand pepper is native to Honduras and is hotter than the pepper discovered in October.
6. The Griffix pepper is not as hot as the Tarawa pepper.
7. The pepper discovered in September is twice as hot as the one discovered in October.

		Chili Peppers				Countries					Months				
		Capacine	Devil's Hand	Griffix	Riki-kuku	Tarawa	Honduras	India	Mexico	Panama	Thailand	February	April	July	September	October
Heat Units	25,000 SHU															
	50,000 SHU															
	100,000 SHU															
	200,000 SHU															
	400,000 SHU															
Months	February															
	April															
	July															
	September															
	October															
Countries	Honduras															
	India															
	Mexico															
	Panama															
	Thailand															

SOLVE RATE
45.2%

AVERAGE TIME
14 min, 48 sec

BEST TIME
5 min, 41 sec by carolinaclaw

Heat Units	Chili Peppers	Countries	Months
25,000 SHU			
50,000 SHU			
100,000 SHU			
200,000 SHU			
400,000 SHU			

Broadband Users

The conversation at Ellie's dinner party eventually drifted toward broadband Internet, the different types that are available in the area, and what sorts of speeds each provided. Of all the guests, five (including Ellie) currently have broadband Internet, each through a different type of service and with a different maximum speed. They each use broadband mainly for a specific purpose. Using only the clues below, match the broadband type, maximum speed, and primary use to each Internet user.

1. The fiber-optic broadband user has a slower maximum download speed than the one who uses power line broadband.

2. The DSL user (who doesn't do video chatting) has a slower broadband connection than Ellie, but it is still twice as fast as Sidney's (whose connection is twice as fast as Jasper's). Ellie's broadband connection isn't 8 Mbps.

3. The person with the slowest connection doesn't use broadband primarily to download movies.

4. Neither Kevin nor the power line broadband user has the slowest broadband speed.

5. The DSL user's connection is half the speed of the person who relies on broadband access for home business.

6. Of Jasper and the one with the fastest broadband, one has cable broadband and the other uses fiber-optic (but not for video chatting).

7. Of the satellite and cable users, one uses broadband primarily for online gaming and the other has the 2 Mbps broadband connection.

		People						Types					Main Uses			
		Ellie	Jasper	Kevin	Riley	Sidney	Cable	DSL	Fiber-optic	Power Line	Satellite	Gaming	Home Business	Movies	Mp3s	Video Chat
Speeds	1 Mbps															
	2 Mbps															
	4 Mbps															
	8 Mbps															
	16 Mbps															
Main Uses	Gaming															
	Home Business															
	Movies															
	Mp3s															
	Video Chat															
Types	Cable															
	DSL															
	Fiber-optic															
	Power Line															
	Satellite															

SOLVE RATE
45.1%

AVERAGE TIME
10 min, 58 sec

BEST TIME
3 min, 34 sec by avecsoleil

Speeds	People	Types	Main Uses
1 Mbps			
2 Mbps			
4 Mbps			
8 Mbps			
16 Mbps			

Dinner Dilemmas

Count Basington is known worldwide for his fine wine collection, housed at his family's castle in the rugged hills of Scotland. To celebrate his birthday this year, he invited five friends to the castle for a weekend dinner and wine tasting. Each guest arrived at the castle on a different day, and each tried a different wine. To further complicate things for Basington's chef, each guest had a different food allergy that had to be skillfully avoided when preparing the menu. Using only the clues below, determine the wine, food allergy, and day of arrival for all five of Count Basington's guests.

1. The five diners were the person who arrived on Monday, Ernesto (who arrived the day before the person with the peanut allergy), Allen (who arrived the day before Brooklyn), the person who was allergic to gluten, and the one who tasted the Bordeaux.
2. Neither the person who arrived on Wednesday nor the one who had the Chianti (who wasn't Allen) was allergic to peanuts.
3. The one who enjoyed the Pinot Noir at dinner arrived at the castle sometime before Skylar.
4. The person who was allergic to dairy, who wasn't Allen, drank neither the Chianti nor the Chardonnay.
5. Of Brooklyn and the person with the mango allergy, one arrived on Monday and the other sipped the Pinot Noir.

		First Names					Wines					Allergies				
		Allen	Brooklyn	Ernesto	Rachel	Skylar	Bordeaux	Burgundy	Chardonnay	Chianti	Pinot Noir	Dairy	Gluten	Mangoes	Peanuts	Seafood
Days	Monday															
	Tuesday															
	Wednesday															
	Thursday															
	Friday															
Allergies	Dairy															
	Gluten															
	Mangoes															
	Peanuts															
	Seafood															
Wines	Bordeaux															
	Burgundy															
	Chardonnay															
	Chianti															
	Pinot Noir															

SOLVE RATE
45%

AVERAGE TIME
13 min, 23 sec

BEST TIME
2 min, 26 sec by jade_3031

Days	First Names	Wines	Allergies
Monday			
Tuesday			
Wednesday			
Thursday			
Friday			

The Most Important Meal ...

Five volunteers took turns making breakfast every weekday last week for the residents of Shady Grove Retirement Home. Each volunteer was assigned a different day, Monday through Friday, and each prepared a different meal and a different beverage. Using only the clues given below, determine which volunteer was assigned to which day, and figure out which person prepared which meal and which beverage.

1. Between Rodrigo and the volunteer who made coffee, one prepared oatmeal for their breakfast and the other was assigned to Thursday.

2. The five volunteers were the one who worked on Friday, the one who served mineral water, the one who prepared oatmeal, Karina, and Rodrigo.

3. Tomato juice (which Timothy refused to serve) wasn't served with the cereal breakfast.

4. Monday morning's breakfast was pancakes.

5. Karina, who didn't serve orange juice, volunteered the day before the waffle breakfast was served.

6. Of Tuesday's breakfast (which wasn't prepared by Timothy) and the one served by Javon, one offered pancakes and the other coffee.

7. Wednesday's breakfast didn't include bacon and eggs.

		First Names					Breakfast Foods					Beverages				
		Javon	Karina	Liana	Rodrigo	Timothy	Bacon and Eggs	Cereal	Oatmeal	Pancakes	Waffles	Coffee	Mineral Water	Orange Juice	Ceylon Tea	Tomato Juice
Days	Monday															
	Tuesday															
	Wednesday															
	Thursday															
	Friday															
Beverages	Coffee															
	Mineral Water															
	Orange Juice															
	Ceylon Tea															
	Tomato Juice															
Breakfast Foods	Bacon and Eggs															
	Cereal															
	Oatmeal															
	Pancakes															
	Waffles															

SOLVE RATE
45%

AVERAGE TIME
13 min, 41 sec

BEST TIME
2 min, 38 sec by darsinewman

Days	First Names	Breakfast Foods	Beverages
Monday			
Tuesday			
Wednesday			
Thursday			
Friday			

Peace Corps

Veronica invited four fellow former Peace Corps volunteers to dinner to reminisce about their experiences. Each volunteered in a different country for the standard 27-month enlistment. Using only the clues below, determine the years during which each person volunteered, where each went, and what each person's primary work focus was.

1. The five volunteers are Luis (who didn't serve in Armenia), Samuel, the one who served in Honduras, the one who focused on environmental issues (but didn't work in Tanzania), and Veronica, who served from 1997 to 1999 but didn't focus on health and medicine.
2. Neither Luis nor the volunteer who went to Cambodia specialized in environmental issues.
3. Either Ezekiel or the volunteer who served in Indonesia was the last of the five to have worked in the Peace Corps.
4. The volunteer who went to Tanzania wasn't there in 1996.
5. Of Arianna and the first to serve in the Peace Corps, one went to Honduras and the other focused on children's education.
6. Either Veronica or Luis served from 1995 to 1997.
7. The one who volunteered in Cambodia served immediately after the one who worked on agricultural projects.

	Arianna	Ezekiel	Luis	Samuel	Veronica	Armenia	Cambodia	Honduras	Indonesia	Tanzania	Agriculture	Education	Environment	Medicine	Water Issues
Volunteers						**Countries**					**Focuses**				
1991–1993															
1993–1995															
1995–1997															
1997–1999															
1999–2001															
Agriculture															
Education															
Environment															
Medicine															
Water Issues															
Armenia															
Cambodia															
Honduras															
Indonesia															
Tanzania															

SOLVE RATE
44.7%

AVERAGE TIME
13 min, 52 sec

BEST TIME
3 min, 32 sec by gulfcoastswimmer

Service Dates	Volunteers	Countries	Focuses
1991–1993			
1993–1995			
1995–1997			
1997–1999			
1999–2001			

Anuakian Kings

A spectacular archaeological discovery on the island of Anuakia has revealed information on five ancient kings who were never mentioned in any other chronicles. Using only the clues below, determine the start and end of each king's reign, the animal he used as his royal symbol, and the number of children he sired.

1. The five kings are those represented by the dolphin and the eagle, the one with four children, Abidonas, and the one who reigned from 1448 to 1432 BC.
2. Minoacam (whose royal symbol wasn't the eagle) held his kingdom sometime after the king who used a dolphin for his royal insignia, who reigned immediately after the king who used the goat as his royal symbol.
3. Cayophalum's reign didn't last from 1511 to 1495 BC.
4. The last of the five kings to rule Anuakia during this period didn't have the fewest children.
5. Of the king with the eagle insignia and the one with the longest reign, one had 7 children and the other has 12.
6. The dolphin king reigned immediately after Darigalus.
7. The king who used the symbol of the bull reigned immediately after the one who wore the eagle insignia.
8. The king who reigned the longest didn't have seven children and didn't use a dolphin as his royal symbol.

		Kings					Symbols					Children				
		Abidonas	Cayophalum	Darigalus	Minoacam	Phylarisea	Bull	Dog	Dolphin	Eagle	Goat	Three	Four	Seven	Nine	Twelve
Reigns	1542–1511 BC															
	1511–1495 BC															
	1495–1491 BC															
	1491–1448 BC															
	1448–1432 BC															
Children	Three															
	Four															
	Seven															
	Nine															
	Twelve															
Symbols	Bull															
	Dog															
	Dolphin															
	Eagle															
	Goat															

Reigns	Kings	Symbols	Children
1542–1511 BC			
1511–1495 BC			
1495–1491 BC			
1491–1448 BC			
1448–1432 BC			

Scholarships

Five students from Wenatchee High School were awarded sizeable scholarships this week, each from a different college. Using only the clues below, determine the size of each scholarship, what college it came from, and in what field of study each student wants to specialize.

1. The five scholarships are the $10,000 scholarship, the one from Beale College (which wasn't awarded to Mitchell), the $20,000 scholarship, the one awarded to Tate (who doesn't want to study law), and the one awarded to the future engineering student.

2. The Hemet College scholarship is larger than the one awarded to the student who intends to study medicine.

3. The smallest scholarship was awarded by Menifee College.

4. Of Kyra and the student who received the Weslaco College scholarship, one was awarded $10,000 and the other intends to study engineering.

5. The $15,000 scholarship wasn't awarded to either Tate or Abigail.

6. Of Mitchell and Kyra, one received the Menifee College scholarship and the other plans to study anthropology.

7. The East Alton College scholarship is worth $5,000 more than the one awarded to Abigail.

		Students					Colleges					Fields				
		Abigail	Chase	Kyra	Mitchell	Tate	Beale	East Alton	Hemet	Menifee	Weslaco	Anthropology	Architecture	Engineering	Law	Medicine
Scholarships	$5,000															
	$10,000															
	$15,000															
	$20,000															
	$25,000															
Fields	Anthropology															
	Architecture															
	Engineering															
	Law															
	Medicine															
Colleges	Beale															
	East Alton															
	Hemet															
	Menifee															
	Weslaco															

SOLVE RATE
44.6%

AVERAGE TIME
15 min

BEST TIME
2 min, 44 sec by Vaughns

Scholarships	Students	Colleges	Fields
$5,000			
$10,000			
$15,000			
$20,000			
$25,000			

Orchid Fever

It was widely known that Sydney's finest orchid shop had just received a shipment of some excellent new orchid specimens, and buyers from all over the world were flying in to snatch them up regardless of price. Five orchid collectors flew in just last week alone, each on a different day, and each bought a different orchid at a different price. Using only the clues below, determine the orchid purchased by each collector, its price, and the day each person flew into Sydney.

1. Between the person who bought the fly orchid and Callie, one paid $220 (but not for the calypso orchid) and the other arrived on Monday.
2. Myles arrived on either Monday or Tuesday.
3. Either the person who paid $160 for their orchid or Alicia arrived on Wednesday.
4. The five collectors were the one who bought the pigeon orchid, Alicia (who paid $20 less for her orchid than did the person who bought the fly orchid), Callie (who didn't fly in on Friday), the person who paid $200 for the orchid, and the one who arrived on Wednesday.
5. The cooktown orchid wasn't bought for either $160 or $220.
6. Either Laura or Callie arrived on Monday.

Disastrous Presentations

Mrs. Hanley's sixth grade class was given an assignment to give a presentation on different kinds of natural disasters and the effects they have on both people and the environment. Five students gave their presentations this week, each on a different kind of natural disaster, and Mrs. Hanley gave each a different grade. Using only the clues below, determine the grade, topic, and presentation day for each student.

1. Eduardo gave his presentation the day before the one on tornados.

2. Keith (who didn't get the A- or the B+) gave his presentation sometime after the one who got the highest grade.

3. Neither the one who got the A nor the student who presented on Wednesday studied volcanoes.

4. Monday's presenter didn't get the A-.

5. The five students were Ricky, the one who studied hurricanes (who didn't present on Thursday), April (who presented the day before Jack), the one who got the B-, and Friday's presenter.

6. Between Eduardo (who didn't give his presentation on Wednesday) and Tuesday's presenter, one focused on hurricanes and the other on earthquakes.

		Students					Topics					Grades				
		April	Eduardo	Jack	Keith	Ricky	Earthquakes	Hurricanes	Tornados	Volcanos	Wildfires	A	A-	B+	B	B-
Days	Monday															
	Tuesday															
	Wednesday															
	Thursday															
	Friday															
Grades	A															
	A-															
	B+															
	B															
	B-															
Topics	Earthquakes															
	Hurricanes															
	Tornados															
	Volcanos															
	Wildfires															

Days	Students	Topics	Grades
Monday			
Tuesday			
Wednesday			
Thursday			
Friday			

SOLVE RATE
44.3%

AVERAGE TIME
14 min, 21 sec

BEST TIME
3 min, 49 sec by riffraff

A Rough Day at the Phone Company

Five people were scheduled to have new telephone numbers installed this week, but a computer crash left the phone company relying on hand-scribbled notes to figure out what the installation schedule was supposed to be. Each customer has a different first name and a different last name and is scheduled for a different day. Using only the clues below, match the names to the proper phone numbers and installation dates.

1. The Brewer family wasn't scheduled for a Wednesday installation.
2. The Venter family wasn't assigned the number 281-0911.
3. David Appleton wasn't scheduled for Thursday.
4. Of the Brewer family and the person whose phone number is 368-9614, one was scheduled for Monday and the other for Wednesday.
5. Amelia's last name isn't Tillman.
6. Of the person whose phone number is 281-0911 and Maurice, one has the last name Venter and the other was scheduled for Tuesday.
7. Either the person whose phone number is 867-5309 or the Tillman family was scheduled for Monday.
8. Either Amelia or the person scheduled for Wednesday is assigned the number 281-0911.
9. Of the person scheduled for the Wednesday installation and the one with the number 589-2812, one was Maurice (whose number wasn't 368-9614) and the other was Trey.

SOLVE RATE
44.2%

AVERAGE TIME
12 min, 46 sec

BEST TIME
4 min, 15 sec by glam86

Horse Stables

Pennington Stables currently houses five horses, each of a different breed and belonging to different owners. The stables consist of five stalls, all next to each other, numbered one through five, in order. Stall #1 is farthest to the left, stall #2 is just to the right of that one, and so on, until the right-most stall #5. Using only the clues below, determine the owner of each horse, its breed, and its stall number.

1. The five owners are Georgia, Keira (whose horse's name isn't Patches), the one who owns the Morgan horse, the one who rents stall #4, and Magdalena's owner.
2. The horse in stall #5 isn't an Arabian or an Appaloosa.
3. Taylor's horse is named either Dario or Flash.
4. Of Keira's horse and the Clydesdale, one is in stall #5 and the other is named Dario.
5. Meredith doesn't rent stall #1.
6. Georgia rents the stall immediately to the left of the one that holds the Clydesdale.
7. Dario is owned by either Keira or Omar.
8. The horse in stall #2 isn't an Arabian.

		Georgia	Keira	Meredith	Omar	Taylor	Appaloosa	Arabian	Clydesdale	Morgan	Thoroughbred	Angel	Dario	Flash	Magdalena	Patches
Stalls	#1															
	#2															
	#3															
	#4															
	#5															
Names	Angel															
	Dario															
	Flash															
	Magdalena															
	Patches															
Horses	Appaloosa															
	Arabian															
	Clydesdale															
	Morgan															
	Thoroughbred															

Stalls	Owners	Horses	Names
#1			
#2			
#3			
#4			
#5			

SOLVE RATE
43.9%

AVERAGE TIME
10 min, 8 sec

BEST TIME
2 min, 53 sec by nvision

Home Run Leaders

It's time for the all-county baseball awards to go out, starting first with the top-five home run leaders of the last season. Each of the winners racked up a different number of home runs, and each played for a different team and had a different batting average. Using only the clues below, find the batting average, team, and number of home runs for each player.

1. Of the Warrior player and the one who hit 17 home runs last season (who didn't play for the Giants), one was Dante and the other had a .419 batting average.
2. The player with the .407 batting average had one more home run than the player from the Ottumwa Outlaws.
3. The Kings player had the .418 batting average, but didn't hit 15 home runs.
4. The player with the .419 batting average (who wasn't Roger) had one more home run last season than the player with the .407 batting average.
5. Jason (who didn't have 16 home runs) had one more home run last season than Walter.
6. The Warriors player, who wasn't Dante, had the most home runs last season.
7. The Giants player didn't have the lowest batting average.

		Players					Teams					Averages				
		Carlos	Dante	Jason	Roger	Walter	Giants	Grizzlies	Kings	Outlaws	Warriors	.400	.407	.418	.419	.439
Home Runs	14															
	15															
	16															
	17															
	18															
Averages	.400															
	.407															
	.418															
	.419															
	.439															
Teams	Giants															
	Grizzlies															
	Kings															
	Outlaws															
	Warriors															

Home Runs	Players	Teams	Averages
14			
15			
16			
17			
18			

SOLVE RATE
43.8%

AVERAGE TIME
11 min, 51 sec

BEST TIME
3 min, 42 sec by Borealis

Buy Low, Sell High

Derrick's investment club held its latest meeting last night, with Derrick and four other investors attending. Each talked a bit about their own favorite stock pick of the week. Using only the clues below, match each stock symbol to the investor who recommended it, and determine the value and sector (financial, technology, and so on) of each.

1. The five investors are Brett, Connor, the one who recommended HOPN, the one whose stock pick is currently valued at $1.50, and the one whose pick-of-the-week is in the pharmaceutical sector.
2. Brett's stock is valued 25¢ lower than GGML.
3. Scott's pick-of-the-week is in either the manufacturing or pharmaceutical sectors.
4. Derrick's stock is valued 25¢ lower than Brett's.
5. Of GGML and the stock Connor recommended (which isn't in the technology sector), one has the highest per-share value and the other is a financial-sector stock.
6. The stock with the highest per-share value is neither AMBR nor CFWT. CFWT isn't currently valued at a dollar per share.
7. Either Leslie or Connor recommended the financial-sector stock.

		Investors					Stock Symbols					Sectors				
		Brett	Connor	Derrick	Leslie	Scott	AMBR	CFWT	GGML	HOPN	TLVU	Energy	Financial	Manufacturing	Pharmaceutical	Technology
Share Values	$0.75															
	$1.00															
	$1.25															
	$1.50															
	$1.75															
Sectors	Energy															
	Financial															
	Manufacturing															
	Pharmaceutical															
	Technology															
Stock Symbols	AMBR															
	CFWT															
	GGML															
	HOPN															
	TLVU															

SOLVE RATE
43.8%

AVERAGE TIME
13 min, 20 sec

BEST TIME
3 min, 32 sec by MsJangle

Share Values	Investors	Stock Symbols	Sectors
$0.75			
$1.00			
$1.25			
$1.50			
$1.75			

Pen Names

It's not unusual in the publishing world for an author to take a pen name or a pseudonym. In fact, five very well-known modern authors each write under a different pen name. Using only the clues below, determine the pen name used by each of the five authors and the year and title of their last published book. (Note: Male writers might use female pen names, and vice versa!)

1. The five authors are Paul Ponts, the one who wrote *Lamentations,* Bev Willard, the one who writes as Chase Kent (who didn't write *Bay of Tears),* and the one who published his or her latest book in 2003.
2. Bev Willard's last book (which isn't *Bay of Tears)* was published sometime after the one by Chase Kent.
3. Guy Coraline's pen name is either Jay Walden or Chase Kent. He didn't write *Persian Days.*
4. Paul Ponts writes as Jay Walden; his last book was published in 2005.
5. *Bay of Tears* wasn't published in 2003.
6. *Agamemnon* wasn't published in 2006.
7. The author who writes as Kyle Clark didn't write *Persian Days.*
8. Nina Knowles' book was published the year before Leslie Lane's book.
9. Of Zach Friese and the author who published his or her last book in 2002, one writes as Leslie Lane and the other wrote *Lamentations.*

		Pen Names					Titles					Real Names				
		Chase Kent	Jay Walden	Kyle Clark	Leslie Lane	Nina Knowles	Agamemnon	Bay of Tears	Ended Dreams	Lamentations	Persian Days	Bev Willard	Guy Coraline	Matt Jenkins	Paul Ponts	Zach Friese
Years	2002															
	2003															
	2004															
	2005															
	2006															
Real Names	Bev Willard															
	Guy Coraline															
	Matt Jenkins															
	Paul Ponts															
	Zach Friese															
Titles	Agamemnon															
	Bay of Tears															
	Ended Dreams															
	Lamentations															
	Persian Days															

Years	Pen Names	Titles	Real Names
2002			
2003			
2004			
2005			
2006			

SOLVE RATE
43.7%

AVERAGE TIME
9 min, 40 sec

BEST TIME
2 min, 1 sec by russelldugan

A Mile in Their Shoes ...

To prepare for the upcoming all-county track meet, five aspiring runners met at the local track for a friendly one-mile competition. Each runner was from a different school (each of which had its own mascot), and each wore a different color uniform. All five ran the mile together, but no one finished at exactly the same time. Using only the clues below, determine the finishing time, uniform color, and mascot associated with each runner.

1. The runner who wore the Marlins logo (who wasn't Esmeralda) finished sometime before the competitor in the red uniform.

2. Jay was not a Spartan, and he didn't wear the silver uniform.

3. Of the runner who finished with a time of 4 minutes and 3 seconds and Esmeralda, one was a Marlin and the other a Hurricane.

4. Among the Wahoo and the runner in the black uniform, one finished with a time of 4 minutes and 11 seconds and the other was Gloria.

5. Of the Spartan and Ramon, one was the last to finish and the other wore the green uniform.

6. The runner in the red uniform finished right after the runner who wore the Hurricanes logo.

7. The Blue Hen (who didn't have the fastest time and didn't wear the green uniform) finished sometime before the Spartan.

	Names					Mascots					Colors				
	Esmeralda	Gloria	Jay	Maddox	Ramon	Blue Hens	Hurricanes	Marlins	Spartans	Wahoos	Black	Blue	Green	Red	Silver
Times 3:59															
4:03															
4:08															
4:11															
4:24															
Colors Black															
Blue															
Green															
Red															
Silver															
Mascots Blue Hens															
Hurricanes															
Marlins															
Spartans															
Wahoos															

SOLVE RATE
43.4%

AVERAGE TIME
14 min, 4 sec

BEST TIME
4 min, 56 sec by Hayden

Times	Names	Mascots	Colors
3:59			
4:03			
4:08			
4:11			
4:24			

Deep Sea Fishing

Five friends chartered the Salty Seadog, a deep-sea fishing vessel known to have good luck in the waters off Belize. Each of the five caught a different kind of fish, each at a different time, and each coming in at a different weight. Using only the clues below, match the fish and its weight to the fisherman (or fisherwoman) and determine what time each was caught.

1. The five friends were the one who caught the sailfish, Gabriela, Grace (who wasn't the last person to catch their fish), the one who caught the 75 pound fish, and the one who caught a fish at 3:35 pm.
2. Nancy's fish was heavier than the sailfish.
3. The barracuda didn't weigh 45 pounds.
4. Mason's fish (which didn't weigh 30 pounds) was 15 pounds lighter than Gabriela's, whose fish was 15 pounds lighter than the marlin.
5. Of Grace and the person who caught the marlin, one caught the heaviest fish (which wasn't a barracuda or an amberjack) and the other caught a fish at 10:48 am.
6. Yesenia caught her fish at either 10:48 am or 1:10 pm.

		Names					Fish					Times				
		Gabriela	Grace	Mason	Nancy	Yesenia	Amberjack	Barracuda	Marlin	Sailfish	Tuna	9:30 am	10:48 am	1:10 pm	3:35 pm	3:59 pm
Weights	30 lb.															
	45 lb.															
	60 lb.															
	75 lb.															
	90 lb.															
Times	9:30 am															
	10:48 am															
	1:10 pm															
	3:35 pm															
	3:59 pm															
Fish	Amberjack															
	Barracuda															
	Marlin															
	Sailfish															
	Tuna															

Weights	Names	Fish	Times
30 lb.			
45 lb.			
60 lb.			
75 lb.			
90 lb.			

SOLVE RATE
43.4%

AVERAGE TIME
14 min, 18 sec

BEST TIME
2 min, 33 sec by urielzet

Leaps and Bounds

Five champion track-and-field athletes put together a short, three-event jumping exhibition to help promote the sport. Each of the five athletes competed in the high jump, the long jump, and the pole vault, back to back, and there were no ties in any of the three events. Using only the clues below, determine the highest high jump, longest long jump, and highest pole vault achieved by each of the five competitors.

1. The athlete who came in first place on the long jump scored better in the high jump than the one who reached 8.2 meters in the long jump.
2. The one who came in second in the long jump finished better in the high jump than the athlete who came in fourth in the pole vault.
3. Of the high jumper who reached 2.33 meters and Alex, when it came time for the long jump event, one came in third and the other came in second.
4. Of the long jumper who finished in last place and the pole vaulter who finished in first place, one was Francis and the other reached 2.25 meters in the high jump.
5. Hadley didn't finish fourth in the long jump, and he didn't finish last in the pole vault.
6. The pole-vaulter who reached 5.0 meters wasn't the competitor who scored the longest long jump (who finished better than Alex in the high jump).
7. The winner of the high jump competition didn't win the long jump event.
8. Alex didn't finish third in the long jump.
9. Of John and the competitor who reached 8.2 meters in the long jump, one came in last on the high jump and the other finished third in the pole vault.

		Competitors					Long Jumps					Pole Vaults				
		Alex	Francis	Hadley	Hugh	John	8.8 meters	8.6 meters	8.5 meters	8.2 meters	8.1 meters	5.4 meters	5.2 meters	5.0 meters	4.9 meters	4.5 meters
High Jumps	2.35 meters															
	2.33 meters															
	2.29 meters															
	2.25 meters															
	2.21 meters															
Pole Vaults	5.4 meters															
	5.2 meters															
	5.0 meters															
	4.9 meters															
	4.5 meters															
Long Jumps	8.8 meters															
	8.6 meters															
	8.5 meters															
	8.2 meters															
	8.1 meters															

SOLVE RATE
43.3%

AVERAGE TIME
10 min, 59 sec

BEST TIME
2 min, 49 sec by urielzet

High Jumps	Competitors	Long Jumps	Pole Vaults
2.35 meters			
2.33 meters			
2.29 meters			
2.25 meters			
2.21 meters			

Genome Sequencing

Once relegated to the realm of science fiction, genetic sequencing—recording every single genetic base pair in an organism's DNA—is now proceeding at a rapid pace across biotechnology labs across the world. At GGNC, five microscopic organisms are currently being sequenced. Using only the clues below, determine which researcher is sequencing which organism, how many base pairs each organism has, and what month and year each project is scheduled to be completed by.

1. The five organisms are the one Ruben is sequencing, the one scheduled to be finished by June 2012, the one with 1.2 million base pairs, *protoforelum,* and *carsonelium.*
2. *Ventrilium* has half as many base pairs as *carsonelium.*
3. Neither the project scheduled for completion in 2014 nor the one studying the organism with the most base pairs is headed by Jose (who, like Brian, isn't studying *mycothelium*). Brian's project isn't scheduled to end in April 2012.
4. The organism Amir is sequencing has 4.8 million base pairs.
5. *Protoforelum* doesn't have the fewest base pairs of all five organisms.
6. The five projects are the one focusing on the organism with the fewest base pairs, the one scheduled to end in May 2012, the one studying the organism with 9.6 million base pairs, Ruben's study, and the one focusing on *carsonelium.*
7. The *nanorudium* sequence is scheduled to be done by June 2012.
8. The organism with 2.4 million base pairs is expected to be fully sequenced at least a year earlier than July 2014.

	Researchers					Organisms					Dates				
	Amir	Brian	Jose	Karla	Ruben	Carsonelium	Mycothelium	Nanorudium	Protoforelum	Ventrilium	May 2012	April 2012	June 2012	March 2013	July 2014
Base Pairs 600,000															
1,200,000															
2,400,000															
4,800,000															
9,600,000															
Dates May 2012															
April 2012															
June 2012															
March 2013															
July 2014															
Organisms Carsonelium															
Mycothelium															
Nanorudium															
Protoforelum															
Ventrilium															

SOLVE RATE
43.1%

AVERAGE TIME
13 min, 56 sec

BEST TIME
2 min, 52 sec by khead

Base Pairs	Researchers	Organisms	Dates
600,000			
1,200,000			
2,400,000			
4,800,000			
9,600,000			

The Town Hall Meeting

More speakers than usual signed up to give brief presentations at this month's town hall meeting in Humberton. Each of the five came from a different street, and each had a different complaint to make before the council members. To keep things moving, each speaker was allowed just 15 minutes to make his or her argument. Using only the clues below, determine the street and complaint associated with each speaker, and the time the speakers gave their presentations to the council.

1. Neither Josephine (who spoke sometime after the person complaining about construction near his or her house) nor Priscilla was there to complain about their unruly neighbors.

2. Masha's only complaint was about the two potholes on her street, which were causing drivers to swerve onto the sidewalk in front of her house. She spoke sometime before the person who was there to complain about dogs barking at all hours of the night.

3. The speaker who began at 7:45 pm doesn't live on Oak Ridge Road and didn't speak about potholes.

4. The five speakers were Nate (who lived on Madison Street and wasn't complaining about his unruly neighbors), the one who complained there weren't any street lights in front of his or her house (who didn't speak at 7:00 pm), the one who lives on Campus Drive (who spoke immediately after the person from Paul Circle), the person who spoke at 7:45 pm, and Josephine.

		Speakers					Streets					Complaints				
		Josephine	Lincoln	Masha	Nate	Priscilla	Bluff Avenue	Campus Drive	Madison Street	Oak Ridge Road	Paul Circle	Construction	Dogs Barking	Neighbors	Potholes	Street Lights
Times	7:00 pm															
	7:15 pm															
	7:30 pm															
	7:45 pm															
	8:00 pm															
Complaints	Construction															
	Dogs Barking															
	Neighbors															
	Potholes															
	Street Lights															
Streets	Bluff Avenue															
	Campus Drive															
	Madison Street															
	Oak Ridge Road															
	Paul Circle															

SOLVE RATE
42.9%

AVERAGE TIME
12 min, 53 sec

BEST TIME
4 min, 25 sec by jb71

Times	Speakers	Streets	Complaints
7:00 pm			
7:15 pm			
7:30 pm			
7:45 pm			
8:00 pm			

The Bridge Era

Spangler County is renowned for its five bridges, all built in the 1930s during an unprecedented infrastructure expansion. Each bridge is considered a work of art in its own right, designed by some of the most famous architects of their day. Using only the clues below, determine what year each bridge was built, the length it spans, and the name of its designer.

1. The five bridges are the one that spans 13,861 yards, the Ingleside Bridge, the Liberty Bridge (which wasn't designed by Victor Valentine), the one built in 1935, and the one designed by Neils Nillith.
2. The Milford Pass Bridge was built the year before the Ingleside Bridge, which was built the year before the bridge that now spans 13,733 yards.
3. Neither the last of the five bridges to be built nor the one that went up in 1933 spans exactly 11,490 yards.
4. Of the Liberty Bridge and the one that spans 13,733 yards, one was built in 1936 and the other was designed by Irving Iampiah.
5. Thurgood Bridge was designed by Joseph Jackson.
6. Irving Iampiah designed either the Ridgewood Bridge or the Liberty Bridge.
7. The shortest bridge wasn't the last to be built.

		Bridges				Lengths					Designers				
		Ingleside	Liberty	Milford Pass	Ridgewood	Thurgood	10,254 yards	11,490 yards	13,733 yards	13,861 yards	16,028 yards	Frederick	Iampiah	Jackson	Nillith	Valentine
Years	1932															
	1933															
	1934															
	1935															
	1936															
Designers	Frederick															
	Iampiah															
	Jackson															
	Nillith															
	Valentine															
Lengths	10,254 yards															
	11,490 yards															
	13,733 yards															
	13,861 yards															
	16,028 yards															

SOLVE RATE
42.8%

AVERAGE TIME
20 min, 6 sec

BEST TIME
4 min, 42 sec by sleepingviper

Years	Bridges	Lengths	Designers
1932			
1933			
1934			
1935			
1936			

Folk Songs

Serendipitea, a hip new tea and music lounge, just had its grand opening last weekend. To help draw in new customers, the owners hired five local folk singers to perform during the opening ceremonies. Using only the clues below, figure out the name and length of the song each musician sang and the order in which the musicians performed.

1. The five songs are "Playtime" (which Jacob didn't sing), the longest song, the song that lasted 3 minutes and 21 seconds, Quinton's song (which was the second longest), and the one that was performed fourth.
2. Neville's song wasn't the shortest.
3. Of Genesis (who didn't perform third) and the musician whose song lasted 3 minutes and 10 seconds, one sang "Winter Wind" and the other performed "Moontide."
4. The song that was performed second (but not by Jacob) was shorter than "Callous Soul."
5. The five singers are Genesis, the one who sang "Callous Soul," the one whose song lasted 3 minutes and 21 seconds, the one who performed first, and the singer of "Winter Wind."

		Singers					Titles					Orders				
		Brittany	Genesis	Jacob	Neville	Quinton	"Callous Soul"	"Moontide"	"Never Again"	"Playtime"	"Winter Wind"	First	Second	Third	Fourth	Fifth
Song Lengths	2:35															
	3:10															
	3:21															
	3:27															
	3:56															
Orders	First															
	Second															
	Third															
	Fourth															
	Fifth															
Titles	"Callous Soul"															
	"Moontide"															
	"Never Again"															
	"Playtime"															
	"Winter Wind"															

SOLVE RATE
42.4%

AVERAGE TIME
13 min, 45 sec

BEST TIME
2 min, 59 sec by khead

Song Lengths	Singers	Titles	Orders
2:35			
3:10			
3:21			
3:27			
3:56			

Auto Insurance

Reese and four of her friends each signed up for new auto insurance policies through a new company that's been advertising widely over the past several months. Each of them drives a different type of car, and each ended up with a different premium (yearly rate) and deductible. Using only the clues below, match each driver to his or her vehicle and figure out what kind of insurance rate and deductible each ended up receiving.

1. The five drivers are Guadalupe, the one with the $1,000 deductible, Herbert (who doesn't drive the SUV), the one with the second-highest premium, and the one who drives a sedan.
2. The $590 premium didn't include a $500 deductible.
3. The $665 insurance policy included a deductible that was higher than its yearly premium.
4. Reese drives either a coupe or a pickup truck.
5. The driver with the $750 deductible pays $25 more per year for insurance than Guadalupe, who pays $25 more per year than Jeffrey.
6. Of Herbert and the person with the $750 deductible, one bought the insurance policy with the highest yearly premium and the other drives the coupe.
7. Either Makenna or Herbert owns the coupe.

		Drivers					Deductibles					Vehicles				
		Guadalupe	Herbert	Jeffrey	Makenna	Reese	$250	$500	$750	$1,000	$1,500	Convertible	Coupe	Pickup	Sedan	SUV
Premiums	$565															
	$590															
	$615															
	$640															
	$665															
Vehicles	Convertible															
	Coupe															
	Pickup															
	Sedan															
	SUV															
Deductibles	$250															
	$500															
	$750															
	$1,000															
	$1,500															

SOLVE RATE
42.4%

AVERAGE TIME
15 min, 47 sec

BEST TIME
6 min, 8 sec by jb71

Premiums	Drivers	Deductibles	Vehicles
$565			
$590			
$615			
$640			
$665			

Speedboats

The Pinckton speed trials—a 25-lap speedboat race—were held today, and the top-five finishers qualified for next month's finals. Each of the top-five racers performed admirably, and each was clocked with a different maximum speed during the race. Of course, the fastest boat doesn't always win (tactics and control are important, too), so using only the clues below, determine the boat that belonged to each racer, the maximum speed each achieved during the race, and the final placement of each among the top-five finishers.

1. The top-five finishers are Jordan, the one who raced the *Odyssey,* the racer in the *Viking* (who isn't Ashton and didn't finish third), the one who finished fourth (who isn't Jules and didn't have a maximum speed of 283 MPH), and the boater who reached the slowest maximum speed (who finished right before the one who reached a maximum speed of 283 MPH).

2. The five top boaters are the one with the slowest maximum speed, the first-place finisher, the fifth-place finisher (who isn't Jules and didn't reach the fastest maximum speed), Hayden, and the boater who raced *Bravery.*

3. Of Jordan and the person who finished fifth, one reached a maximum speed of 285 MPH and the other was the only one to break the 300 MPH barrier during the race.

4. The *Sea Giant* finished sometime after the *Great Western.*

	Racers					Places					Speedboats				
	Ashton	Hanson	Hayden	Jordan	Jules	271 MPH	279 MPH	283 MPH	285 MPH	302 MPH	Bravery	Odyssey	Great Western	Sea Giant	Viking
First															
Second															
Third															
Fourth															
Fifth															
Bravery															
Odyssey															
Great Western															
Sea Giant															
Viking															
271 MPH															
279 MPH															
283 MPH															
285 MPH															
302 MPH															

SOLVE RATE
42.2%

AVERAGE TIME
13 min, 29 sec

BEST TIME
3 min, 35 sec by carolinaclaw

Max Speeds	Racers	Places	Speedboats
First			
Second			
Third			
Fourth			
Fifth			

Census Numbers

It's time again for the 10-year census, and already the results for five different cities have come in, tallying the total number of people (population) and the total number of households in each city. The census bureau put a different worker in charge of confirming the numbers for each city. Using only the clues below, determine the city verified by each worker and the final tally for population and number of households in each.

1. Destiny wasn't in charge of verifying the numbers for the city of Tyrone. The final tally she came up with for her city wasn't 19,001.

2. The five cities are Conyers, the ones with the smallest and largest populations, the city Addison was assigned to verify, and the one with 12,019 households.

3. Between Hinesville and Alpharetta, one was verified by Emma and the other was found to have had 11,984 households.

4. The city of Eastman is next highest in population after the city that has 11,513 households.

5. The city Emma was assigned to verify (which wasn't Alpharetta) didn't have the smallest population.

6. Of Eastman and the city with 19,001 inhabitants, one was verified by Addison and the other had 11,513 households (but wasn't verified by Ali).

7. Not surprisingly, the city with the fewest number of households also had the smallest population.

		Workers					Cities					Households				
		Addison	Ali	Destiny	Emma	Titus	Alpharetta	Conyers	Eastman	Hinesville	Tyrone	11,021	11,513	11,984	12,019	12,440
Populations	18,728															
	19,001															
	19,222															
	19,310															
	20,197															
Households	11,021															
	11,513															
	11,984															
	12,019															
	12,440															
Cities	Alpharetta															
	Conyers															
	Eastman															
	Hinesville															
	Tyrone															

SOLVE RATE
42.2%

AVERAGE TIME
14 min, 13 sec

BEST TIME
3 min, 30 sec by avecsoleil

Populations	Workers	Cities	Households
18,728			
19,001			
19,222			
19,310			
20,197			

Coast Guard Calls

The Coast Guard received five distress calls last night from different ships in the Bering Sea. Each was at a different latitude (north-to-south coordinate) and a different longitude (east-to-west coordinate). Using only the clues below, determine the name of each ship, its coordinates (latitude and longitude), and the time each made its distress call. In this part of the sea, just as an example, 60 degrees latitude is farther to the *north* than 59 degrees, and -170 degrees longitude is farther to the *west* than -169 degrees.

1. The five ships are *Heaven Sent* (which wasn't the westernmost boat), the southernmost boat, the one at 56.5° latitude, the one that made the fourth distress call of the evening, and the easternmost boat (which was at 57.5° latitude).

2. *Tied for Life* was one degree farther south than the boat that made the second distress call, which wasn't the *Captain Pride*.

3. The third distress call wasn't made from -164.7° longitude.

4. *Bayford Skol* made its distress call at 11:20 pm.

5. The ship that was at 58.5° latitude wasn't at -166.0° longitude.

6. Of the *Bayford Skol* and the ship that made the final distress call, one was at 55.5° latitude and the other was farther to the west than any other ship.

7. The ship that made the fourth distress call was one degree farther south than the one that was at -164.7° longitude.

8. The ship that made the first distress call was one degree farther south than the one that called the Coast Guard at 10:52 pm.

		Ships					Longitudes					Times				
		Bayford Skol	Captain Pride	Heaven Sent	Jessie's Girl	Tied for Life	-168.2°	-166.0°	-165.3°	-164.7°	-163.1°	10:08 pm	10:52 pm	10:59 pm	11:20 pm	11:43 pm
Latitudes	54.5°															
	55.5°															
	56.5°															
	57.5°															
	58.5°															
Times	10:08 pm															
	10:52 pm															
	10:59 pm															
	11:20 pm															
	11:43 pm															
Longitudes	-168.2°															
	-166.0°															
	-165.3°															
	-164.7°															
	-163.1°															

Latitudes	Ships	Longitudes	Times
54.5°			
55.5°			
56.5°			
57.5°			
58.5°			

SOLVE RATE
42.1%

AVERAGE TIME
15 min, 3 sec

BEST TIME
4 min, 14 sec by CherylRwfm

Ceramics Class

Mrs. Jolsen's ceramics class was drawing to a close, and five students rushed to finish their final projects in time for the deadline. Each of the five created a different item (such as a coffee mug or an ashtray) and each glazed her final piece in a different color. Using only the clues below, determine the color and type of ceramic made by each student and the day each turned the project in to Mrs. Jolsen.

1. The five students are the one who submitted her project on Wednesday, the two who chose the blue and orange glazes, Kaitlynn (who didn't make an ashtray), and the one who crafted a vase.
2. The student who created the vase (who isn't Isabelle) submitted her project the day before the student who chose the blue glaze, who submitted her project sometime before Jalen.
3. Of the person who finished her project on Wednesday and the one who made the coffee mug, one chose a purple glaze and the other was Brenda.
4. The coffee mug project was submitted to Mrs. Jolsen the day after Kaitlynn finished her project.
5. Monday's submission wasn't in a white glaze.
6. The bowl isn't white and wasn't submitted on Tuesday.

		Brenda	Caroline	Isabelle	Jalen	Kaitlynn	Ashtray	Bowl	Coffee Mug	Flower Pot	Vase	Blue	Green	Orange	Purple	White
Days	Monday															
	Tuesday															
	Wednesday															
	Thursday															
	Friday															
Glazes	Blue															
	Green															
	Orange															
	Purple															
	White															
Ceramics	Ashtray															
	Bowl															
	Coffee Mug															
	Flower Pot															
	Vase															

SOLVE RATE
41.9%

AVERAGE TIME
14 min, 13 sec

BEST TIME
2 min, 54 sec by urielzet

Days	Students	Ceramics	Glazes
Monday			
Tuesday			
Wednesday			
Thursday			
Friday			

Having a Whale of a Time

The Sea Spirit research vessel just returned from a five-month scientific expedition, during which five different species of whales were intensively studied by a team of marine biologists. The trip was broken into month-long segments, with each month devoted to a specific type of whale and headed by a different researcher. Each segment had a different investigative focus, such as whale songs, diet, maximum diving depth, and so on. Using only the clues below, determine which whales were studied in which months, what the focus of each investigation was, and the name of the biologist who headed each investigation.

1. The five investigations are the one headed by Madelynn (which studied right whales), the one concerned with diet, the one that studied maximum range, the one on pilot whales, and the one that took place in September.

2. Jasper didn't head the study on whale songs.

3. Of the birthing investigation and the one that took place in July, one involved right whales and the other focused on pilot whales.

4. The study concerned with the maximum range of humpback whales took place the month after the study involving right whales.

5. The birthing study took place one month before the investigation into how deep a certain whale species could dive.

6. The study of blue whales didn't concern their songs.

7. Neither Dennis's investigation (which didn't involve blue whales) nor the one on sperm whales took place in June.

8. Rowan headed the June investigation.

SOLVE RATE
41.8%

AVERAGE TIME
13 min, 37 sec

BEST TIME
3 min, 27 sec by Hayden

Months	Scientists	Study Subjects	Whales
June			
July			
August			
September			
October			

Everything Went Swimmingly ...

The competition was fierce at the women's 200m freestyle race. Although there were eight women in the race, only those who finished in the top five (who were all from different countries) made it to the post-race press conference and posed for photographs. Using only the clues below, determine which swimmers came from which countries, which lane each swam in, and what order they finished.

1. The Swedish swimmer finished sometime after Cali, who did not take third place. The third place finisher didn't swim in lane seven.
2. The Canadian, who finished just after the Swede, wasn't Natalie.
3. The Danish swimmer finished just before Megan.
4. The winner of the race was in either lane three or lane one.
5. Between the swimmer in lane number one and Megan, one finished in second place and the other was Swedish.
6. The swimmer in lane six, who wasn't Kaitlyn, finished sometime after the swimmer in lane one, who wasn't Natalie.
7. Of the swimmer in lane seven and the swimmer who placed fourth, one was Swedish and the other Italian.

	Names					Lanes					Countries				
	Cali	Kaitlyn	Megan	Natalie	Parker	1	3	4	6	7	Canada	Denmark	Italy	Sweden	United States
First															
Second															
Third															
Fourth															
Fifth															
Canada															
Denmark															
Italy															
Sweden															
United States															
1															
3															
4															
6															
7															

Finishes / Countries / Lanes (row group labels)

Finishes	Names	Lanes	Countries
First			
Second			
Third			
Fourth			
Fifth			

SOLVE RATE
41.6%

AVERAGE TIME
17 min, 26 sec

BEST TIME
5 min, 9 sec by ejagfan25

The Sweet Taste of Success

Fralington High School recently put on a bake sale to raise money for the football team, which needs some new equipment this year. Five kitchen connoisseurs volunteered their skills; each brought different desserts and set up his or her own table at the sale. At the end of the day, they counted their earnings, and all together, they raised an impressive $175! Using only the clues below, find the dessert, table number, and total earnings for each of the five volunteers.

1. The person who brought the carrot cake earned five dollars more than Brenda.
2. Gary didn't have table #5.
3. The brownie seller didn't earn exactly $30.
4. Either Linda or Gary was stationed at table #2.
5. The person who earned the most didn't bring brownies or apple pie.
6. Jayson didn't earn the least of the five volunteers.
7. Morgan was at table #3.
8. The five volunteers were the person who brought the lemon bars, Brenda, Gary, the person who earned $40, and sellers at table #4.
9. Of the person who brought the carrot cake and Gary, one earned the most money and the other was stationed at table #2.

		Brenda	Gary	Jayson	Linda	Morgan	Apple Pie	Brownies	Carrot Cake	Lemon Bars	Pecan Sandies	Table 1	Table 2	Table 3	Table 4	Table 5
Earnings	$25															
	$30															
	$35															
	$40															
	$45															
Tables	Table 1															
	Table 2															
	Table 3															
	Table 4															
	Table 5															
Baked Goods	Apple Pie															
	Brownies															
	Carrot Cake															
	Lemon Bars															
	Pecan Sandies															

Earnings	Sellers	Baked Goods	Tables
$25			
$30			
$35			
$40			
$45			

SOLVE RATE
41.6%

AVERAGE TIME
12 min, 4 sec

BEST TIME
3 min, 3 sec by moodymom

Cross-Country Kitsch

Five friends set out on a cross-country drive from Delaware to Arizona. Along the way, each of the five had one silly roadside attraction they wanted to visit, each in a different state. Using only the clues below, determine the attraction each friend insisted on stopping at, what state it was in, and what its admission fee was.

1. Of the attraction with the $13.00 ticket fee and the one in Oklahoma, one is the wax museum and the other is suggested by Hannah.
2. The Oklahoma roadside attraction (which isn't the most expensive of the five) cost $4.00 more per ticket than the one they stopped at in Ohio.
3. The place Jenna insisted on seeing cost $4.00 more than Hannah's attraction (which isn't the mystery hole).
4. The house decorated entirely by pennies didn't charge a $9.00 admission fee.
5. Neither the place Michaela wanted to see nor the one that charged $17.00 per ticket is in Texas.
6. Of the Pennsylvania attraction and the one suggested by Andrew, one charges $9.00 per ticket and the other is a pricey $21.00 per person (but isn't the world's second largest ball of twine).
7. Of Michaela's attraction (which isn't the mystery hole) and the second largest ball of twine, one charges a $9.00 admission fee and the other is in Texas.

	Andrew	Hannah	Jenna	Michaela	Nicholas	Aluminum Cow	Ball of Twine	Mystery Hole	Penny House	Wax Museum	Indiana	Ohio	Oklahoma	Pennsylvania	Texas
Admissions $5.00															
$9.00															
$13.00															
$17.00															
$21.00															
States Indiana															
Ohio															
Oklahoma															
Pennsylvania															
Texas															
Attractions Aluminum Cow															
Ball of Twine															
Mystery Hole															
Penny House															
Wax Museum															

SOLVE RATE
41.4%

AVERAGE TIME
15 min, 19 sec

BEST TIME
6 min, 10 sec by rxs98

Admissions	Travelers	Attractions	States
$5.00			
$9.00			
$13.00			
$17.00			
$21.00			

Clever Inventions

A number of local inventors established an online support group to help inventors and potential inventors get their ideas patented. Five members of the group were awarded patents for their ideas this year. Using only the clues below, determine which invention was made by each, what patent number it was granted, and how many total patents each inventor now holds.

1. The five inventors are Mekhi, the one who was assigned patent #9,450,183, the inventor who (literally) made a better mousetrap, Davis, and the inventor who currently holds three patents in his or her name.
2. The inventor with 11 total patents doesn't hold patent #9,412,210.
3. The inventor with the most patents was awarded a higher patent number this year than the one Jesse received for his invention.
4. The five inventors are the one who designed the autonomous lawn mower, the one with eight total patents, the one who was awarded patent #9,412,210, Jesse, and Luna (who doesn't own patent #9,599,672 and didn't invent a squeak-proof door hinge).
5. Of Davis and the inventor who owns patent #9,599,672, one invented a new type of engine coolant and the other has three total patents.
6. The person who invented the autonomous lawn mower (which received a lower patent number than the engine coolant patent) has the most patents of anyone in the group.

	Inventors					Inventions					Total Patents				
	Dane	Davis	Jesse	Luna	Mekhi	Door Hinge	Engine Coolant	Lawn Mower	Mousetrap	Pool Cover	1	3	8	11	16
9,412,210															
9,450,183															
9,599,672															
9,608,495															
9,671,336															
1															
3															
8															
11															
16															
Door Hinge															
Engine Coolant															
Lawn Mower															
Mousetrap															
Pool Cover															

SOLVE RATE
41.2%

AVERAGE TIME
17 min

BEST TIME
4 min, 44 sec by DCF

Patent Numbers	Inventors	Inventions	Total Patents
9,412,210			
9,450,183			
9,599,672			
9,608,495			
9,671,336			

Car Shopping

Kyle has been car shopping for a while now, and he's narrowed it down to five possibilities. Price and fuel efficiency are both important criteria, but Kyle is also interested in some extra features each car has to offer. Using only the clues below, determine the price and fuel efficiency (in miles per gallon, or MPG) of each vehicle and the extra feature each offers.

1. The five cars are the Finestra (which costs $6,000 more than the Marcuzza), the Goromati IV (which doesn't offer an in-dash navigation system), the one with the second-highest fuel efficiency rating, the one with the mp3 player, and the one with the second-highest price.

2. The car that gets 25 miles per gallon costs $6,000 more than the Finestra.

3. Neither the most expensive car nor the one that costs $45,000 gets exactly 22 miles per gallon.

4. The Wendtfar standard model includes keyless entry.

5. Either the Poltron or the Goromati IV offers heated seats, perfect for those cold Wisconsin winters.

6. The most expensive car doesn't get the worst gas mileage.

7. Of the Goromati IV and the car that gets 25 MPG, one is the most expensive of all five vehicles and the other includes heated seats.

		Cars					Mileage					Extras				
		Finestra	Goromati	Marcuzza	Poltron	Wendtfar	19 MPG	22 MPG	25 MPG	28 MPG	30 MPG	Convertible	Heated Seats	Keyless Entry	MP3 Player	Nav. System
Prices	$39,000															
	$45,000															
	$51,000															
	$57,000															
	$63,000															
Extras	Convertible															
	Heated Seats															
	Keyless Entry															
	MP3 Player															
	Nav. System															
Mileage	19 MPG															
	22 MPG															
	25 MPG															
	28 MPG															
	30 MPG															

SOLVE RATE
41.2%

AVERAGE TIME
15 min, 57 sec

BEST TIME
4 min, 55 sec by jb71

Prices	Cars	Mileage	Extras
$39,000			
$45,000			
$51,000			
$57,000			
$63,000			

Almost as Good as the Real Thing ...

The weekly outdoor market has something of a back room down a side alley, where unscrupulous vendors sell cheap knock-offs (fakes) of expensive brand-name merchandise. Although not strictly a legal enterprise, the back room has become popular with bargain-hunting fashionistas who want the best looks for the best prices. Five such friends visited the market today, and each came away with a different piece of knock-off merchandise. Each was labeled with a different brand name and each cost a different amount of money. Using only the clues below, determine the brand and purchase made by each of the five friends and what each paid for the knock-off.

1. Between the girl who bought the skirt and the one who came away with an Effendi item, one paid $40 and the other was Elly.

2. The one who bought the Gupshie piece paid more for her knock-off than the one who bought the pantsuit (who wasn't Alyssa).

3. The blouse (which didn't cost $25) sold for less than the purse. Estelle (who didn't buy the purse) didn't buy anything from the Hugh Bosch vendor.

4. The girl who bought the dress paid $5 less for her purchase than the one who bought the Gupshie brand item.

5. Of Alyssa and the one who spent $30, one bought the pantsuit and the other bought the dress.

6. Between Rochelle and the girl who bought the purse, one paid the most money of all five friends and the other bought something other than a blouse from the Guy Vanchy seller.

		Alyssa	Elly	Estelle	Marcy	Rochelle	Blouse	Dress	Pantsuit	Purse	Skirt	Effendi	Georgia Manni	Guy Vanchy	Gupshie	Hugh Bosch
Prices	$25															
	$30															
	$35															
	$40															
	$45															
Knock-offs	Effendi															
	Georgia Manni															
	Guy Vanchy															
	Gupshie															
	Hugh Bosch															
Purchases	Blouse															
	Dress															
	Pantsuit															
	Purse															
	Skirt															

SOLVE RATE
41.1%

AVERAGE TIME
14 min, 54 sec

BEST TIME
5 min, 10 sec by michellek_cm

Prices	Customers	Purchases	Knock-offs
$25			
$30			
$35			
$40			
$45			

The Petting Zoo

Adriana's parents took her and four friends to the local petting zoo today. They visited five different enclosures, each with a different type of animal inside. Each enclosure held a different number of animals as well. Using only the clues below, determine each child's favorite animal, the order in which each visited each enclosure, and how many animals were in each pen.

1. The rabbits weren't inside the fourth enclosure.
2. The group saw Adriana's favorite animal sometime after the group visited the pen that held the fewest number of animals.
3. The group visited the sheep enclosure right before the goats.
4. The first animal pen didn't hold the most animals.
5. The enclosure that held eight animals was Ally's favorite.
6. The children visited the pen that held 10 animals (which were Angelo's favorite) before they saw the pen that held six.
7. Camille's favorite animals were the llamas.
8. The five enclosures are Camille's favorite, Adriana's favorite, the fourth enclosure (which didn't hold 10 animals), the one that held 13 animals, and the goat pen.

		Children					Animals					Numbers				
		Adriana	Ally	Angelo	Camille	Christopher	Calves	Goats	Llamas	Rabbits	Sheep	Five	Six	Eight	Ten	Thirteen
Enclosures	First															
	Second															
	Third															
	Fourth															
	Fifth															
Numbers	Five															
	Six															
	Eight															
	Ten															
	Thirteen															
Animals	Calves															
	Goats															
	Llamas															
	Rabbits															
	Sheep															

SOLVE RATE
41.0%

AVERAGE TIME
13 min, 43 sec

BEST TIME
3 min, 30 sec by myerslite

Enclosures	Children	Animals	Numbers
First			
Second			
Third			
Fourth			
Fifth			

Gold Fever

Sadie and four of her friends recently got interested in gold prospecting among the streams and river beds of Northern California. Each recently returned from their own separate prospecting trips. Using only the clues below, determine how much gold each prospector found, where each was searching, and how long each spent looking for gold.

1. The five prospectors are Francesca, the one whose trip lasted six days (who didn't go to Captain Creek), the one who went up to the Middle River, the one who found the most gold, and the one who spent five days prospecting.

2. The prospector who went to Seneca Stream found more than 0.02 ounces of gold.

3. Either the Captain Creek prospector (who found 0.03 ounces of gold) or the one who found the least gold was Sadie (who didn't spend five days on her claim).

4. Maximilian found more gold than Emanuel.

5. Of the person who found 0.08 ounces of gold and the one who went to Vindal Pass, one spent four days searching and the other lasted an entire week.

6. Neither Sadie nor the prospector who spent an entire week on his or her claim found the most gold.

7. Emanuel didn't find exactly 0.03 ounces of gold.

8. The person who found 0.08 ounces of gold spent less than five days searching.

		Prospectors					Durations					Locations				
		Angel	Emanuel	Francesca	Maximilian	Sadie	3 days	4 days	5 days	6 days	7 days	Balder's Bend	Captain Creek	Middle River	Seneca Stream	Vindal Pass
Gold Found	0.02 ounces															
	0.03 ounces															
	0.05 ounces															
	0.08 ounces															
	0.12 ounces															
Locations	Balder's Bend															
	Captain Creek															
	Middle River															
	Seneca Stream															
	Vindal Pass															
Durations	3 days															
	4 days															
	5 days															
	6 days															
	7 days															

SOLVE RATE
41.0%

AVERAGE TIME
15 min, 47 sec

BEST TIME
3 min, 52 sec by Tamar

Gold Found	Prospectors	Durations	Locations
0.02 ounces			
0.03 ounces			
0.05 ounces			
0.08 ounces			
0.12 ounces			

Hardwood Floors

Jeff is working every day this week, installing hardwood floors for five different people. Each job is scheduled for a different day and involves installation of a different type of wood flooring in a different room or section of each home. Using only the clues below, determine which person Jeff is working for on each day, and what type of flooring each customer has requested and for which rooms or areas of the customer's home.

1. The dining room job doesn't involve cherry wood.

2. Neither Athena nor the customer scheduled for Friday wants to have just their bedroom or the entire first floor redone in hardwood.

3. The five customers are Leilani, the one who chose oak flooring, the one who's having the entire house refloored, Athena (who isn't redoing her dining room floor), and the Friday appointment.

4. The oak flooring (which won't be used on Tuesday's job) will be installed the day before the cherry flooring (which was chosen by Chad).

5. Of Anthony and the customer who chose mahogany, one is redoing the living room and the other is reflooring the entire first floor of the house.

6. Of Monday's job and the living room project, one is in Athena's house and the other involves pine flooring.

	Customers					Woods					Areas				
	Anthony	Athena	Chad	Leilani	Stephanie	Cherry	Mahogany	Maple	Oak	Pine	Bedroom	Dining Room	First Floor	Living Room	Whole House
Days Monday															
Tuesday															
Wednesday															
Thursday															
Friday															
Areas Bedroom															
Dining Room															
First Floor															
Living Room															
Whole House															
Woods Cherry															
Mahogany															
Maple															
Oak															
Pine															

Days	Customers	Woods	Areas
Monday			
Tuesday			
Wednesday			
Thursday			
Friday			

SOLVE RATE
40.8%

AVERAGE TIME
10 min, 26 sec

BEST TIME
4 min, 35 sec by roxieC

Philatelists

Five philatelists—or stamp collectors—visited their local collectibles shop today to see what rare new stamps were in stock. Each was pleased to find and purchase a new stamp for his or her collection. Using only the clues below, determine the year and original value of each stamp, who purchased it, and for how much.

1. The five philatelists were Jackie, Kadence (who didn't buy the 12¢ stamp), the collector who bought the 1931 stamp, the one who paid $750 for the new acquisition, and the one who bought the 11¢ stamp.

2. Neither the stamp that sold for the highest price today nor the one that sold for $600 was originally issued in 1923.

3. Talon bought either the 8¢ or the 5¢ stamp.

4. Of Kadence and the person who bought the 1927 stamp, one paid the most of all five collectors and the other bought the 5¢ stamp.

5. Either Jackie or the collector who spent $600 today bought the 11¢ stamp.

6. The 1912 stamp didn't fetch the highest price today.

7. Either Reece or Kadence bought the 5¢ stamp.

8. The stamp issued in 1927 cost its purchaser $75 more than the stamp Jackie purchased today.

		Jackie	Kadence	Kimberly	Reece	Talon	1912	1923	1927	1931	1934	3¢	5¢	8¢	11¢	12¢
Prices	$525															
	$600															
	$675															
	$750															
	$825															
Orig. Values	3¢															
	5¢															
	8¢															
	11¢															
	12¢															
Issue Years	1912															
	1923															
	1927															
	1931															
	1934															

Prices	Collectors	Issue Years	Orig. Values
$525			
$600			
$675			
$750			
$825			

Antarctic Adventure

To help raise awareness about climate change at the poles, an environmental group sponsored five different American teams in a race (on foot!) across the continent of Antarctica. Each of the five teams came from a different state, and each team was of a different size. All five teams successfully crossed the continent, and although they each began at the same time, they each took a different number of days to make the passage. Using only the clues below, find out how long it took each team to cross Antarctica, how many members were in each team, and from what state each originated.

1. The team that completed the trek in 295 days isn't from Oregon.
2. Of the team that finished in 275 days (which isn't from Wisconsin) and the one with 7 members (which isn't the Parker team), one is the Timberton team and the other came from Kansas.
3. The Jackson team isn't the smallest of the five, but it was the last to finish.
4. The five teams are the one that finished first, the one from South Carolina, the team from Oregon, the Parker expedition (which finished exactly 10 days after the Timberton team), and the team with exactly 9 members (which isn't the Blankley team).
5. Of the Blankley team (which wasn't the first to finish) and the one that finished in 275 days, one has 6 members and the other has 9 members.

		Expeditions					Home States					Team Sizes				
		Blankley	Daugherty	Jackson	Parker	Timberton	Kansas	Louisiana	Oregon	South Carolina	Wisconsin	4	6	7	9	12
Lengths	265 days															
	275 days															
	285 days															
	295 days															
	305 days															
Team Sizes	4															
	6															
	7															
	9															
	12															
Home States	Kansas															
	Louisiana															
	Oregon															
	South Carolina															
	Wisconsin															

Lengths	Expeditions	Home States	Team Sizes
265 days			
275 days			
285 days			
295 days			
305 days			

SOLVE RATE
40.6%

AVERAGE TIME
13 min, 49 sec

BEST TIME
2 min, 39 sec by darsinewman

Talk, Talk, Talk

Jaylen and her four best friends love to keep in touch with each other on their cell phones, but sometimes their mobile bills can get a bit out of hand! Each girl has a different type of phone; each phone has a special extra feature and is a different color. Using only the clues below, figure out how many minutes each girl used on her cell phone plan last month, and determine the color and special feature of each girl's phone.

1. The five girls are the two who used 500 and 600 minutes last month, the one with the hands-free cell phone, Talia (who didn't use 550 minutes last month and doesn't have an mp3 player on her phone), and the one with the blue phone (who isn't Rebekah).

2. Jaylen didn't use 550 minutes last month.

3. Of Linda and the girl with the white phone, one used 500 minutes and the other has a hands-free phone.

4. The girl with the pink phone used 50 more minutes than Jaylen.

5. The girl who used the fewest minutes last month has the violet phone.

6. Between Rebekah and Linda, one has the violet phone and the other has the camera phone.

7. The girl with the smart phone used fewer minutes than the one with the silver-colored phone.

	Talkers					Colors					Features				
	Jaylen	Kaden	Linda	Rebekah	Talia	Blue	Pink	Silver	Violet	White	Camera	Flip Phone	Hands Free	MP3 Player	Smart Phone
450															
500															
550															
600															
650															
Camera															
Flip Phone															
Hands Free															
MP3 Player															
Smart Phone															
Blue															
Pink															
Silver															
Violet															
White															

SOLVE RATE
40.6%

AVERAGE TIME
12 min, 57 sec

BEST TIME
2 min, 48 sec by urielzet

Minutes	Talkers	Colors	Features
450			
500			
550			
600			
650			

New Stars

Astronomers announced the discovery of five new stars this week. Each star is a different distance from Earth (measured in parsecs), and each has a different mass relative to our sun (referred to as solar mass). Using only the clues below, determine the distance and solar mass of each new star, its name, and the astronomer who discovered it.

1. The star Roy discovered has a mass of either 2.5 or 5.0 solar masses.
2. Dendricle II isn't 12 or 96 parsecs away from Earth.
3. Of Minitarius and the star discovered by Esmerelda, one has a mass of 2.5 solar masses and the other is the most distant of the five.
4. The five stars are the one discovered by Blake, Phylarian, Esmerelda's discovery (which isn't the most massive star), the one that is 48 parsecs from Earth, and the one that has a mass of 8.1 solar masses.
5. Minitarius is twice as far from Earth as the star Blake discovered.
6. Keaton's discovery isn't the nearest star of the five.
7. The star with a mass of 2.5 solar masses was discovered by either Pierce or Esmerelda.
8. Beta Colaris isn't the most distant of the five stars.

		Astronomers					Stars					Solar Masses				
		Blake	Esmerelda	Keaton	Pierce	Roy	Beta Colaris	Dendricle II	Minitarius	Phylarian	Zinfadron	1.2	2.5	5.0	8.1	9.4
Distances	6 parsecs															
	12 parsecs															
	24 parsecs															
	48 parsecs															
	96 parsecs															
Solar Masses	1.2															
	2.5															
	5.0															
	8.1															
	9.4															
Stars	Beta Colaris															
	Dendricle II															
	Minitarius															
	Phylarian															
	Zinfadron															

SOLVE RATE
40.4%

AVERAGE TIME
12 min, 49 sec

BEST TIME
3 min, 55 sec by myerslite

Distances	Astronomers	Stars	Solar Masses
6 parsecs			
12 parsecs			
24 parsecs			
48 parsecs			
96 parsecs			

Checking Accounts

Palmerston Savings and Loan had five new customers sign up this morning for checking accounts. Each customer selected a different type of account, and each chose a different customized style for their checkbooks. Using only the clues below, determine the first and last name of each customer, his or her account type, and checkbook illustrations.

1. Of Carter and Julius, one (Mr. Neville) chose the economy-level checking account and the other (who didn't have the surname Pollis) opted for the multi-colored balloon checkbook.

2. Between Braden and the customer who chose the dog-themed checkbook, one got the premium-level checking account and the other had the last name Garston.

3. Spencer didn't sign up for a retirement checking account.

4. Of Emma and the customer who got the balloon-themed checkbook, one signed up for the student checking account and the other had Lipton as a surname.

5. The customer with the horse-themed checkbook signed up for a premium-level account.

6. The retirement customer ordered the clown-themed checkbook.

		First Names					Last Names					Account Types				
		Braden	Carter	Emma	Julius	Spencer	Farmar	Garston	Lipton	Neville	Pollis	Economy	Premium	Super-Saver	Retirement	Student
Styles	Balloons															
	Clowns															
	Dogs															
	Horses															
	Sunset															
Account Types	Economy															
	Premium															
	Super-Saver															
	Retirement															
	Student															
Last Names	Farmar															
	Garston															
	Lipton															
	Neville															
	Pollis															

Styles	First Names	Last Names	Account Types
Balloons			
Clowns			
Dogs			
Horses			
Sunset			

SOLVE RATE
40%

AVERAGE TIME
11 min, 22 sec

BEST TIME
3 min, 36 sec by haley

Keeping Up with the Joneses ...

Spooner Street isn't very large (there are only five houses on it, each numbered consecutively), and each of the five inhabitants wants to differentiate his or her home from the others. Each homeowner builds a different type of house and paints it a different color to ensure that each home is not at all like any of the neighbors' homes. Using only the clues below, can you determine the street number, color, and type of construction chosen by each homeowner?

1. Of the owner of 4157 Spooner Street and the owner of the indigo house, one is Jason and the other lives in the Victorian house.
2. The street number of the country house comes immediately after the street number for the bungalow.
3. The street number for the violet house (which isn't the duplex) comes immediately after the street number for the ranch home.
4. 4160 Spooner Street isn't pink.
5. The five homes are Laura's (which isn't the indigo house), 4156 Spooner Street, the ranch house, 4158 Spooner Street, and the white house (which is at 4159 Spooner Street).
6. Theodore's street number comes immediately before that of the country house (which wasn't Kamryn's).

		Jason	Kamryn	Laura	Roberto	Theodore	Indigo	Pink	Tan	Violet	White	Bungalow	Country House	Duplex	Ranch House	Victorian House
House Numbers	4156															
	4157															
	4158															
	4159															
	4160															
Houses	Bungalow															
	Country House															
	Duplex															
	Ranch House															
	Victorian House															
House Colors	Indigo															
	Pink															
	Tan															
	Violet															
	White															

House Numbers	First Names	House Colors	Houses
4156			
4157			
4158			
4159			
4160			

SOLVE RATE
39.8%

AVERAGE TIME
16 min, 42 sec

BEST TIME
3 min, 35 sec by Vaughns

The Barbershop

Five customers arrived all at once at Tyler's barbershop, A Cut Above the Rest. Using only the clues below, figure out the order in which each customer was served, what type of haircut each received, and what color hair each had.

1. The five customers are the one who was served first, the one who got the flat-top, Matthew, the customer who requested a crew cut (who wasn't served fourth), and the one who has prematurely gray hair (who isn't Alan).

2. The second customer to be served didn't get the Mohawk.

3. Trevor got his haircut before Matthew (who doesn't have brown hair).

4. Of Alan (who wasn't served first) and the person who was served second, one has blond hair and the other has gray hair.

5. Jay (who didn't have black hair) was served last.

6. Darren got either a Mohawk or a bowl cut.

7. Of the brown-haired customer and the one who was served second, one is Trevor and the other got a bowl cut.

		Customers					Haircuts					Hair Colors				
		Alan	Darren	Jay	Matthew	Trevor	Bowl Cut	Caesar Cut	Crew Cut	Flattop	Mohawk	Black	Blond	Brown	Gray	Red
Orders	First															
	Second															
	Third															
	Fourth															
	Fifth															
Hair Colors	Black															
	Blond															
	Brown															
	Gray															
	Red															
Haircuts	Bowl Cut															
	Caesar Cut															
	Crew Cut															
	Flattop															
	Mohawk															

Orders	Customers	Haircuts	Hair Colors
First			
Second			
Third			
Fourth			
Fifth			

Wacky Water Bills

There have been problems lately with the water bills for certain residents of Penrose Tower Apartments. Five different residents in the span of the past six months have each been vastly overcharged on one of their bills. Using only the clues below, determine the month in which each resident was overcharged, the total amount of the faulty bill, and the apartment number each resides in.

1. The five residents are Max (who was overcharged on his May bill), the occupant of apartment #302 (who wasn't billed $135 by the water company), Eliza, the one whose faulty bill was for $159, and the one who was overcharged in April.
2. Neither Max nor Owen lives in apartment #255.
3. The resident who received the faulty bill in April was charged $8 more than the one who was most recently overcharged.
4. The resident who was billed erroneously for $159 (but not in June) doesn't live in apartment #280.
5. The faulty bill that was sent to apartment #280 was for a smaller amount than the one that was mistakenly sent to Eliza (who doesn't live in apartment #255).
6. The faulty bill sent to apartment #192 was larger than the one received by Lillian in apartment #280.

		People					Months					Apt. Numbers				
		Eliza	Kassandra	Lillian	Max	Owen	March	April	May	June	July	#134	#192	#255	#280	#302
Water Bills	$135															
	$143															
	$151															
	$159															
	$167															
Apt. Numbers	#134															
	#192															
	#255															
	#280															
	#302															
Months	March															
	April															
	May															
	June															
	July															

Water Bills	People	Months	Apt. Numbers
$135			
$143			
$151			
$159			
$167			

Incunabula

In the world of antiquarian book-dealing, some of the rarest and most desired books are called incunabula—a term that refers to any printer book published before 1501. A small auction was held this week in which five incunabula were put up for bids. Using only the clues below, determine the title and publication year of each book, who won it, and how much the person paid for it.

1. *Chronicon* was published in 1497.
2. Mrs. Solomon didn't make a final bid of $4,250 and didn't win the *Infortiatum* auction.
3. Neither the book published in 1498 nor one that sold for $4,250 (which isn't *Chronicon*) was won by Dr. Horwitz.
4. The 1496 book didn't have the highest final bid.
5. The five incunabula are the ones published in 1496 and 1497, *Missale Romanum,* the one that sold for $5,600, and the book won by Marguerite Mellon (which didn't have the lowest final auction price).
6. Somewhat confusingly for collectors of incunabula, *Chronicon* was published just one year after the similarly titled *Polycronicon.*
7. Of the book won by Lucius Payton and the one published in 1498, one was *Aquila Volante* and the other was *Chronicon.*
8. The book that fetched the highest final bid was published one year after the book that sold for $5,600.

	Bidders					Incunabula					Final Bids				
	Horwitz	Lilliford	Mellon	Payton	Solomon	Aquila Volante	Chronicon	Infortiatum	Mis. Romanum	Polycronicon	$3,500	$4,250	$5,600	$9,800	$14,950
1494															
1495															
1496															
1497															
1498															
$3,500															
$4,250															
$5,600															
$9,800															
$14,950															
Aquila Volante															
Chronicon															
Infortiatum															
Mis. Romanum															
Polycronicon															

Years — left axis label. Final Bids — left axis label. Incunabula — left axis label.

Years	Bidders	Incunabula	Final Bids
1494			
1495			
1496			
1497			
1498			

Stormy Seas

Thankfully, none of the first five hurricanes of this year's big storm season made landfall near any populated areas. Each storm formed—and dissipated—over the Atlantic Ocean. Using only the clues below, determine the name and maximum size of each storm (Category 1 is weakest and Category 5 is strongest), the date it formed, and how many days it lasted as a hurricane before it dissipated.

1. The five storms are the ones that lasted three and five days, Charlotte, the one that formed on September 28, and the biggest of them all—the Category 5 hurricane (which wasn't named Angie).
2. Of the Category 3 hurricane and the one that lasted for only a day, one is named Charlotte and the other Eustis.
3. The five storms are the ones that lasted two and six days, Hurricane Darla, the one that formed on August 29, and the Category 4 storm.
4. Either the largest storm or the one that formed on September 28 lasted as a hurricane for six straight days.
5. The Category 5 storm didn't form on October 6.
6. The storm that began on September 15 was one category smaller than the one that formed on August 29, which was one category smaller than the storm that formed on September 28.
7. The hurricane that lasted for two days was stronger than the one that lasted for the longest amount of time.
8. The hurricane that formed on October 6 isn't named Charlotte and didn't last for three days.

	Names					Dates					Durations				
	Angie	Becka	Charlotte	Darla	Eustis	August 29	September 15	September 28	October 6	October 17	1 day	2 days	3 days	5 days	6 days
Storm Sizes Category 1															
Category 2															
Category 3															
Category 4															
Category 5															
Durations 1 day															
2 days															
3 days															
5 days															
6 days															
Dates August 29															
September 15															
September 28															
October 6															
October 17															

SOLVE RATE
38.8%

AVERAGE TIME
15 min, 9 sec

BEST TIME
2 min, 54 sec by urielzet

Storm Sizes	Names	Dates	Durations
Category 1			
Category 2			
Category 3			
Category 4			
Category 5			

Teachers' Pets

Five different classrooms, each in a different grade, have recently acquired class pets—small animals of one type or another that the students care for and observe as part of their daily class work. Each class has a different type of pet, and each class is held in a different room in the school (and is taught by a different teacher). Using only the clues below, figure out what type of animal(s) are being studied by each class, the name of the teacher, the room number, and its associated grade level.

1. The second grade class isn't held in either room 115 or 222.
2. Neither Mrs. Harmon's class nor the one held in room 209 is in the fourth grade.
3. The class that has the mouse is one grade higher than the one taught by Mrs. Ashley (which isn't in room 209).
4. The third grade class doesn't have the snake.
5. Mr. Tarkle's class, which is one grade lower than Mr. Carson's, doesn't have the ant farm.
6. The class with the snake (which isn't in room 222) is in a lower grade than the class with the spider, which is in a lower grade than the class held in room 118.
7. Of the class with the ant farm and Mrs. Ashley's class, one is in the second grade and the other is held in room 102.

		Mrs. Ashley	Mr. Carson	Mrs. Graves	Mrs. Harmon	Mr. Tarkle	Room 102	Room 115	Room 118	Room 209	Room 222	Ant Farm	Frog	Mouse	Snake	Spider
Grades	2nd grade															
	3rd grade															
	4th grade															
	5th grade															
	6th grade															
Class Pets	Ant Farm															
	Frog															
	Mouse															
	Snake															
	Spider															
Rooms	Room 102															
	Room 115															
	Room 118															
	Room 209															
	Room 222															

SOLVE RATE
38.7%

AVERAGE TIME
18 min, 11 sec

BEST TIME
3 min, 44 sec by khead

Grades	Teachers	Rooms	Class Pets
2nd grade			
3rd grade			
4th grade			
5th grade			
6th grade			

waterfalls

Terrence Tenford is one of the few nature photographers who can rightfully claim to have photographed five of the world's highest and most inaccessible waterfalls. Using only the clues below, determine the height of each of these waterfalls, the name of the river that forms it, and the year in which Terrence photographed it.

1. The waterfall Terrence photographed in 1998 was taller than Julamongry Falls (which he visited in 2005).
2. The five waterfalls are Kassandra Falls, the waterfall Terrence photographed most recently (which wasn't the shortest of the five), the waterfall formed by the Comarongo River, the second-highest waterfall, and Clarafin Falls (which Terrence didn't visit in 2002).
3. The waterfall formed by the Miraclee River isn't 496 meters high.
4. Kassandra Falls (which Terrence didn't visit in 2002) is formed by the majestic Ejibou River.
5. The waterfall Terrence photographed in 2005 (which wasn't exactly 496 meters high) wasn't as tall as Clarafin Falls.
6. The waterfall formed by the Tambaroon River is just 7 meters shorter than the one on the Comarongo River.
7. Terrence didn't photograph Ryland Falls in 2002.

	Waterfalls					Rivers					Years				
	Clarafin	Diamond Drop	Julamongry	Kassandra	Ryland	Brahmatan	Comarongo	Ejibou	Miraclee	Tambaroon	1995	1998	2002	2005	2007
Heights 475 meters															
482 meters															
489 meters															
496 meters															
503 meters															
Years 1995															
1998															
2002															
2005															
2007															
Rivers Brahmatan															
Comarongo															
Ejibou															
Miraclee															
Tambaroon															

Heights	Waterfalls	Rivers	Years
475 meters			
482 meters			
489 meters			
496 meters			
503 meters			

Good Fences Take Good Laborers ...

Krista needs to have a new fence built around her house in order to keep her dogs safely in her yard. Always looking for the best deal, she calls five different contractors and receives a different estimate from each. Each contractor also requires a different number of days to complete the fence and wants to hire a different number of laborers for the project. Using only the clues below, determine the estimate, project length, and number of laborers offered by each contractor.

1. The estimate that required four days was neither the $800 nor the $1,400 estimate.
2. Either the contractor with the $800 estimate or Bob Roth requires exactly five laborers.
3. The estimate that included three laborers came from either Mike Green or Ed Jones. Ed Jones did not submit the estimate requiring six laborers.
4. Tom Lane's estimate required either three or four laborers.
5. The five contractors were the one who needed 6 days to finish the project, Bob Roth, Ed Jones, the one who gave the $1,200 estimate and the one who required five laborers.
6. The $1,400 estimate didn't have a 3-day schedule.
7. Bob Roth's estimate was $200 less than the estimate with the 5-day schedule.
8. Of Ed Jones and the contractor with the 5-day schedule, one came back with the highest estimate and the other required three laborers to complete the job.

		Bob Roth	Ed Jones	Jim Beall	Mike Green	Tom Lane	3 days	4 days	5 days	6 days	7 days	Two	Three	Four	Five	Six
Estimates	$600															
	$800															
	$1,000															
	$1,200															
	$1,400															
Workers	Two															
	Three															
	Four															
	Five															
	Six															
Lengths	3 days															
	4 days															
	5 days															
	6 days															
	7 days															

SOLVE RATE
38.1%

AVERAGE TIME
16 min, 36 sec

BEST TIME
2 min, 33 sec by urielzet

Estimates	Contractors	Lengths	Workers
$600			
$800			
$1,000			
$1,200			
$1,400			

A Five-Alarm Catastrophe

The local fire department was flummoxed when they received five separate CIT (cat-in-tree) calls, at five different locations, at almost exactly the same time. The dispatcher quickly mapped out all five locations and determined the quickest route in which to reach all five, in some specific order. Using only the clues below, match the pet owner to his or her cat, the location of the tree, and the order in which the cats were rescued.

1. Between Wesley's cat (who was rescued just after the cat on Brook Street) and the one stuck up in an oak tree on Racine Street, one is named Whiskers and the other Princess.
2. Louis's cat was rescued immediately before the cat at Cape Court.
3. Felix's cat wasn't rescued last.
4. The five cats are Whiskers (who wasn't up a tree at Topper Way), Griffin's cat (who wasn't Princess), the one that was rescued second, the one at Hyde Lane, and the one that belongs to Louis.
5. Between Whiskers and Mittens (who was rescued right before Cardamom), one is Jackie's cat and the other was rescued last.

		Felix	Griffin	Jackie	Louis	Wesley	Cardamom	Dimples	Mittens	Princess	Whiskers	Brook Street	Cape Court	Hyde Lane	Racine Street	Topper Way
Orders	First															
	Second															
	Third															
	Fourth															
	Fifth															
Locations	Brook Street															
	Cape Court															
	Hyde Lane															
	Racine Street															
	Topper Way															
Cats	Cardamom															
	Dimples															
	Mittens															
	Princess															
	Whiskers															

Owners / Cats / Locations

Orders	Owners	Cats	Locations
First			
Second			
Third			
Fourth			
Fifth			

SOLVE RATE
38.1%

AVERAGE TIME
15 min, 45 sec

BEST TIME
4 min, 52 sec by jade_3031

Lawyers

Paula and Bobby Beacham couldn't be prouder of their five children, all of whom became lawyers in different states and with different focuses. Using only the clues below, figure out what type of law each practices, what state each practices in, and the year in which each passed the bar exam.

1. The five Beacham children are the one who practices in California (who doesn't focus on criminal law), the lawyer who practices in Tennessee (who passed the bar in 2008), Damian, the malpractice lawyer, and the one who passed the bar exam in 2006 (who also doesn't practice criminal law).
2. Kaylin passed her bar exam earlier than Leilani.
3. Either Kaylin or Damian (who doesn't practice criminal law) live and work in sunny Florida.
4. Damian passed his bar exam sometime before the sibling who practices in California.
5. The tax lawyer doesn't work in Florida and isn't Leilani.
6. Of the Wisconsin lawyer and the sibling who was the first Beacham to pass the bar exam, one is Selena and the other is a malpractice lawyer.
7. Selena passed her bar exam one year after Zion.
8. The most recent Beacham to pass the bar exam doesn't practice bankruptcy law.

		Damian	Kaylin	Leilani	Selena	Zion	Bankruptcy	Criminal	Immigration	Malpractice	Tax	California	Florida	Ohio	Tennessee	Wisconsin
Years	2005															
	2006															
	2007															
	2008															
	2009															
States	California															
	Florida															
	Ohio															
	Tennessee															
	Wisconsin															
Types	Bankruptcy															
	Criminal															
	Immigration															
	Malpractice															
	Tax															

Years	Lawyers	Types	States
2005			
2006			
2007			
2008			
2009			

SOLVE RATE
38.0%

AVERAGE TIME
11 min, 47 sec

BEST TIME
2 min, 50 sec by gulfcoastswimmer

In Walt's Wallet

Walt's been trying to pay down his debt this year, and part of that requires him to re-examine his wallet—specifically, the credit cards within it. Using only the clues below, determine the credit limit, interest rates, and expiration dates for all five of Walt's credit cards.

1. The card with the highest interest rate doesn't expire in June and doesn't have a $4,500 credit limit.
2. The credit card with the earliest expiration date has a credit limit that's $1,000 lower than the one with the 4.9% interest rate.
3. Neither Walt's Fidelis card (which doesn't have the lowest interest rate) nor the one with the 4.9% interest rate expires in June 2013.
4. Of the card with the 9.5% interest rate and the one that expires in February, one is from Crident Corporation and the other has the smallest credit limit.
5. Either Walt's Deltron card or the one with the second-highest interest rate has the largest credit limit.
6. Either the Primocarte or Fidelis card has a $4,500 credit limit.
7. The five cards are Fidelis, Mordett, the one with the 9.5% interest rate, the one that expires in June, and the card with the $5,500 credit limit (which is from Primocarte Inc. but doesn't expire in 2014).

		Crident	Deltron	Fidelis	Mordett	Primocarte	2.9%	4.9%	9.5%	12.9%	19.5%	09/2012	02/2013	06/2013	12/2014	04/2015
	Card Brands						**Interest Rates**					**Exp. Dates**				
Credit Limits	$2,500															
	$3,500															
	$4,500															
	$5,500															
	$6,500															
Exp. Dates	09/2012															
	02/2013															
	06/2013															
	12/2014															
	04/2015															
Interest Rates	2.9%															
	4.9%															
	9.5%															
	12.9%															
	19.5%															

Credit Limits	Card Brands	Interest Rates	Exp. Dates
$2,500			
$3,500			
$4,500			
$5,500			
$6,500			

SOLVE RATE
37.7%

AVERAGE TIME
19 min, 11.3 sec

BEST TIME
3 min, 7 sec by khead

Providing Some Illumination

Paige was still pretty new at working customer service at Lightbulb Emporium, so when five customers came in all at once and each asked for five different types of lights, she felt like she might be in a little over her head. Her training kicked in, however, and she expertly showed the customers to the appropriate aisle in which the lights they were searching for could be found. Using only the clues below, match the customers to the type of light they were shopping for, what aisle Paige directed them to, and the final price they paid.

1. The sodium-vapor light wasn't the most expensive.
2. The mercury-vapor light cost $2.50 more than the LED light.
3. The five customers were James, the one who spent exactly $35, Jenna (whose light didn't cost $40), the one Paige sent to aisle four, and the one who bought the LED light.
4. Jenna's light cost $2.50 less than the shopper who went to aisle four.
5. Of Kelvin and the customer who spent $37.50, one bought the halogen light and the other found a quarry in aisle three.
6. Of the person that spent the least (who wasn't sent to aisle one) and Caleb, one spent a good 15 minutes examining lights in aisle four and the other bought the halogen light.
7. Aisle seven housed either neon lights or sodium-vapor lights.
8. Paige didn't send Clara to aisle one.

SOLVE RATE
37.5%

AVERAGE TIME
15 min, 29 sec

BEST TIME
5 min, 6 sec by CherylRwfm

Island Cruise

To celebrate their 20th wedding anniversary, John and Veronica treated themselves to a two-week-long South Pacific island-hopping cruise. From June 8 through the 20th the cruise ship stopped at five different islands. Always the adventurous couple, John and Veronica made the most of each excursion by participating in a different outdoor activity on each island. Using only the clues below, try to piece together their cruise itinerary.

1. The five island landings are the one made at 8:30 am, the 6:00 pm landing, the one on June 20 (which didn't happen at 10:45 am), the stop at Ephrata, and the one where John and Veronica hiked a massive volcano on the island of Puyallup.
2. The June 14 landing occurred at precisely 12 noon.
3. John and Veronica enjoyed their rainforest tour on Barnhart Island.
4. The zip line excursion took place three days before the volcano hike.
5. There are no horses on the island of Isanti.
6. The couple went snorkeling three days before the landing that occurred at 6:00 pm.
7. The Barnhart excursion took place sometime after the landing on the exotic isle of Watonga.
8. The June 17 landing wasn't on Puyallup.

	Times					Islands					Activities				
	8:30 am	10:45 am	12 Noon	2:30 pm	6:00 pm	Barnhart	Ephrata	Isanti	Puyallup	Watonga	Horseback	Rainforest	Snorkeling	Volcano	Zip Line
June 8															
June 11															
June 14															
June 17															
June 20															
Horseback															
Rainforest															
Snorkeling															
Volcano															
Zip Line															
Barnhart															
Ephrata															
Isanti															
Puyallup															
Watonga															

SOLVE RATE
37.1%

AVERAGE TIME
15 min, 5 sec

BEST TIME
3 min, 7 sec by Hayden

Dates	Times	Islands	Activities
June 8			
June 11			
June 14			
June 17			
June 20			

Serving Their Country

The principal of Fletcher High School had a plaque installed in the school's trophy case, commemorating all Fletcher High alumni who enlisted in the military. The plaque lists each person's name, the year each graduated Fletcher High, the branch of the military each chose to enter, and the state each now calls home. Using only the clues below, determine which alumni joined each military branch, when each graduated, and where each currently lives.

1. The graduate of the class of 1993 doesn't live in New Jersey.
2. Melissa graduated four years after Jocelyn.
3. The five alumni are the Alaskan, Natasha (who didn't join the Marines), the one who lives in New Jersey, the one who joined the Coast Guard, and the 2001 graduate (who was either Brooklyn or Beau).
4. The alumnus who joined the Coast Guard graduated four years after the one who now lives in Texas.
5. Brooklyn joined the Air Force.
6. Of the class of 2001 graduate and the one who joined the Coast Guard, one is Beau and the other lives in Texas.
7. The Californian graduated four years after the one who joined the Navy.

		Beau	Brooklyn	Jocelyn	Melissa	Natasha	Air Force	Army	Coast Guard	Marines	Navy	Alabama	Alaska	California	New Jersey	Texas
Years	1989															
	1993															
	1997															
	2001															
	2005															
States	Alabama															
	Alaska															
	California															
	New Jersey															
	Texas															
Branches	Air Force															
	Army															
	Coast Guard															
	Marines															
	Navy															

Years	Alumni	Branches	States
1989			
1993			
1997			
2001			
2005			

SOLVE RATE
37.0%

AVERAGE TIME
14 min, 10 sec

BEST TIME
4 min, 15 sec by urielzet

Fruits of Their Labor ...

The Wedgefield County Fruit Stand is a popular stop for most shoppers, because some of the best fruit growers in the area use it to sell their produce. This week, five competing fruit growers decided to hold a little competition to see who could bring in the most money from their fruit. Each seller offered only one type of fruit, and each was allowed only one full day (Monday through Friday) at the stand. Using only the clues below, determine the day, type of fruit, and total earnings associated with each fruit grower.

1. Tuesday's seller didn't offer pineapples.
2. Of the kiwi seller (who wasn't at the stand on Friday) and Mary, one sold his or her fruit on Tuesday and the other won the competition, earning more than all the other sellers.
3. Neither the seller who earned $37 nor the watermelon vendor was Paige.
4. Of Dante (who didn't sell limes) and the fruit vendor who sold watermelons, one was at the fruit stand on Wednesday and the other earned $55.
5. Among Anahi and the person who earned $89, one sold his or her fruit on Tuesday and the other sold on Friday.
6. Neither Mary (who didn't sell limes) nor Thursday's seller won the competition.
7. The seller who earned $55 (who wasn't at the market on Friday) set up his or her table at the fruit stand the day after the person who earned $37.

	First Names					Fruits					Earnings				
	Anahi	Dante	Heidi	Mary	Paige	Apricots	Kiwis	Limes	Pineapples	Watermelons	$24	$37	$55	$89	$120
Monday															
Tuesday															
Wednesday															
Thursday															
Friday															
$24															
$37															
$55															
$89															
$120															
Apricots															
Kiwis															
Limes															
Pineapples															
Watermelons															

Days	First Names	Fruits	Earnings
Monday			
Tuesday			
Wednesday			
Thursday			
Friday			

SOLVE RATE
36.9%

AVERAGE TIME
16 min, 54 sec

BEST TIME
6 min, 10 sec by urielzet

Time for a Test ...

Five students at Parmoose High School each took an end-of-year final exam this week; each student is in a different class taught by a different teacher. All of them passed, though some did better than others, and no one got the same exact score. Using only the clues below, determine the teacher, subject, and test score for each of the five students.

1. Of Mr. Reinsford's student and Isaiah, one scored an impressive 96 and the other took the chemistry test.
2. Trevor took his final in either English or chemistry.
3. The person who got the highest test score of all five students didn't have Mr. Ackerman or Mr. Mockel as a teacher.
4. Either London or Isaiah took the chemistry exam.
5. The five students were Mrs. Koralis's student, Gage, Isaiah (who didn't take the physics exam), the one who scored an 89, and the one who took the geometry final exam.
6. The student who got a 76 didn't have Mr. Mockel as a teacher.
7. Mr. Reinsford's student's score was the next highest after Gage's, whose score was the next highest after Kayla's.

		First Names					Teachers					Subjects				
		Gage	Isaiah	Kayla	London	Trevor	Mr. Ackerman	Mr. Mockel	Mr. Reinsford	Mrs. Koralis	Mrs. Rocek	Biology	Chemistry	English	Geometry	Physics
Test Scores	72															
	76															
	81															
	89															
	96															
Subjects	Biology															
	Chemistry															
	English															
	Geometry															
	Physics															
Teachers	Mr. Ackerman															
	Mr. Mockel															
	Mr. Reinsford															
	Mrs. Koralis															
	Mrs. Rocek															

Test Scores	First Names	Teachers	Subjects
72			
76			
81			
89			
96			

SOLVE RATE
36.7%

AVERAGE TIME
19 min, 2 sec

BEST TIME
6 min, 13 sec by hard2beatme

Track and Field

Oviedo's track-and-field team came in first place in an impressive five events during the county finals! Each of the five events was won by a different team member, each of whom trained intensively for this competition for a different number of months. All contestants were given a randomly assigned number at the beginning of the competition. Using only the clues below, determine the event won by each athlete, the number that was assigned to each, and how long each trained for the competition.

1. #26 trained one month longer than #80.
2. The five athletes are the one who trained for 8 months, #54, the one who trained for 7 months (who didn't win the pole vault competition), the team member who came in first in the javelin throw, and Karla.
3. #12 trained longer for his or her event than did the athlete who won the 400m race (who wasn't #26).
4. Landon wasn't #49 and didn't win the 400m race.
5. Karla didn't compete in the 100m hurdles.
6. Either the athlete who trained for 6 months or the one who won the javelin competition was Braydon.
7. The winner of the pole vault trained 1 month longer than the athlete who placed first in the javelin throw.
8. Of Layla and the athlete who trained the longest, one wore #12 and the other wore #26.

		Athletes					Numbers					Events				
		Braydon	Joshua	Karla	Layla	Landon	12	26	49	54	80	100 m Hurdle	400 m Race	Javelin	Long Jump	Pole Vault
Training	5 months															
	6 months															
	7 months															
	8 months															
	9 months															
Events	100 m Hurdle															
	400 m Race															
	Javelin															
	Long Jump															
	Pole Vault															
Numbers	12															
	26															
	49															
	54															
	80															

Training	Athletes	Numbers	Events
5 months			
6 months			
7 months			
8 months			
9 months			

SOLVE RATE
36.6%

AVERAGE TIME
13 min, 28 sec

BEST TIME
4 min, 8 sec by pzlkari

The Dart Toss

Melody and four of her friends went to the carnival, where each of them bought a different number of turns at the dart toss game. By the end of the night, they each earned a different number of total points, which they could then use to claim a prize. Using only the clues below, determine how many turns each player took, how many total points each accumulated, and what prize each eventually selected.

1. The five players are the one who won the water pistol (who didn't take the most turns), the player who accumulated the least points, the one who took the fewest turns (and ended up winning the stuffed bear), Stella (who finished with five fewer points than the player who took five turns), and Kendra.

2. The player who took 20 turns at the dart toss accumulated fewer points than Kendra (who didn't end up with exactly 20 points).

3. The player who won the cowboy hat (who didn't take 10 total turns) finished with five more points than the one who won the stuffed bear, but fewer points than the player who won the water pistol.

4. Kendra's total number of turns was neither 10 nor 25.

5. Of James and the one who won the disposable camera, one had the last accumulated points by the end of the night and the other took the fewest turns.

6. No one ended up with the same number of points and turns.

7. Nivena didn't end the night with 15 total points.

		James	Kendra	Melody	Nivena	Stella	5	10	15	20	25	Camera	Cowboy Hat	Rubber Ball	Stuffed Bear	Water Pistol
Points	15															
	20															
	25															
	30															
	35															
Prizes	Camera															
	Cowboy Hat															
	Rubber Ball															
	Stuffed Bear															
	Water Pistol															
Turns	5															
	10															
	15															
	20															
	25															

SOLVE RATE
35.6%

AVERAGE TIME
16 min, 31 sec

BEST TIME
4 min, 48 sec by russelldugan

Points	Players	Turns	Prizes
15			
20			
25			
30			
35			

Extreme Gardening

Petra is what some would call an extreme gardener—she only works with plants and flowers that are notoriously difficult to grow outside of their natural habitats. This year she is working with five different exotic flowers, each of which requires an exact soil pH level to survive. Using only the clues below, determine the pH level required for each plant, the color of its flowers, and how long it took each to successfully germinate from seeds.

1. The plant that took four weeks to germinate doesn't have yellow flowers.
2. The five plants were the *gelundias,* the *estrellias,* the one that requires a 5.9 pH level, the one that germinated in six weeks, and the one with pink flowers.
3. Of the *gelundias* and the plant that was quickest to successfully germinate (which was neither the *aprilias* nor the *farabelles*), one requires the lowest pH level of all five and the other has pink flowers.
4. The plant with red flowers requires either a pH level of 5.5 or 7.0.
5. Neither the plant that requires a 5.9 soil pH nor the one with the longest germination period is the *gelundias* (which has yellow flowers).
6. The plant that needs a soil pH of 5.5 successfully germinated one week after the one that thrives in a 6.4 pH (which doesn't have orange flowers and isn't *farabelles*).

	Angelines	Aprilias	Estrellias	Farabelles	Gelundias	Orange	Pink	Red	White	Yellow	5.2	5.5	5.9	6.4	7.0
3 weeks															
4 weeks															
5 weeks															
6 weeks															
7 weeks															
5.2															
5.5															
5.9															
6.4															
7.0															
Orange															
Pink															
Red															
White															
Yellow															

SOLVE RATE
35.0%

AVERAGE TIME
19 min, 32 sec

BEST TIME
3 min, 13 sec by urielzet

Germinations	Flowers	Colors	Soil PHs
3 weeks			
4 weeks			
5 weeks			
6 weeks			
7 weeks			

The Halloween Weigh-In

Five friends decided to hold a little trick-or-treating competition this year to see who could bring in the most candy at the end of the night. Each trick-or-treater left at a different time, and each was dressed in a different costume. After the candy weigh-in, there was a clear winner, and none of the five children brought in the same amount of candy. Using only the clues below, determine the costume worn by each child, the time each child left, and the amount of candy each brought in by the end of the night.

1. The five children were Cameron, the one who brought in 1.9 pounds of candy (who left 15 minutes before Adrianna), Angelina, the one who dressed up as a mummy (who didn't bring in the least amount of candy), and the person who left at 7:30 pm (who didn't dress up as a witch).

2. Between the one who left at 7:00 pm and the trick-or-treater who dressed up as a mummy, one was Adrianna and the other collected the most candy.

3. The child who collected 1.5 pounds of candy (who didn't dress up as a vampire or a zombie) left 15 minutes before the person who brought in 1.9 pounds of treats.

4. The five trick-or-treaters were the one who dressed up as a vampire (who didn't bring in 1.5 pounds of candy), Aden, the one who brought in the most candy, the one who left the latest, and Cameron (who wasn't the zombie).

		Children				Costumes					Weights				
		Aden	Adrianna	Angelina	Cameron	Julissa	Mummy	Vampire	Werewolf	Witch	Zombie	1.1 pounds	1.5 pounds	1.9 pounds	2.3 pounds	2.6 pounds
Times	7:00 pm															
	7:15 pm															
	7:30 pm															
	7:45 pm															
	8:00 pm															
Weights	1.1 pounds															
	1.5 pounds															
	1.9 pounds															
	2.3 pounds															
	2.6 pounds															
Costumes	Mummy															
	Vampire															
	Werewolf															
	Witch															
	Zombie															

SOLVE RATE
34.9%

AVERAGE TIME
13 min, 46 sec

BEST TIME
3 min, 22 sec by darsinewman

Times	Children	Costumes	Weights
7:00 pm			
7:15 pm			
7:30 pm			
7:45 pm			
8:00 pm			

Free-Diving

The sport of free-diving, where competitors dive to extreme depths using no breathing apparatus, has become quite popular in recent years. The current top five women competitors in the field each come from different countries and have managed to achieve maximum depths between 92 and 104 meters. Using only the clues below, determine which country each diver is from, each diver's personal-best dive depth, and how long it took each to complete it.

1. The five divers are the one who achieved 101 meters, the one who took 3 minutes and 15 seconds on her best dive, the one who reached 98 meters (who isn't German), Myra (who isn't Canadian), and the English diver.

2. The Danish diver didn't take precisely 3 minutes and 10 seconds on her personal best dive. Neither the woman who reached 104 meters deep nor the Danish competitor is Josephine.

3. The diver whose best dive took the longest reached a maximum depth of just three meters less than the diver who took exactly 3 minutes and 10 seconds.

4. Priscilla's personal best dive depth didn't keep her underwater for precisely 3 minutes and 13 seconds.

5. The German competitor's best dive is three meters deeper than the English diver's personal best.

6. Of Natasha and the competitor with the deepest depth record, neither of them took more than 3 minutes and 11 seconds to complete their best dives.

7. The competitor with the shortest dive time reached a deeper maximum depth than the Danish diver (who isn't Priscilla).

		Josephine	Mackenna	Myra	Natasha	Priscilla	3:02	3:10	3:13	3:15	3:18	Canada	Denmark	England	France	Germany
Depths	92 meters															
	95 meters															
	98 meters															
	101 meters															
	104 meters															
Countries	Canada															
	Denmark															
	England															
	France															
	Germany															
Times	3:02															
	3:10															
	3:13															
	3:15															
	3:18															

SOLVE RATE
34.6%

AVERAGE TIME
15 min, 33 sec

BEST TIME
2 min, 49 sec by Vaughns

Depths	Divers	Times	Countries
92 meters			
95 meters			
98 meters			
101 meters			
104 meters			

It's Knot as Easy as It Looks

The local scouts had a treat today! They'd been studying knot tying for a while now, and pretty soon they would all get a chance to earn their merit badges in the field. Today, five experts in the art of knot tying came in and gave presentations to the entire troop. Each demonstrated how to tie a specific type of knot. Afterward, the troop split into five smaller groups, with each expert joining a different group to help the group learn the process first-hand. Using only the clues below, determine the type of knot demonstrated by each expert, the order in which the experts gave their presentations, and the individual study groups to which each gave hands-on training.

1. Dustin didn't give the first or second presentation and didn't give hands-on instruction to Group E.

2. The first presentation was about bowline knots.

3. The expert who worked with Group D gave a presentation sometime after the one who demonstrated how to make a sheet knot, who in turn gave a presentation sometime after the one who demonstrated the half-hitch (who wasn't Avery).

4. Between Ashton and the one who demonstrated how to make a half-hitch knot, one worked with Group C and the other gave their presentation second.

5. Norbert worked with Group D.

6. The five experts were the one who worked with Group B, the ones who gave the first and last presentations, Ashton, and the one who demonstrated the sheep shank.

		Experts					Groups					Knots				
		Ashton	Avery	Dustin	Norbert	Sam	Group A	Group B	Group C	Group D	Group E	Bowline	Half-Hitch	Halyard	Sheep Shank	Sheet
Orders	First															
	Second																
	Third																
	Fourth																
	Fifth																
Knots	Bowline																
	Half-Hitch																
	Halyard																
	Sheep Shank																
	Sheet																
Groups	Group A																
	Group B																
	Group C																
	Group D																
	Group E																

SOLVE RATE
34.5%

AVERAGE TIME
13 min, 26 sec

BEST TIME
3 min, 33 sec by Vaughns

Orders	Experts	Groups	Knots
First			
Second			
Third			
Fourth			
Fifth			

The Meteorite Hunters ...

Meteor ME-52109 struck Earth's atmosphere last Sunday and exploded into countless tiny fragments somewhere over Cedar Rapids. Five volunteers decided to help find as many of these fragments as they could. Each volunteer started his or her search from the same central location but at different times, and each went off in a different direction. Using only the clues below, determine how many fragments each discovered, what time each volunteer began his or her search, and what direction he or she went off in.

1. Either the volunteer who headed south or the one who went east of base camp started his or her search at 1:30 pm.

2. Of the volunteer who headed west of base camp and the one who started at 2:15 pm, one found three fragments, and the other discovered six.

3. Of Dustin and the volunteer who headed east, one started at 1:45 pm and the other found six meteorite fragments.

4. The volunteer who headed east (who wasn't John) started his or her search sometime before the person who headed off in a southwesterly direction (who wasn't Brenda).

5. Dustin started 15 minutes after the volunteer who discovered two fragments.

6. Of the person who arrived on 2:30 pm and the person who headed west, one is Dustin and the other found no meteorite fragments.

7. Anya (who didn't start at 2:00 pm) began her search sometime before the volunteer who found six meteorite fragments, who started off 15 minutes before the only volunteer who didn't find any meteorite fragments (who wasn't John).

		Searchers					Directions					Fragments				
		Anya	Brenda	Dustin	John	Ken	East	South	Southeast	Southwest	West	None	Two	Three	Six	Twelve
Times	1:30 pm															
	1:45 pm															
	2:00 pm															
	2:15 pm															
	2:30 pm															
Fragments	None															
	Two															
	Three															
	Six															
	Twelve															
Directions	East															
	South															
	Southeast															
	Southwest															
	West															

SOLVE RATE
34.1%

AVERAGE TIME
19 min, 47 sec

BEST TIME
3 min, 34 sec by khead

Times	Searchers	Directions	Fragments
1:30 pm			
1:45 pm			
2:00 pm			
2:15 pm			
2:30 pm			

On Line at the Music Store

Five customers were in line at the local music shop waiting to buy some CDs, when the fire alarm went off and everyone had to evacuate the building. Fortunately, it was a false alarm, and within just 10 minutes, everyone was allowed back in, but now no one remembers what order the original line had been in! Using only the clues below, determine the proper order of the line before the evacuation and the price and genre of the CD each customer wanted to purchase.

1. The five customers were the one with the hip hop CD, the one with the $12.99 CD (who wasn't first in line), Xander, and the people who were third and fourth in line.

2. The person who was second in line didn't have the country music CD.

3. Between the classical music customer and the one who was last in line (who wasn't Marc), one was Ricardo and the other had the most expensive CD.

4. The five shoppers were the one who was first in line, the hip hop fan, Brenna, and the ones with the $10.49 and $13.49 CDs.

5. Ricardo didn't have the $13.49 CD, which wasn't country music.

6. The classical music fan was third in line.

7. The person who was fourth in line didn't have the blues CD.

		Shoppers					Genres					Prices				
		Brenna	Marc	Ricardo	Valentina	Xander	Blues	Classical	Country	Hip Hop	Jazz	$9.99	$10.49	$12.99	$13.49	$13.99
Orders	First															
	Second															
	Third															
	Fourth															
	Fifth															
Prices	$9.99															
	$10.49															
	$12.99															
	$13.49															
	$13.99															
Genres	Blues															
	Classical															
	Country															
	Hip Hop															
	Jazz															

SOLVE RATE
33.6%

AVERAGE TIME
14 min, 8 sec

BEST TIME
4 min, 37 sec by khead

Orders	Shoppers	Genres	Prices
First			
Second			
Third			
Fourth			
Fifth			

The Science Fair

Students from all over the country were invited to participate in a week-long, national science fair competition. Each student presented a unique project on a certain theme, and all projects would be judged at the end of each day, when a single blue ribbon winner would be selected. A new winner was chosen each day during the first five days of the fair. Each winner was from a different state, and each submitted a project concerned with a different natural phenomenon. Using only the clues below, match the students to their project, their home state, and the day in which they were selected as a blue ribbon winner.

1. The five winners were the one chosen on Friday, the student from Wyoming, the one who submitted a project on earthquakes, Allison (who didn't win on Thursday), and Nicole.

2. The person who won on Thursday didn't study cloud formation.

3. Of the student from Michigan and the one who studied earthquakes, one won on Wednesday and the other on Tuesday.

4. The five winning entries were the one on volcanos, the one submitted by the Connecticut student, Braden's entry, and the two winning submissions from Thursday and Friday.

5. Of the student who submitted the electricity project and Francisco, one is from South Carolina and the other won Friday's competition.

6. The earthquake project won a blue ribbon one day after the magnetism project was selected to win.

		Winners					Subjects					States				
	Allison	Braden	Carson	Francisco	Nicole	Cloud Form.	Earthquakes	Electricity	Magnetism	Volcanos	Connecticut	Kentucky	Michigan	South Carolina	Wyoming
Days	Monday															
	Tuesday															
	Wednesday															
	Thursday															
	Friday															
States	Connecticut															
	Kentucky															
	Michigan															
	South Carolina															
	Wyoming															
Subjects	Cloud Form.															
	Earthquakes															
	Electricity															
	Magnetism															
	Volcanos															

SOLVE RATE
33.3%

AVERAGE TIME
15 min, 56 sec

BEST TIME
2 min, 20 sec by urielzet

Days	Winners	Subjects	States
Monday			
Tuesday			
Wednesday			
Thursday			
Friday			

Greener Grass

It can be tricky to get a healthy looking lawn in Whartonville. Numerous local pests love to dig up grass, and the rapidly shifting and unpredictable weather can be particularly punishing. Five neighbors decide to each reseed their entire lawns with a different type of grass, to see which of the five would work out best. Each of the five have different-size lawns, and each scheduled the reseeding on a different day. Using only the clues below, determine the size of each homeowner's lawn, when the homeowner scheduled the reseeding, and what type of grass each selected.

1. Of Cadence and the homeowner with the 1-acre lawn, one is scheduled for Tuesday and the other is scheduled for Sunday.

2. The homeowner who scheduled the reseeding for Saturday (which won't be with red fescue) has a smaller lawn than Cadence, who isn't scheduled for Tuesday.

3. Jamie's reseeding (which won't be with Zoysia grass) won't take place on Thursday. The homeowner with the smallest lawn isn't scheduled for reseeding on Saturday.

4. Between Tyler and the homeowner scheduled for a Thursday reseeding, one has the largest lawn and the other chose red fescue.

5. The person who's reseeding on Sunday has a smaller lawn than the homeowner who is switching to ryegrass.

6. Of Dakota and the person with the 2.5-acre lawn, one is scheduled for Friday and the other has chosen to try Bermuda grass on the new lawn.

		Cadence	Dakota	Jamie	Reid	Tyler	Saturday	Sunday	Tuesday	Thursday	Friday	Bermuda	Bluegrass	Red Fescue	Ryegrass	Zoysia
Lawn Sizes	1/2 acre															
	1 acre															
	2 acres															
	2.5 acres															
	4 acres															
Grasses	Bermuda															
	Bluegrass															
	Red Fescue															
	Ryegrass															
	Zoysia															
Days	Saturday															
	Sunday															
	Tuesday															
	Thursday															
	Friday															

Lawn Sizes	Homeowners	Days	Grasses
1/2 acre			
1 acre			
2 acres			
2.5 acres			
4 acres			

SOLVE RATE
32.9%

AVERAGE TIME
13 min, 29 sec

BEST TIME
3 min, 13 sec by russelldugan

Best Ball

Five friends went to the driving range to try out their new golf clubs. They decided to each hit 10 balls with the club of their choice and compare their best drives—the one with the shortest drive would pay for dinner later that night. Using only the clues below, determine what brand of golf club each player used, how far each player's longest drive was, and what type of club each used.

1. Between Chevy and the player who used his 5 wood, one had the longest drive of all and the other used Greenford clubs.
2. The five players were the one who used his 1 iron, Abel, Chevy (who doesn't use Triple Play clubs), the player whose best drive was 260 yards, and the one who used Pinseeker clubs.
3. The player who used his 3 wood didn't hit the longest drive, nor did his best shot go exactly 230 yards.
4. Either Matthew or Chevy has always used Greenford brand clubs.
5. Abel's best shot went 15 yards farther than Lebron's, and 15 yards shorter than the player who used his 5 wood.
6. Surprisingly enough, the longest shot wasn't hit with a driver!
7. Tate used either Greenford or Irvington clubs.

SOLVE RATE 32.6%

AVERAGE TIME 16 min, 30 sec

BEST TIME 3 min, 58 sec by pfuffer13

Prom Night

Alice and four of her girlfriends had a great time at their high school prom, though they each arrived separately and at different times. They'd gone shopping for dresses together weeks before to ensure that none of them would wear anything even remotely similar to any of the others. Using only the clues below, figure out the name of each girl's date, the color of her prom dress, and the time she arrived at the dance.

1. The five girls are Jennifer, the one who arrived right on time at 8:00 pm exactly (who didn't wear the silver dress), the one who went as Maxwell's date, the one with the black dress, and Denise (who wore the purple dress).

2. Alice didn't wear the red dress.

3. The first girl to arrive at the dance was with either Stephen or Kevin.

4. Of Kevin's date and the girl with the purple dress, one was Felicity and the other was the last of the five girls to arrive.

5. Jennifer arrived sometime before the girl who went with Stephen and immediately after Cathy.

6. Of Cathy and the girl who went with Nicholas, one wore the navy blue dress and the other wore the silver dress.

		Boys					Girls					Dress Colors				
		Franklin	Kevin	Maxwell	Nicholas	Stephen	Alice	Cathy	Denise	Felicity	Jennifer	Black	Navy Blue	Purple	Red	Silver
Arrivals	7:58 pm															
	8:00 pm															
	8:02 pm															
	8:04 pm															
	8:06 pm															
Dress Colors	Black															
	Navy Blue															
	Purple															
	Red															
	Silver															
Girls	Alice															
	Cathy															
	Denise															
	Felicity															
	Jennifer															

SOLVE RATE
32.4%

AVERAGE TIME
23 min, 10 sec

BEST TIME
4 min by darsinewman

Arrivals	Boys	Girls	Dress Colors
7:58 pm			
8:00 pm			
8:02 pm			
8:04 pm			
8:06 pm			

154

Busy Day at Court

Jason Menendez was a skilled public defender, but even he was a bit overwhelmed to have to try five cases on the same day! Each case was for a different client and was in front of a different judge. Using only the clues below, determine which judge heard which case, what time each trial was held, and how many years each judge has been presiding on the bench.

1. The client accused of starting a bar fight didn't have his trial presided over by Judge Emmis.
2. The judge who scheduled the 9:00 am trial hasn't been on the bench for a total of 15 years.
3. Judge Powers held his trial immediately after Judge Kelso's.
4. Of the judge with the fewest years of experience and the one who held the 10:25 am trial, one presided over the client accused of starting a bar fight and the other passed sentence on the bank robbery suspect.
5. The five judges are Judge Soros, the two with the most years on the bench, the one who presided over the earliest trial, and the one who presided over the forgery trial.
6. The judge with 15 years on the bench held his trial sometime before the one with more than 30 years experience.
7. The forgery trial was held sometime before Judge Mackey's trial.
8. The reckless driving trial wasn't scheduled for 11:50 am.
9. The most senior judge of all five held his trial right before Judge Powers's trial.

		Judges					Offenses					Years				
		Judge Emmis	Judge Kelso	Judge Mackey	Judge Powers	Judge Soros	Bank Robbery	Bar Fight	Car Theft	Forgery	Reck. Driving	12	15	19	24	32
Court Times	9:00 am															
	10:25 am															
	11:50 am															
	1:15 pm															
	3:40 pm															
Years	12															
	15															
	19															
	24															
	32															
Offenses	Bank Robbery															
	Bar Fight															
	Car Theft															
	Forgery															
	Reck. Driving															

SOLVE RATE
32.1%

AVERAGE TIME
13 min, 28 sec

BEST TIME
4 min, 59 sec by jasper_320_

Court Times	Judges	Offenses	Years
9:00 am			
10:25 am			
11:50 am			
1:15 pm			
3:40 pm			

Radio Winners

By a strange stroke of luck, five students at Wallingford High School each won a different radio call-in contest the night before, each on a different station. To win, each had to be a certain caller in a certain order (such as the 11th caller, 100th caller, and so on). Using only the clues below, figure out who won each station's contest, what the call letters and frequency are for each station, and what number caller the student had to be to win. Hint: Higher radio frequency numbers are higher up on the dial.

1. The five stations were WKPC, the one that gave away a trip to Paris to the 21st caller, the station where Roman won the contest, the station at 101.1 on the dial, and WOLD.

2. WSPR didn't give away a prize for the 3rd caller.

3. Among the five stations, WRFT is the next highest frequency on the dial after WKPC, and WTLD is the next highest on the dial after WSPR. WSPR is next highest on the dial after the station where Jennifer won her contest.

4. Between Roman and the person who won the contest on 101.1, one got a prize from WSPR and the other was the 11th caller.

5. Either the 100th caller winner or the 21st caller winner was Andrew.

6. Dorian didn't win the WTLD call-in contest, which wasn't on 104.5.

7. Either the 100th caller or Jennifer won WKPC's contest.

		Winners					Call Letters					Callers				
		Amber	Andrew	Dorian	Jennifer	Roman	WKPC	WTLD	WOLD	WRFT	WSPR	3rd caller	11th caller	21st caller	49th caller	100th caller
Frequencies	89.3															
	94.6															
	99.1															
	101.1															
	104.5															
Callers	3rd caller															
	11th caller															
	21st caller															
	49th caller															
	100th caller															
Call Letters	WKPC															
	WTLD															
	WOLD															
	WRFT															
	WSPR															

Frequencies	Winners	Call Letters	Callers
89.3			
94.6			
99.1			
101.1			
104.5			

SOLVE RATE
31.7%

AVERAGE TIME
12 min, 20 sec

BEST TIME
3 min, 10 sec by Vaughns

Deli Delight

Mac's Deli is the most popular place in town for lunch, so it was no surprise that when five co-workers came in just after noon, the place was packed. They each grabbed a number and waited their turn to be called to the counter, lowest numbers going first. It took a while, but within about 10 minutes, all five had ordered sandwiches, though no one selected the same type of meat or the same type of bread. Using only the clues below, determine what type of sandwich each co-worker ordered and what number each picked while waiting in line.

1. Of the one who ordered a sandwich on white bread (who got #148) and the co-worker who was served first, one selected roast beef and the other was Arthur.

2. Abigail, who didn't get her sandwich on wheat bread, didn't get #147.

3. Michael always orders a salami sandwich for lunch, but never on wheat bread.

4. Whoever ordered the roast beef was served immediately before the person who ordered the liverwurst sandwich.

5. Between the co-worker who ordered pastrami (who wasn't Mario) and Arthur, one got a sandwich on pumpernickel and the other was served first.

6. The person who ordered a sandwich on sourdough was served right before Michael.

		Customers					Meats					Breads				
		Abigail	Arthur	Casey	Mario	Michael	Corned Beef	Liverwurst	Pastrami	Roast Beef	Salami	Pumpernickel	Rye	Sourdough	Wheat	White
Numbers	145															
	146															
	147															
	148															
	149															
Breads	Pumpernickel															
	Rye															
	Sourdough															
	Wheat															
	White															
Meats	Corned Beef															
	Liverwurst															
	Pastrami															
	Roast Beef															
	Salami															

Numbers	Customers	Meats	Breads
145			
146			
147			
148			
149			

Earth Tremors

Californians are no strangers to earthquakes. In fact, Shaker County experienced five just this morning alone! (None of them were too serious, though, and thankfully no damage or injuries were reported.) Using only the clues below, determine the magnitude of each quake (on the Richter scale), what time it began, how long it lasted, and the name of the town in which each quake was centered.

1. The five quakes are the one that lasted 10 seconds, the 2.8 magnitude quake, the one that began at 6:42 am, the quake with the longest duration, and the one whose epicenter was beneath the town of Chrisville, CA.
2. The smallest-magnitude earthquake was centered in Saravello, CA, but it didn't strike at 9:03 am.
3. The 5:04 am earthquake (which didn't last the longest) was next highest in magnitude after the Saravello earthquake.
4. The 6:42 am quake was next highest in magnitude after the 4:59 am incident.
5. Neither the quake that lasted for exactly 23 seconds nor the one that struck at 9:03 am was centered in Yosalinda.
6. The Amaya Hills quake was the second one to strike this morning.
7. The quake that lasted precisely 23 seconds was next highest in magnitude after the Yosalinda quake.
8. Of the Amaya Hills quake and the one that lasted 17 seconds, one was largest in magnitude and the other struck at 4:59 am.

	Amaya Hills	Chrisville	Leonardi	Saravello	Yosalinda	4 seconds	10 seconds	17 seconds	23 seconds	25 seconds	3:25 am	4:59 am	5:04 am	6:42 am	9:03 am
Epicenters						**Durations**					**Times**				
Magnitudes 2.3															
2.6															
2.8															
3.1															
3.6															
Times 3:25 am															
4:59 am															
5:04 am															
6:42 am															
9:03 am															
Durations 4 seconds															
10 seconds															
17 seconds															
23 seconds															
25 seconds															

Magnitudes	Epicenters	Durations	Times
2.3			
2.6			
2.8			
3.1			
3.6			

SOLVE RATE
30.3%
AVERAGE TIME
20 min, 52 sec
BEST TIME
6 min, 8 sec by ballerina1031

Pizza Pandemonium

It was Mandy's first day at the Pizza Shack, and the dinner rush almost got the best of her. Five different people called in their pizza orders back-to-back, each within a minute of the last, and as luck would have it, each wanted a different topping and a different type of pizza. Mandy dutifully scribbled down each order, but she was in such a rush, she could barely make out her own writing! Using only the clues below, match each customer to the type of pizza each ordered, the topping each wanted, and the time each phoned in.

1. Scott didn't order onions on his pizza (which wasn't hand tossed).
2. The five customers were the one who called at 6:08 pm (but didn't want a wheat crust pizza), the one who phoned in an order one minute later, the one who wanted pepperoni, the one who ordered the Sicilian pizza, and Liam (who didn't want a deep-dish pizza).
3. Of Paola and the person who called at 6:10 pm, one wanted green peppers and the other mushrooms (but not on a hand-tossed pizza).
4. The customer who ordered the hand-tossed pizza called sometime before the one who asked for green peppers.
5. The one who ordered mushrooms called immediately after the one who asked for sausage.
6. Either the person who called at 6:07 pm or the one who ordered the Sicilian pizza was Dakota.
7. The person who ordered the wheat crust pizza phoned immediately after the person who ordered the Sicilian pizza.

	Customers					Toppings					Pizza Types				
	Dakota	Gregory	Liam	Paola	Scott	Green Peppers	Mushrooms	Onions	Pepperoni	Sausage	Deep Dish	Hand Tossed	Sicilian	Thin Crust	Wheat Crust
Times 6:06 pm															
6:07 pm															
6:08 pm															
6:09 pm															
6:10 pm															
Pizza Types Deep Dish															
Hand Tossed															
Sicilian															
Thin Crust															
Wheat Crust															
Toppings Green Peppers															
Mushrooms															
Onions															
Pepperoni															
Sausage															

SOLVE RATE
29.7%

AVERAGE TIME
20 min, 58 sec

BEST TIME
2 min, 55 sec by jade_3031

Times	Customers	Toppings	Pizza Types
6:06 pm			
6:07 pm			
6:08 pm			
6:09 pm			
6:10 pm			

We All Scream for Ice Cream

It was a banner day at the Olde Towne Ice Cream Shoppe. The line went out the door and snaked entirely around the corner! The first group of customers consisted of five friends, each of whom ordered a different ice cream flavor and a different topping. Although Javier was kind enough to pay the bill for everyone, each individual ice cream concoction came out to a different price. Using only the clues below, determine what flavor and toppings each friend ordered and the resulting price for each treat.

1. Of the one who ordered mint ice cream and Connor, one opted for sprinkles and the other ordered the most expensive of the five treats.

2. Between Joanna and the one who ordered the hot fudge topping, one got coffee-flavored ice cream and the other went for strawberry.

3. The one who ordered pistachio ice cream didn't top it with maraschino cherries.

4. The five friends are the one who got the whipped cream topping, the person whose ice cream treat cost $2.59, Javier, the one who ordered chocolate ice cream, and the one who opted for the peanut topping.

5. Either Kimberly or Connor ordered the cheapest concoction of the group.

6. Carly's custom combination didn't cost $2.89.

7. The person who ordered mint ice cream topped it with peanuts.

8. The ice cream topped with hot fudge cost 10¢ less than the one topped with whipped cream.

9. The strawberry ice cream combination didn't cost $2.59.

Prices	Customers	Toppings	Flavors
$2.49			
$2.59			
$2.69			
$2.79			
$2.89			

SOLVE RATE
29%

AVERAGE TIME
18 min, 51 sec

BEST TIME
4 min, 49 sec by DCF

Credit Cards

Five co-workers each recently got new credit cards, each from a different bank. Personalized cards are all the rage these days, so of course, each person chose a custom design for his or her new card. Using only the clues below, determine the company that provided each credit card, the design chosen for each, and each applicant's credit score.

1. Of the applicant with the 700 credit score (who didn't choose the card with puppies on it) and the one who chose the Van Gogh design, one received a Purple Card credit card and the other was Rafael.

2. Between Cole and the one who got the Tenth Bank credit card, one chose the flower design and the other had the 625 credit score (but didn't choose the sailboat design).

3. Of Cole and the applicant with the 700 credit score, one got their card from Purple Card and the other from the Bank of Lima.

4. The five applicants are Sarai (who didn't choose the sailboat design for her card), the one who chose the Van Gogh design, the one who got the Bank of Lima credit card, the one with the lowest credit score, and the one with the 625 credit score.

5. Makayla's credit score is higher than Philip's.

6. The applicant who got the Minute Card credit card has a credit score that's 75 points lower than the score of the person who got the Tenth Bank credit card.

		Applicants					Companies					Designs				
		Cole	Makayla	Philip	Rafael	Sarai	Bank of Lima	Evening Trust	Minute Card	Purple Card	Tenth Bank	Flowers	Puppy	Sailboat	Snowman	Van Gogh
Credit Scores	475															
	550															
	625															
	700															
	775															
Designs	Flowers															
	Puppy															
	Sailboat															
	Snowman															
	Van Gogh															
Companies	Bank of Lima															
	Evening Trust															
	Minute Card															
	Purple Card															
	Tenth Bank															

SOLVE RATE
28.3%

AVERAGE TIME
24 min, 13 sec

BEST TIME
3 min, 7 sec by urielzet

Credit Scores	Applicants	Companies	Designs
475			
550			
625			
700			
775			

Positive Cash Flow

It was a good year for Consolidated Widgets, and when it came time for annual reviews, just about every employee got a good-size raise as a result. Five co-workers, each of whom works under a different boss and in a different department, and each of whom got a raise, decided to go out and celebrate. Using only the clues below, determine the size of each employee's raise, the department each works in, and the name of each person's boss.

1. The employee who received the smallest raise works under either Mr. Perkins or Mrs. Fowler.
2. Between Mrs. Fowler's employee and the one who got the $4,000 raise, one works in human resources and the other is Pierce.
3. Irma's raise was $2,000 higher than that of the employee who works in the operations department (who didn't get the $8,000 raise). The operations employee's raise was $2,000 higher than that of the person in human resources.
4. Either Rodney or the human resources employee works under Mr. Perkins.
5. The employee who received the largest raise doesn't work in accounting.
6. Irma's raise was larger than the one given to the employee who works for Mr. Baldwin.
7. Carmen's raise was $2,000 less than what Mrs. Fowler's employee was awarded.
8. Mrs. Carr's employee (who isn't Orlando) doesn't work in accounting.
9. The $8,000 raise wasn't given to the person who works in the sales department.

		Employees					Bosses					Departments				
		Carmen	Irma	Pierce	Orlando	Rodney	Mr. Baldwin	Mrs. Carr	Mrs. Fowler	Mr. Lawson	Mr. Perkins	Accounting	H.R.	Operations	Reception	Sales
Raises	$2,000															
	$4,000															
	$6,000															
	$8,000															
	$10,000															
Departments	Accounting															
	H.R.															
	Operations															
	Reception															
	Sales															
Bosses	Mr. Baldwin															
	Mrs. Carr															
	Mrs. Fowler															
	Mr. Lawson															
	Mr. Perkins															

SOLVE RATE
28.2%

AVERAGE TIME
21 min, 46 sec

BEST TIME
3 min, 30 sec by khead

Raises	Employees	Bosses	Departments
$2,000			
$4,000			
$6,000			
$8,000			
$10,000			

Rocket Man

Dennis, an expert in satellite launches, has five launches scheduled this year, each in a different location and in a different month. Each rocket has a unique name and each is carrying a satellite intended for a different purpose. Using only the clues below, determine which rockets are launching when and where and what sort of satellites each will carry into space.

1. The Seltron V rocket will launch one month before Ares II.
2. The five rockets are the Celera III (which launches earliest), the one carrying the telescopic satellite, the one scheduled to launch out of Florida, the Triton II, and the October launch.
3. Of the Ares II rocket and the one that will launch in California, one is last on the launch scheduled and the other is part of a secret government satellite project.
4. The GPS-satellite will go up sometime after the Florida launch and sometime before the California launch.
5. The five satellites are the radio and GPS satellites, the one on the Ares II rocket, the one that launches latest, and the one that will launch from New Mexico.
6. The Arizona launch isn't scheduled for November.

		Rockets					Locations					Satellites				
		Ares II	Celera III	Seltron V	Triton II	Vesta I	Arizona	California	Florida	New Mexico	Texas	GPS	Radio	Secret Gov't	Telescope	Television
Months	August															
	September															
	October															
	November															
	December															
Satellites	GPS															
	Radio															
	Secret Gov't															
	Telescope															
	Television															
Locations	Arizona															
	California															
	Florida															
	New Mexico															
	Texas															

SOLVE RATE
27.9%

AVERAGE TIME
14 min, 3 sec

BEST TIME
2 min, 37 sec by Vaughns

Months	Rockets	Locations	Satellites
August			
September			
October			
November			
December			

Gold Medalists

Five gold medalists from the last Winter Olympics came to speak at Chumley College this weekend. Each was from a different country, and each had won a gold medal in a different sport. Using only the clues below, determine the sport in which each athlete won the medal, what country each is from, and the order in which each spoke during Saturday's presentation.

1. The five medalists are the figure skater (who spoke fourth), Zachary (who spoke second), Clayton, the one from Finland, and the Swedish athlete.
2. Nicholas didn't speak third and isn't from the United States.
3. The snowboarder isn't Danish.
4. The speed skater isn't Finnish.
5. Either the snowboarder or the figure skater is from the United States.
6. Of the luge medalist and the one who spoke last, one is Canadian and the other is Danish.
7. Of the Finn and the one who spoke last, one is Terry and the other is the snowboarder.

| SOLVE RATE |
| 27.8% |
| AVERAGE TIME |
| 25 min, 9 sec |
| BEST TIME |
| 8 min, 18 sec by amywalls |

Sports	Athletes	Orders	Countries
Figure Skating			
Luge			
Ski Jump			
Snowboarding			
Speed Skating			

Cookies for a Cause

This is Public Service Week at the local high school, and five students decided to sell homemade cookies out of the cafeteria to raise money for different causes. Each student bakes a different kind of cookie, and each sells her cookies on the lunch line on a different day of the week. Each girl also chose a different charity that would receive all proceeds from her sales. Using only the clues below, match the cookies and causes to each student and determine which day she participated in the sale.

1. The almond cookies didn't raise money for environmental issues.
2. The five students are the one who made peanut butter cookies (which didn't benefit local schools), the one who gave her proceeds to the homeless shelter, the one who made chocolate chip cookies, Brenda, and Monday's seller (who didn't donate her proceeds to benefit the elderly).
3. Kailey sold her cookies the day before Janiyah (who baked gingerbread cookies).
4. Of Ariel and the one who helped raise money for local schools, one baked chocolate chip cookies and the other had her sale on Wednesday.
5. The five girls are the one whose cookies benefited the city orphanage (which weren't sold on Thursday), Brenda, Monday's seller, and the bakers who made gingerbread and peanut butter cookies.
6. Caitlyn didn't bake black and white cookies.

		Students					Cookies					Fund Raisers				
		Ariel	Brenda	Caitlyn	Janiyah	Kailey	Almond	Black and White	Chocolate Chip	Gingerbread	Peanut Butter	Elderly	Environment	Homeless	Orphanage	School
Days	Monday															
	Tuesday															
	Wednesday															
	Thursday															
	Friday															
Fund Raisers	Elderly															
	Environment															
	Homeless															
	Orphanage															
	School															
Cookies	Almond															
	Black and White															
	Chocolate Chip															
	Gingerbread															
	Peanut Butter															

Days	Students	Cookies	Fund Raisers
Monday			
Tuesday			
Wednesday			
Thursday			
Friday			

SOLVE RATE
27.4%

AVERAGE TIME
22 min, 27 sec

BEST TIME
4 min, 53 sec by urielzet

Christmas Gifts

Santa knew just what to get the five Brewster boys for Christmas. Each boy received a different video game, each of which was wrapped in a different kind of wrapping paper to make it easy to tell which child should receive which gift. Using only the clues below, determine the age of each of the Brewster boys, the video game each received, and the colors it was wrapped in.

1. The five Brewster boys are the 12 and 14 year olds, Matthew, the one who received *Stalactia,* and Xavier (whose gift was wrapped in blue and white paper).
2. The oldest boy received either *Stalactia* or *Robot Wars.*
3. The 13 year old got *Mega Rally.*
4. *Astroboy* wasn't wrapped in red and white paper.
5. The boy whose gift was wrapped in red and green paper was two years younger than the boy who received *Stalactia.*
6. Uri was older than the boy who received *Robot Wars.*
7. The gift that was wrapped in red and white paper wasn't *Stalactia* and didn't go to Russell.
8. The boy who got *Demon Guild* wrapped in gold and silver paper was one year younger than Uri.

		Brian	Matthew	Russell	Uri	Xavier	Robot Wars	Stalactia	Demon Guild	Astroboy	Mega Rally	Blue & White	Blue & Gold	Gold & Silver	Red & Green	Red & White
Ages	11															
	12															
	13															
	14															
	15															
Wrappings	Blue & White															
	Blue & Gold															
	Gold & Silver															
	Red & Green															
	Red & White															
Video Games	Robot Wars															
	Stalactia															
	Demon Guild															
	Astroboy															
	Mega Rally															

SOLVE RATE
27.0%

AVERAGE TIME
15 min, 43 sec

BEST TIME
2 min, 51 sec by gulfcoastswimmer

Ages	Boys	Video Games	Wrappings
11			
12			
13			
14			
15			

Maternity Ward

Five babies were born this week at the Fogelma Hospital maternity ward, each on a different day. Using only the clues below, figure out which baby was born to which family, how much each weighed, and what day each was delivered.

1. The five babies are the one that weighed 8 pounds and 7 ounces, the one born on May 4 (who isn't part of the Thomas family), Kristopher, the one that weighed 8 pounds and 2 ounces (whose last name is Giatris), and the one born to the Bellamy family.
2. Either Steven or Janiyah was born on May 3.
3. The heaviest baby was born the day after the baby who weighed 7 pounds, 11 ounces.
4. Of Janiyah and the newest member of the Giatris family, one weighed 8 pounds, 6 ounces and the other was the last of the five to be born (but isn't Cesar).
5. Of Miguel and the baby who weighed 7 pounds, 11 ounces, one was born to the Francones and the other is the newest member of the Thomas family.
6. The Hilbern baby isn't the lightest of the five.

		Baby Names					Weights					Families			
		Cesar	Janiyah	Kristopher	Miguel	Steven	7 lb. 9 oz.	7 lb. 11 oz.	8 lb. 2 oz.	8 lb. 6 oz.	8 lb. 7 oz.	Bellamy	Francone	Giatris	Hilbern	Thomas
Birthdays	May 3															
	May 4															
	May 5															
	May 6															
	May 7															
Families	Bellamy															
	Francone															
	Giatris															
	Hilbern															
	Thomas															
Weights	7 lb. 9 oz.															
	7 lb. 11 oz.															
	8 lb. 2 oz.															
	8 lb. 6 oz.															
	8 lb. 7 oz.															

Birthdays	Baby Names	Weights	Families
May 3			
May 4			
May 5			
May 6			
May 7			

SOLVE RATE
26.9%

AVERAGE TIME
17 min, 26 sec

BEST TIME
4 min, 46 sec by kenbrikim

On the Lecture Circuit ...

The art department at Fort Duquesne Academy has decided to showcase five of its top students in a traveling lecture circuit. Each of the five students will give a presentation on the work and influences of a different famous artist, and each presentation will be in a different, consecutive month and in a different U.S. city. Using only the clues below, determine which lecturer is presenting in each month and the location and subject of each presentation.

1. Between Serenity and the person who will give their lecture in San Francisco, one is scheduled for September and the other will discuss the works of Jackson Pollock.

2. The earliest lecture on the schedule will not be devoted to a study of Paul Cezanne.

3. Neither Emily (who will not give her presentation in Miami) nor the artist who will speak about Pablo Picasso is scheduled to give a presentation in Austin.

4. The lecture on Paul Cezanne will not be held in San Francisco.

5. Makenna will give her lecture in Chicago.

6. The Austin lecture will not be held in September.

7. The Miami lecture will take place sometime after the New York lecture.

8. Between Matthew and the November lecturer, one is scheduled to give a presentation in San Francisco and the other will discuss the many works of Claude Monet.

9. Between the final lecturer (who is scheduled to be in Chicago) and Emily, one will discuss Pablo Picasso and the other will discuss Paul Cezanne.

	Lecturers					Subjects					Locations				
	Emily	Keegan	Makenna	Matthew	Serenity	Claude Monet	Gustav Klimt	Jackson Pollock	Pablo Picasso	Paul Cezanne	Austin	Chicago	Miami	New York	San Francisco
August															
September															
October															
November															
December															
Austin															
Chicago															
Miami															
New York															
San Francisco															
Claude Monet															
Gustav Klimt															
Jackson Pollock															
Pablo Picasso															
Paul Cezanne															

SOLVE RATE
26.5%

AVERAGE TIME
25 min, 17 sec

BEST TIME
6 min, 19 sec by Sublime75

Months	Lecturers	Subjects	Locations
August			
September			
October			
November			
December			

Quiz Show

The latest quiz show sensation to sweep the country is *The Devil You Say!*, a smart and quirky competition between five trivia buffs to see who can accrue the most points. Using only the clues below, determine the career, home state, and total points won by each contestant on last week's show.

1. The five contestants are Tatum, the one from Virginia, the artist, the one who got the fewest points, and the player who ended with 200 points (who isn't from Montana).
2. Of the Virginia native and the musician, one is Kaitlyn and the other ended with 225 points.
3. The engineer ended the show with 25 fewer points than the teacher.
4. Tatum isn't from Montana.
5. Between Brendan and the teacher, one is from Alabama and the other ended the game with 200 points.
6. The Delaware native didn't finish with the second-highest score.
7. Of Brendan and the player who finished with 225 points, one is the artist and the other is the musician.
8. Estrella ended the game with more points than Chandler.

		Contestants					Careers					Home States				
		Brendan	Chandler	Estrella	Kaitlyn	Tatum	Artist	Biologist	Engineer	Musician	Teacher	Alabama	Delaware	Montana	South Dakota	Virginia
Total Points	150 points															
	175 points															
	200 points															
	225 points															
	250 points															
Home States	Alabama															
	Delaware															
	Montana															
	South Dakota															
	Virginia															
Careers	Artist															
	Biologist															
	Engineer															
	Musician															
	Teacher															

SOLVE RATE
26.4%

AVERAGE TIME
17 min, 45 sec

BEST TIME
2 min, 34 sec by urielzet

Total Points	Contestants	Careers	Home States
150 points			
175 points			
200 points			
225 points			
250 points			

New Holidays

The House of Representatives recently voted on the establishment of five new holidays, each proposed by a different representative from a different state. Using only the clues below, figure out which representative proposed each holiday, what state each is from, and what day it would fall on.

1. Of the representative from Arkansas and the one who suggested the July 28 holiday, one proposed the establishment of Mechanic Day and the other was Representative McCabe.
2. Janitor Day was to be scheduled three days after Mayor Day.
3. The Florida representative didn't propose a new holiday on July 25.
4. Neither Waitress Day nor Mailman Day will be held on July 19.
5. Of the Virginian and the one who proposed the July 25 holiday, one was Representative Ritter and the other put forth the suggestion for Janitor Day.
6. Between the Nevadan and Representative Ritter, one proposed Waitress Day and the other proposed Mayor Day.
7. Waitress Day will be held sometime earlier in the month than Mailman Day.
8. Representative Webber isn't from Arkansas, and he didn't propose Waitress Day.
9. Neither the Virginian nor Representative Ritter suggested Waitress Day.
10. Representative Simms didn't propose Mechanic Day.

	Janitor Day	Mailman Day	Mechanic Day	Mayor Day	Waitress Day	Rep. McCabe	Rep. Novak	Rep. Ritter	Rep. Simms	Rep. Webber	Arkansas	Florida	Nevada	New Jersey	Virginia
July 16															
July 19															
July 22															
July 25															
July 28															
Arkansas															
Florida															
Nevada															
New Jersey															
Virginia															
Rep. McCabe															
Rep. Novak															
Rep. Ritter															
Rep. Simms															
Rep. Webber															

SOLVE RATE 25.1%

AVERAGE TIME 24 min, 3 sec

BEST TIME 8 min, 54 sec by spignesi

Days	Holidays	Politicians	States
July 16			
July 19			
July 22			
July 25			
July 28			

Shipping Rates

Natalie's new business—selling antique trinkets via online auctions—is thriving, and she had five new packages to send out this morning via the local shipping company, DPS. They determine shipping costs based on three factors: the weight and dimensions of the package and its final destination. Using only the clues below, determine all three factors for each package and the final shipping cost for each.

1. The five packages are the one that measured 6" × 10" × 8", the two going to zip codes 30218 and 44592, the one that weighs 24 ounces, and the one that cost $6.57 to ship.

2. The package that is a perfect cube (meaning the same width in all dimensions) is neither 16 ounces nor 28 ounces in weight.

3. Of the 6" × 8" × 6" package and the one going to zip code 44592, one is the heaviest of the five and the other cost $5.68 to ship.

4. The lightest package wasn't going to the 56253 zip code.

5. The heaviest package isn't the smallest one.

6. The most expensive package isn't going to 44592.

7. The package going to 30218 weighs 4 ounces less than the one that is 6" × 8" × 6".

8. The shipment to zip code 90296 cost either $5.68 or $6.05 to ship.

9. The package that cost $5.68 to ship was going to either the 81125 or the 44592 zip code.

	30218	44592	56253	81125	90296	4" x 6" x 6"	6" x 6" x 6"	6" x 8" x 6"	6" x 10" x 8"	6" x 12" x 8"	$5.29	$5.68	$6.05	$6.57	$7.13
12 ounces															
16 ounces															
20 ounces															
24 ounces															
28 ounces															
$5.29															
$5.68															
$6.05															
$6.57															
$7.13															
4" x 6" x 6"															
6" x 6" x 6"															
6" x 8" x 6"															
6" x 10" x 8"															
6" x 12" x 8"															

Weights	Zip Codes	Sizes	Prices
12 ounces			
16 ounces			
20 ounces			
24 ounces			
28 ounces			

SOLVE RATE
23.7%

AVERAGE TIME
16 min, 22 sec

BEST TIME
7 min, 7 sec by boxyroxy

Healthy Eating

Five friends, each of whom were diagnosed with elevated cholesterol levels, decided to each try eating more of a specific type of cholesterol-fighting food in order to reduce their numbers. All five successfully lowered their cholesterol by different amounts and over different periods of time. Using only the clues below, determine what food each person ate, how much each person's cholesterol dropped, and how long it took to achieve.

1. Of the person who lost 13 cholesterol points and the one whose diet lasted the longest, one ate lots of salmon and the other was Madison.
2. The person whose cholesterol dropped the most didn't eat oatmeal and is a life-long vegetarian (so the fish-focused diets were not an option).
3. The tuna diet didn't last for exactly 12 weeks.
4. The person whose cholesterol dropped by the smallest amount wasn't Perla.
5. The person whose diet lasted the longest dropped his or her cholesterol by four more points than the person who tried the shortest diet.
6. The 10-week dieter successfully dropped his or her cholesterol levels by either 5 or 17 points.
7. Of Clayton and the 12-week dieter (who wasn't Quinton), one dropped his or her cholesterol by 9 points and the other by 21.
8. Quinton lost four more cholesterol points than Madison.
9. Of Perla and the almond-dieter, one dropped his or her cholesterol by 9 points and the other dieted for 10 weeks.

		Clayton	Madison	Perla	Quinton	Saniya	Almonds	Oatmeal	Salmon	Tuna	Walnuts	6 weeks	8 weeks	10 weeks	12 weeks	14 weeks
Chol. Dropped	5 points															
	9 points															
	13 points															
	17 points															
	21 points															
Durations	6 weeks															
	8 weeks															
	10 weeks															
	12 weeks															
	14 weeks															
Foods	Almonds															
	Oatmeal															
	Salmon															
	Tuna															
	Walnuts															

SOLVE RATE
23.4%

AVERAGE TIME
18 min, 47 sec

BEST TIME
5 min, 22 sec by urielzet

Chol. Dropped	People	Foods	Durations
5 points			
9 points			
13 points			
17 points			
21 points			

WWI Airshow

The world-famous Bennington's World War I Airshow was held today in Richtenberg. Five original WWI-era fighter planes each had their own segment of the show, flown by pilots and historical aviation experts from five different countries. Using only the clues below, determine the order in which each plane flew, who flew it, and what country each pilot is from.

1. Of Littleton and the pilot who flew fourth, one was from New Zealand and the other was from Germany.
2. Neither Grayson nor Parisien flew the Sopwith Camel.
3. Either Sennford (who wasn't American) or the Sopwith Camel pilot was from Sweden.
4. Of the Swede and the fourth pilot, one flew the Fokker Dr.I and the other was Grayson.
5. Of the first pilot and the one who flew the Nieuport 28 (which wasn't third on the program), one was Sennford and the other hailed from Denmark.
6. The pilot of the Albatros D.II flew immediately after the German pilot. The German pilot flew sometime before Littleton.

		Pilots				Planes					Countries				
		Davids	Grayson	Littleton	Parisien	Sennford	Albatros D.II	Fokker Dr.I	Nieuport 28	Sopwith Camel	Spad S.VII	Denmark	Germany	New Zealand	Sweden	United States
Orders	First															
	Second															
	Third															
	Fourth															
	Fifth															
Countries	Denmark															
	Germany															
	New Zealand															
	Sweden															
	United States															
Planes	Albatros D.II															
	Fokker Dr.I															
	Nieuport 28															
	Sopwith Camel															
	Spad S.VII															

Orders	Pilots	Planes	Countries
First			
Second			
Third			
Fourth			
Fifth			

SOLVE RATE
23.2%

AVERAGE TIME
18 min, 32 sec

BEST TIME
7 min, 5 sec by jade_3031

Maid Services

The Magical Maids house-cleaning company services five families on Breakwater Drive. Although it would be more efficient to simply service all five families on the same day, Magical Maids schedule simply doesn't allow it. So now a different house cleaner services each of the five families, and the families have scheduled their services for a different day and a different time. Using only the clues below, determine which cleaner services which family and the time and day scheduled for each.

1. Neither April nor the cleaner scheduled for 2:30 pm works for the Cantrell family (which doesn't have service scheduled for Tuesdays).

2. Charlie's schedule has him working later in the week than the cleaner who services the Holland family (who isn't April), who is scheduled later in the week than the house cleaner who services the Lane family.

3. The 4:30 pm appointment isn't on Mondays and isn't for the Williams family.

4. Between Summer and the person who services the Williams family, one works on Tuesdays and the other is scheduled for 1:00 pm cleanings.

5. Of April and the cleaner who works on Fridays, one is scheduled for 2:30 pm and the other for 4:30 pm.

6. Charlie works for the Downs family.

7. Between Leo and the Thursday cleaner, one works for the Williams family and the other has an early 8:00 am schedule.

		April	Audrey	Charlie	Leo	Summer	8:00 am	10:00 am	1:00 pm	2:30 pm	4:30 pm	Cantrell	Downs	Holland	Lane	Williams
Days	Monday															
	Tuesday															
	Wednesday															
	Thursday															
	Friday															
Homeowners	Cantrell															
	Downs															
	Holland															
	Lane															
	Williams															
Times	8:00 am															
	10:00 am															
	1:00 pm															
	2:30 pm															
	4:30 pm															

SOLVE RATE
23%

AVERAGE TIME
22 min, 15 sec

BEST TIME
8 min, 45 sec by janiebrock

Days	Maids	Times	Homeowners
Monday			
Tuesday			
Wednesday			
Thursday			
Friday			

Athletic Amphibians

The Fastest Frog Finale is a tradition at the state fair, and this year's competitors didn't disappoint. Five different contestants raced their frogs (each with a different name), but only one came out on top. Using only the clues below, find the owner of each frog, the order the frogs finished, and the lanes in which each frog raced.

1. Between Sydney's frog and the one in lane four, one won the race and the other finished fourth.
2. Neither Hopping Hank (who doesn't belong to Catherine) nor Froggy Fred won the race.
3. Neither the frog in lane five (who wasn't Froggy Fred) nor the frog that finished third belongs to Kaitlyn.
4. Green Gus finished just before the frog in lane two (who wasn't Roger Ribbit).
5. The frog in lane one (which wasn't Kaitlyn's or Catherine's) finished in second place.
6. Between Froggy Fred and Braxton's frog, one came in last place and the other ran in lane three.
7. The frog that finished last ran in either lane one or lane five.

		Contestants					Frogs					Lanes				
		Braxton	Catherine	Erik	Kaitlyn	Sydney	Froggy Fred	Green Gus	Hopping Hank	Leaping Larry	Roger Ribbit	Lane One	Lane Two	Lane Three	Lane Four	Lane Five
Finishes	First															
	Second															
	Third															
	Fourth															
	Fifth															
Lanes	Lane One															
	Lane Two															
	Lane Three															
	Lane Four															
	Lane Five															
Frogs	Froggy Fred															
	Green Gus															
	Hopping Hank															
	Leaping Larry															
	Roger Ribbit															

SOLVE RATE
22.5%

AVERAGE TIME
17 min

BEST TIME
3 min, 39 sec by glam86

Finishes	Contestants	Frogs	Lanes
First			
Second			
Third			
Fourth			
Fifth			

If You're Going to San Francisco ...

Varion, a technology firm based in New York City, holds its yearly marketing meeting for a week each July in San Francisco. Five of the attendees booked their own hotels, because they wanted to have specific amenities available while they were traveling. Using only the clues below, determine the location and price-per-night for each hotel chosen by the five co-workers and the specific amenity that convinced each to book stays there.

1. The five hotels are the one on Telegraph Hill, the one that charged $150/night (which doesn't offer free shuttle bus service), Brielle's hotel, the one that offered free parking to all guests, and the hotel on Potrero Hill.
2. Of Brayden's hotel and the one that offered complimentary use of an in-house gym and spa, one is in the SOMA district and the other is the most expensive of the five.
3. The Noe Valley hotel (which didn't cost $200/night) doesn't offer rooms with kitchenettes.
4. The Telegraph Hill hotel cost $25 more per night than the one in North Beach, but it was still less expensive than the one Noel chose to stay at.
5. Either Noel or Brayden stayed at the most inexpensive of all five hotels.
6. The hotel on Potrero Hill offers free use of its gym and spa facilities.
7. Of Gage's hotel and the one at North Beach, one offers free Wi-Fi Internet access and the other offers free shuttle bus pickup and drop-off at any local airport.
8. Alondra's hotel room didn't cost $200/night.

		Travelers					Neighborhoods					Amenities				
		Alondra	Brayden	Brielle	Gage	Noel	Noe Valley	North Beach	Potrero Hill	SOMA	Telegraph Hill	Free Parking	Free Wi-Fi	Gym and Spa	Kitchenette	Shuttle Bus
Prices	$125															
	$150															
	$175															
	$200															
	$225															
Amenities	Free Parking															
	Free Wi-Fi															
	Gym and Spa															
	Kitchenette															
	Shuttle Bus															
Neighborhoods	Noe Valley															
	North Beach															
	Potrero Hill															
	SOMA															
	Telegraph Hill															

SOLVE RATE
22.4%
AVERAGE TIME
23 min, 21 sec
BEST TIME
7 min, 54 sec by ingleside81

Prices	Travelers	Neighborhoods	Amenities
$125			
$150			
$175			
$200			
$225			

Land for Sale

Walter Welch, a prominent real estate developer, has been searching for some land for his next project. He has a budget of $2 million to spend and is considering five different parcels of land, each in a different county. Using only the clues below, determine the price and size of each parcel, the name of the seller, and the county in which it is located. And remember, land values vary widely depending on location, so larger parcels don't always mean larger prices!

1. The $1.6 million parcel of land is half the size of the one in Hidalgo County, which is half the size of the one in Orrville County.
2. Of the 200 acre property and the most expensive one (which is also the largest of the five), one is in Orrville County (but isn't owned by Lilly Lyre) and the other is currently owned by Jack Jones.
3. The Leander County property (which isn't 50 acres) is priced at $1.5 million.
4. Mark Medine's property is half the size of Kyle Kip's (which isn't 100 acres).
5. The Conover County parcel isn't the least expensive.
6. The 200 acre property isn't priced at $1.2 million.
7. The Orrville County property is larger than the one currently priced at $1.4 million.

	Sellers					Prices					Counties				
	Chad Colt	Jack Jones	Kyle Kip	Lilly Lyre	Mark Medine	$1.2 million	$1.4 million	$1.5 million	$1.6 million	$1.8 million	Conover	Hidalgo	Leander	Orrville	Roxboro
25 acres															
50 acres															
100 acres															
200 acres															
400 acres															
Conover															
Hidalgo															
Leander															
Orrville															
Roxboro															
$1.2 million															
$1.4 million															
$1.5 million															
$1.6 million															
$1.8 million															

SOLVE RATE
21.9%

AVERAGE TIME
23 min, 5 sec

BEST TIME
3 min, 42 sec by khead

Acreages	Sellers	Prices	Counties
25 acres			
50 acres			
100 acres			
200 acres			
400 acres			

Fill 'Er Up!

The computer system at Mader's Fuel Depot was acting up today, so when five customers all tried to pay at once, Mr. Mader had to do some quick thinking to keep all five transactions straight! Using only the clues below, help Mader out by determining which customers used which fuel pumps, how many gallons each person pumped, and the price per gallon for each type of fuel selected.

1. Of Ella and the driver who chose the cheapest type of gasoline, one used pump #3 and the other used pump #4.

2. The five customers are Ella, the ones at pump #1 and pump #4, the one who filled up with gasoline priced at $2.16 per gallon, and the one who pumped the most gasoline.

3. Of the driver who pumped 10 gallons of gasoline and the one at pump #5, one was Madalyn and the other chose the gasoline priced at $2.16 per gallon.

4. The five drivers are Dennis, Ella, the one who pumped nine gallons of gasoline, the one who used pump #1, and the one who selected the gas that was $2.10 per gallon.

5. The customer at pump #2 chose gasoline that was 6¢ more expensive, per gallon, than the gasoline chosen by the customer who purchased 10 gallons of fuel.

6. The customer at pump #3 didn't pump 12 gallons of gas.

7. Raegan (who didn't pump exactly nine gallons of gas) chose a more inexpensive type of gasoline than Dennis.

		Alessandra	Dennis	Ella	Madalyn	Raegan	#1	#2	#3	#4	#5	5 gallons	9 gallons	10 gallons	12 gallons	15 gallons
Prices	$1.98/gal.															
	$2.04/gal.															
	$2.10/gal.															
	$2.16/gal.															
	$2.22/gal.															
Gallons	5 gallons															
	9 gallons															
	10 gallons															
	12 gallons															
	15 gallons															
Pumps	#1															
	#2															
	#3															
	#4															
	#5															

Prices	Drivers	Pumps	Gallons
$1.98/gal.			
$2.04/gal.			
$2.10/gal.			
$2.16/gal.			
$2.22/gal.			

SOLVE RATE
21.5%

AVERAGE TIME
25 min, 45 sec

BEST TIME
4 min, 52 sec by khead

Dieters Delight

A local weight-loss support group formed recently to help those who want to shed a few pounds find the diet that is right for them. Five dieters shared their success stories at the last meeting. Each lost a different number of pounds (and kept them off) after trying a different diet for a specific length of time. Using only the clues below, determine which diet each person tried, how many pounds each lost, and how long it took to lose the weight.

1. The five dieters are the ones who lost 11 and 17 pounds, the one that was on a diet for 3 months, Spencer (who didn't lose 14 pounds and didn't diet for 5 months), and the one that tried the "all juice" diet (who isn't Nicholas).

2. Of the raw-foods dieter and the one who spent the least amount of time dieting, one is Nicholas and the other is Maxine.

3. Between Maxine (who didn't diet for only 6 weeks) and the vegan dieter, one lost 11 pounds and the other stayed on the diet for 3 months.

4. Francisco (who didn't lose 14 pounds) lost three fewer pounds than the person who tried the low-carb diet.

5. The dieter who stuck to small portion sizes for every meal lost more weight than the person who stuck to the diet for the longest amount of time.

6. Either the vegan or the raw-foods dieter lost the least amount of weight.

		Dieters					Diets					Lengths				
		Francisco	Katelyn	Maxine	Nicholas	Spencer	Juicing	Low Carb	Portioning	Raw Foods	Vegan	6 weeks	2 months	3 months	5 months	6 months
Weight Loss	8 pounds															
	11 pounds															
	14 pounds															
	17 pounds															
	20 pounds															
Lengths	6 weeks															
	2 months															
	3 months															
	5 months															
	6 months															
Diets	Juicing															
	Low Carb															
	Portioning															
	Raw Foods															
	Vegan															

SOLVE RATE
21.3%

AVERAGE TIME
17 min, 28 sec

BEST TIME
5 min, 48 sec by leighe

Weight Loss	Dieters	Diets	Lengths
8 pounds			
11 pounds			
14 pounds			
17 pounds			
20 pounds			

Concert Week

Greenfield Auditorium just started selling tickets for five concerts, all of which are held on a different day and a different time next week. Tickets for each show vary in price from $25 to $65 per person. Using only the clues below, figure out which bands are playing on which nights, what time the curtains go up, and how much each ticket costs.

1. The Monday concert costs either $39 or $45 per ticket.
2. Orange Rain has its concert the day before the show that charges $30 per ticket.
3. Either Tuesday's concert or the one that starts at 7:45 pm has a ticket price of $30.
4. Between Instinct's show and the one that starts at 7:15 pm, one costs $45 per person and the other is scheduled for Wednesday evening.
5. Orange Rain's concert, scheduled for 7:00 pm on Thursday, isn't the cheapest of the five.
6. Tickets for the Cindy Fall performance don't cost $30 per ticket.
7. Monday's show doesn't start at 7:15 pm.
8. The show that costs $39 per person doesn't begin at 8:00 pm.
9. Either Terminus or Instinct plays on Wednesday.
10. Neither Belle Curves nor the $30-per-ticket show is scheduled for Monday.

	Belle Curves	Cindy Fall	Instinct	Orange Rain	Terminus	7:00 pm	7:15 pm	7:45 pm	8:00 pm	8:30 pm	$25	$30	$39	$45	$65
Monday															
Tuesday															
Wednesday															
Thursday															
Friday															
$25											
$30											
$39											
$45											
$65											
7:00 pm						
7:15 pm						
7:45 pm						
8:00 pm						
8:30 pm						

SOLVE RATE
20.9%

AVERAGE TIME
23 min, 8 sec

BEST TIME
3 min, 32 sec by gulfcoastswimmer

Days	Bands	Times	Prices
Monday			
Tuesday			
Wednesday			
Thursday			
Friday			

The People Have Spoken

The sixteenth district congressional race had five first-time candidates on the ballot, each from a different political party, and each with a different background and career. The race was far from predictable, and many were astounded with the results! Using only the clues below, determine each candidate's political party, previous career, and how many votes each received in the final tally.

1. Jackson was a lawyer before he decided to run for Congress.
2. Of Richards and the candidate who came in with the second-highest number of votes, one was a teacher and the other was a member of the Constitution Party.
3. Of Ulbright and the candidate who was previously a teacher, one got the second-lowest number of votes (and isn't the judge) and the other is a lifetime member of the Green Party.
4. The candidate who was previously a state senator received fewer votes than the candidate who had been mayor of Casterville.
5. The Republican didn't get the fewest votes of all five candidates and isn't a teacher.
6. Of Cowling (who isn't the mayor) and the winner of the election (who is a lawyer), one is a Republican and the other a Libertarian.
7. Neither Cowling nor the Libertarian has been a judge.

		Campaigns					Parties					Positions				
		Cowling	Dalton	Jackson	Richards	Ulbright	Constitution	Democrat	Green	Libertarian	Republican	Judge	Lawyer	Mayor	State Senator	Teacher
Votes	182															
	42,918															
	59,222															
	326,717															
	450,013															
Positions	Judge															
	Lawyer															
	Mayor															
	State Senator															
	Teacher															
Parties	Constitution															
	Democrat															
	Green															
	Libertarian															
	Republican															

Votes	Campaigns	Parties	Positions
182			
42,918			
59,222			
326,717			
450,013			

SOLVE RATE
20.5%

AVERAGE TIME
21 min, 7 sec

BEST TIME
7 min, 40 sec by debracut

The SATs

Lindsay and four of her friends each took the SATs two months ago, and their scores just came back today. All five of them did extremely well! SAT scores range from 600–2400 points, and combine the scores of three individual exams (math, critical reading, and writing) of 800 points each. Using only the clues below, determine the total score (up to 2400) and the math score (up to 800) received by each student and the high school each attends.

1. The five students are the ones who scored totals of 1920 and 1980, the one who scored 730 on the math exam, Samara, and the Sikeston High student.

2. The student with the lowest math score earned a higher total score than the Byram High student.

3. Rowan's total score was 20 points lower than Davis's.

4. Samara's total score was 20 points lower than that earned by the Anoka High student.

5. The five students are Ava, the one with the 780 math score, Davis, the Edina High student, and the one with the 1960 total score.

6. The student with the lowest total score (who wasn't Ava) didn't get 750 on the math exam.

7. The student with the lowest math score earned a total score 20 points lower than the student who got 780 on the math exam (who wasn't Lindsay).

		Test Takers					Math Scores					Towns				
		Ava	Davis	Lindsay	Rowan	Samara	690	730	750	780	800	Anoka High	Byram High	Edina High	Moberly High	Sikeston High
Total Scores	1920															
	1940															
	1960															
	1980															
	2000															
Towns	Anoka High															
	Byram High															
	Edina High															
	Moberly High															
	Sikeston High															
Math Scores	690															
	730															
	750															
	780															
	800															

Total Scores	Test Takers	Math Scores	Towns
1920			
1940			
1960			
1980			
2000			

SOLVE RATE
20.1%

AVERAGE TIME
19 min, 7 sec

BEST TIME
3 min, 31 sec by kenbrikim

Clam Diggers of Ochiauoato

The clam diggers of Ochiauoato Island have known for centuries that low tide is the optimum time to hunt for clams. Luckily for them, modern technology now makes it easy to find out precisely when low tide will be each morning. Using only the clues below, figure out when the lowest tide will occur on each morning, how much the sea level will drop, and which of the five clam diggers will be working that day.

1. The five low tides are Tuesday's, the one that will drop the sea level by 2.33 feet, Thursday's tide, the 6:30 am tide (which won't happen on the morning when Pablo goes clamming), and the one on which Walter will go clamming.

2. Of Pablo and Marvin, one will go out clamming on the 8:49 am low tide, and the other is scheduled to go out on the morning of the deepest drop in sea level.

3. Walter won't be fishing the morning when low tide is expected to drop to -2.32 feet. Neither Walter nor Charley will be clamming on Wednesday.

4. The low tide at 8:03 am is scheduled for later in the week than the one that will drop the sea level by 2.30 feet.

5. The 7:17 am low tide is scheduled to occur the morning after Charley goes fishing. Monday's low tide will occur sometime after 8:30 am.

6. Of the 9:34 am low tide and the one on which Marvin is scheduled to go clamming, one will drop the sea level by 2.33 feet and the other will happen on Tuesday morning.

7. Marvin won't be clamming during the lowest low tide.

	Charley	Dennis	Marvin	Pablo	Walter	6:30 am	7:17 am	8:03 am	8:49 am	9:34 am	-2.40 feet	-2.37 feet	-2.33 feet	-2.32 feet	-2.30 feet
Monday															
Tuesday															
Wednesday															
Thursday															
Friday															
-2.40 feet															
-2.37 feet															
-2.33 feet															
-2.32 feet															
-2.30 feet															
6:30 am															
7:17 am															
8:03 am															
8:49 am															
9:34 am															

SOLVE RATE
19.7%

AVERAGE TIME
22 min, 20 sec

BEST TIME
8 min, 9 sec by philbo

Days	Clam Diggers	Low Tides	Sea Levels
Monday			
Tuesday			
Wednesday			
Thursday			
Friday			

Tapas Crawl

Five friends decided to do a traditional tapas crawl in Granada, Spain, where they traveled from tapas bar to tapas bar, sampling different tapas (appetizers) at each restaurant. They went to five different tapas bars, with each friend picking up one bill at one bar. None of the bars served the same tapas. Using only the clues below, determine the order in which the friends visited each establishment, which tapas they ate there, and who paid for each.

1. The five friends are Pierce (who treated at the third tapas bar, which wasn't Los Diamantes or Bar Sevilla), the one who paid the bill at Ermita, Roberta, the one who paid for the empanadas (which weren't served at Los Diamantes), and the one who covered the bill at the fourth tapas bar.
2. The fourth tapas bar didn't serve pork stew.
3. Neither Pierce nor the person who treated at Café Elvira paid for empanadas.
4. Rose treated at the fourth tapas bar; Marley didn't pay the bill for the fifth one.
5. The friends ate bacalao just before they went to Café Elvira.
6. Of Ermita and the bar that served croquetas, one was the first bar the friends visited and the other was where Marley paid the bill.

		Marley	Nayeli	Pierce	Roberto	Rose	Bar Sevilla	Café Elvira	Ermita	La Flauta	Los Diamantes	Bacalao	Croquetas	Empanadas	Pork Stew	Roast Ham
Orders	First															
	Second															
	Third															
	Fourth															
	Fifth															
Tapas	Bacalao															
	Croquetas															
	Empanadas															
	Pork Stew															
	Roast Ham															
Bars	Bar Sevilla															
	Café Elvira															
	Ermita															
	La Flauta															
	Los Diamantes															

SOLVE RATE
19.3%

AVERAGE TIME
15 min, 55 sec

BEST TIME
4 min, 23 sec by khead

Orders	Friends	Bars	Tapas
First			
Second			
Third			
Fourth			
Fifth			

The Sky's the Limit

This week, five different astronomers each announced a new discovery relating to a different planet. None of the astronomers studied the same planet, and each of the astronomer's discoveries related to completely different fields of study. Using only the clues below, determine the planet and discovery made by each astronomer and the day the astronomer announced the discovery.

1. Either the astronomer who studied Mercury or the one who made the announcement on Friday (who wasn't Felix) made the orbital discovery.

2. The Saturn announcement, which wasn't made on Friday, had nothing to do with Mateo. The Mars astronomer made the announcement the day before the Jupiter announcement was made.

3. The Jupiter announcement was made the the day before the one about Mercury.

4. Among Mateo and Skyler, one made Wednesday's announcement and the other discovered an impending asteroid impact.

5. The five astronomers were the one who made the gravitational discovery (which had nothing to do with Saturn), the one who studied Mercury, Mateo, Friday's announcer, and the one who made the magnetic field discovery.

6. The five astronomers were the one whose discovery was announced on Thursday, Nathaniel, the astronomer who studied Jupiter, the one who discovered something new about the composition of the planet he or she was studying, and the one whose discovery related to the orbital path of a certain planet.

7. Neither the astronomer who studied Mars nor the one whose discovery had to do with a planetary orbit was Karen.

SOLVE RATE
19.2%
AVERAGE TIME
25 min, 24 sec
BEST TIME
7 min, 40 sec by janiebrock

Message in a Bottle

Just over a year ago, a group of schoolchildren in the Azores (an island chain in the middle of the Atlantic Ocean) each wrote a message that included his or her e-mail address, enclosed it in an airtight bottle, and then threw it into the ocean to see if anyone would respond. Amazingly, five children did eventually get responses! Using only the clues below, figure out where each child's bottle washed ashore, the name of the person who responded, and how long it took each response to arrive back.

1. Of Beatrice (who doesn't live in Spain) and the person who responded after 11 months, one answered Phillip's message and the other discovered the bottle on a beach in Brazil.
2. Marisol received her response two months after Rila received his.
3. The response that took nine months to arrive wasn't from Carole.
4. Neither Natano's nor Roman's response took exactly five months.
5. Of Valence and the person who responded after nine months, one answered Marisol's message and the other found the bottle on a Moroccan shoreline.
6. Between Roman (whose bottle didn't end up in Spain) and Rila, one got a response from Jean and the other person's bottle went all the way to Morocco.
7. Neither Valence nor the Moroccan responder answered Roman (whose response came back sometime before Natano's).
8. Phillip's bottle didn't end up in Portugal.

		Children					Countries					Responders				
		Marisol	Natano	Phillip	Rila	Roman	Brazil	France	Morocco	Portugal	Spain	Beatrice	Carole	Jean	Tennery	Valence
Lengths	3 months															
	5 months															
	7 months															
	9 months															
	11 months															
Responders	Beatrice															
	Carole															
	Jean															
	Tennery															
	Valence															
Countries	Brazil															
	France															
	Morocco															
	Portugal															
	Spain															

SOLVE RATE
18.6%

AVERAGE TIME
26 min, 9 sec

BEST TIME
10 min, 12 sec by khead

Lengths	Children	Countries	Responders
3 months			
5 months			
7 months			
9 months			
11 months			

To the Rescue ...

Ed's bird rescue often cares for wild birds, releasing them back into their natural habitats after they heal. Last month, five volunteers released five different birds (each of a different species). Each bird was marked with a small tracking tag, and each has since been tracked at different distances (and different directions) from its point of release. Using only the clues below, determine which volunteer released which bird, how far the bird went, and in which direction.

1. The bird Francesca released traveled farther from the release point than the brown pelican. The snowy egret traveled father than the wood stork.

2. The bird that was found 200 miles from the release point didn't go in a westerly or northeasterly direction.

3. Either the wood stork or the snowy egret was the bird found closest to the original release point (which wasn't released by Lucas).

4. The bird that was found northeast of the release point traveled 50 miles less than the bid released by Francesca.

5. Between the snowy egret and the bird that traveled 100 miles from the release point, one went in a northerly direction and the other was released by Hudson.

6. The bird that traveled northeast went 50 miles farther than the bird that went directly north.

7. Lucas didn't release the roseate tern, which wasn't found precisely east of the release point.

8. The snowy egret traveled 50 miles farther than the bird that Cash released.

9. The bird that traveled the farthest didn't go in a precisely easterly direction.

		Volunteers					Birds					Directions				
		Cash	Francesca	Hudson	Lucas	Melany	Brown Pelican	Roseate Tern	Snowy Egret	White Ibis	Wood Stork	East	North	Northeast	Southwest	West
Distances	50 miles															
	100 miles															
	150 miles															
	200 miles															
	250 miles															
Directions	East															
	North															
	Northeast															
	Southwest															
	West															
Birds	Brown Pelican															
	Roseate Tern															
	Snowy Egret															
	White Ibis															
	Wood Stork															

SOLVE RATE
18%

AVERAGE TIME
23 min, 59 sec

BEST TIME
3 min, 7 sec by Kazemizu

Distances	Volunteers	Birds	Directions
50 miles			
100 miles			
150 miles			
200 miles			
250 miles			

Exploring the Explorers

Mr. Grambling's history class has been studying the great explorers this month, and each student's final grade for the semester depends on a presentation each would give (with a partner) on a particular explorer. Five groups (of two students each) gave their presentations today, each on a different explorer. All five presentations were outstanding, and each incorporated a unique visual aid to help bring the topic to life. Using only the clues below, figure out which students were paired with each other, which explorers they discussed, and what visual aid each pair used in each presentation.

1. The five pairs were the one that gave a talk on John Cabot (which included Peter), Denton and Zoe's team, Clayton's group, the one that created a diorama for the presentation (which wasn't about Giovanni da Verrazzano), and the one that brought in some old maps depicting the routes taken by the explorer.

2. Marcy wasn't paired with Nehemiah.

3. The two students that gave the presentation on Magellan didn't dress up in period costumes when they got up in front of the class.

4. Either the presentation on Ferdinand Magellan or the one on John Cabot included a homemade web video, which wasn't done by Nehemiah's team.

5. Of Templeton's team and the one that gave the Columbus talk, one brought in an antique coin depicting the explorer and the other wore period costumes while giving the presentation.

6. Between Templeton's group and the one that created a detailed diorama, one included Talia and the other gave a presentation on Ferdinand Magellan.

		Students					Students				Presentations				
		Clayton	Nehemiah	Sophie	Talia	Zoe	Aliyah	Denton	Marcy	Peter	Templeton	Antique Coin	Costumes	Diorama	Old Maps	Web Video
Explorers	Cabot															
	Columbus															
	Drake															
	Magellan															
	Verrazzano															
Presentations	Antique Coin															
	Costumes															
	Diorama															
	Old Maps															
	Web Video															
Students	Aliyah															
	Denton															
	Marcy															
	Peter															
	Templeton															

SOLVE RATE
16.6%

AVERAGE TIME
28 min, 21 sec

BEST TIME
8 min, 52 sec by Gus

Explorers	Students	Students	Presentations
Cabot			
Columbus			
Drake			
Magellan			
Verrazzano			

Computer Club

Although only five students showed up for the inaugural Computer Club meeting, everyone had a great time and couldn't wait for the next get-together. Each of the five participants was thrilled to show off the latest and greatest laptops each had just ordered online. Each laptop came with a different-size hard drive (measured in gigabytes, or GB, with higher numbers meaning more size) and a different processor speed (measured in gigahertz, or GHz, with higher numbers meaning more speed), and each came with a different extra or upgrade. Using only the clues below, determine the hard drive and processor specs for each student's computer and the extra or upgrade each received.

1. The 2.5-GHz computer doesn't have the smallest hard drive. The computer with the 2.2-GHz processor has a hard drive that's twice as big as Kayleigh's.
2. Of Julian and the student with the slowest processor speed on his or her computer, one loves watching movies on the 18" monitor (which was received as a free upgrade) and the other has a 50-GB hard drive.
3. The student who received the free webcam has a hard drive that's only half the size of the one on Cesar's computer (which didn't come with a free scanner).
4. The student with the 2.0-GHz processor got a matching bag free with purchase, but didn't end up getting the 200-GB hard drive.
5. Neither Madison nor the person with the 2.2-GHz processor has the smallest hard drive.
6. Of Julian and the person with the 25-GB hard drive, one has the fastest processor of all five students and the other has the second fastest.

		Cesar	Janelle	Julian	Kayleigh	Madison	1.6 GHz	2.0 GHz	2.2 GHz	2.5 GHz	3.0 GHz	18" Monitor	DVD Burner	Matching Bag	Scanner	Webcam
Hard Drives	25 GB															
	50 GB															
	100 GB															
	200 GB															
	400 GB															
Extras	18" Monitor															
	DVD Burner															
	Matching Bag															
	Scanner															
	Webcam															
Processors	1.6 GHz															
	2.0 GHz															
	2.2 GHz															
	2.5 GHz															
	3.0 GHz															

SOLVE RATE
15.9%

AVERAGE TIME
25 min, 13 sec

BEST TIME
7 min, 39 sec by Laura

Hard Drives	Students	Processors	Extras
25 GB			
50 GB			
100 GB			
200 GB			
400 GB			

Skee Ball Tournament

It was a bit warm out today on the beach, so a small group of five friends decided to get out of the heat of the boardwalk and into the air-conditioned arcade for an impromptu skee ball competition. Each of the five played one game, each on a different lane. They all ended up with different scores, but one of them was the clear winner. After congratulating the skee ball champion, they each collected their tickets and redeemed them for small prizes at the exit counter. Using only the clues below, determine the final score for each player, which lane each was in, and what prize each received when redeeming their tickets.

1. The five friends were the player in lane 3, Jenny (who didn't play in lane 9), Kaitlyn, the one who scored 150, and the one who turned in tickets for a plastic comb.

2. Of the player with the second-highest score (who didn't get the toy horse) and the one who was in lane 3, one is Jenny and the other got a pencil case.

3. Between Delaney and the one with the highest score (who didn't get the toy horse), one redeemed tickets for a water gun and the other played in lane 4 (but isn't Chase).

4. The player in lane 4 scored higher than the player in lane 1.

5. Chase didn't finish with 140 points.

6. Of Jenny and the player in lane 6, one left the arcade with a water gun and the other scored 260 points.

		Players					Lanes					Prizes			
	Chase	Delaney	Jenny	Kaitlyn	Ronald	Lane 1	Lane 3	Lane 4	Lane 6	Lane 9	Comb	Eraser	Pencil Case	Toy Horse	Water Gun
Scores 110															
140															
150															
260															
350															
Prizes Comb															
Eraser															
Pencil Case															
Toy Horse															
Water Gun															
Lanes Lane 1															
Lane 3															
Lane 4															
Lane 6															
Lane 9															

SOLVE RATE
15.8%

AVERAGE TIME
21 min, 4 sec

BEST TIME
4 min, 36 sec by jade_3031

Scores	Players	Lanes	Prizes
110			
140			
150			
260			
350			

Conference Calls

Jeff's appointment calendar software is corrupted, and he has to rebuild his schedule for next week to make sure he doesn't miss any important meetings. He has a conference call scheduled for each day of the workweek, each with a different company and at a different time. Using only the clues below, figure out which company Jeff is supposed to meet with on each day, what time the conference call is set to begin, and what the access number is for each meeting.

1. Of the 3:30 pm meeting and the one with the access number starting with #445, one is with Mateo Limited and the other is with the sales department at Ellcom Plus.
2. The call with the access number #9790533 is scheduled for the day after the call with the access number #1827181.
3. Of the 10:45 am meeting and Wednesday's conference call, one is with Zilcro Industries and the other has the access number #4450190.
4. Neither the 9:30 am call nor the one with the #5367917 access number is scheduled for Wednesday.
5. Of Tuesday's call and the 2:15 pm meeting, one is with Ferico Financials and the other has the #4450190 access code.
6. The conference call with the #1827181 code is scheduled for the day after the meeting with Mateo Limited.
7. The access code for Monday's meeting isn't #5367917.
8. Of Wednesday's meeting and the call with the #9790533 access code, one is scheduled for 4:45 pm and the other is with Ellcom Plus.

	Ellcom Plus	Ferico Fin.	Lukale Inc.	Mateo Ltd.	Zilcro Ind.	#1827181	#4450190	#5367917	#6558345	#9790533	9:30 am	10:45 am	2:15 pm	3:30 pm	4:45 pm
Monday															
Tuesday															
Wednesday															
Thursday															
Friday															
9:30 am															
10:45 am															
2:15 pm															
3:30 pm															
4:45 pm															
#1827181															
#4450190															
#5367917															
#6558345															
#9790533															

Days	Companies	Conf. Numbers	Times
Monday			
Tuesday			
Wednesday			
Thursday			
Friday			

SOLVE RATE
15.7%

AVERAGE TIME
25 min, 26 sec

BEST TIME
5 min, 17 sec by Kazemizu

Musical Prodigies

The Metroville Symphony Orchestra recently featured a concert in which five different young musical prodigies from across the country performed. Each prodigy was a different age and from a different state, and each played a different instrument. Using only the clues below, determine the age, home state, and instrument associated with each musician.

1. The youngest prodigy was from either Vermont or Washington.
2. The 13-year-old musician was neither Kiley nor Bailey.
3. Of Kevin and Isabella, one was from Vermont and the other played the clarinet.
4. The viola prodigy is younger than the musician from Oklahoma.
5. The Georgia native is one year older than Bailey.
6. Of Isabella and the musician from Washington, one was 12 years old and the other played piano.
7. The five prodigies were the 12 year old, the pianist, the 14 year old, Kiley (who didn't play the piccolo), and the musician from Alabama (who wasn't Kevin).
8. Isabella didn't play the clarinet.

		Names					States					Instruments				
		Bailey	Dan	Isabella	Kevin	Kiley	Alabama	Georgia	Oklahoma	Vermont	Washington	Clarinet	French Horn	Piano	Piccolo	Viola
Ages	11															
	12															
	13															
	14															
	15															
Instruments	Clarinet															
	French Horn															
	Piano															
	Piccolo															
	Viola															
States	Alabama															
	Georgia															
	Oklahoma															
	Vermont															
	Washington															

Ages	Names	States	Instruments
11			
12			
13			
14			
15			

SOLVE RATE
15.4%

AVERAGE TIME
21 min, 26 sec

BEST TIME
7 min, 11 sec by logicfan

Egyptian Tattoos

A team of five archaeologists just finished an intense season of digging in the hot Egyptian desert. To celebrate and commemorate their experience, they each decided to get a different Egyptian-themed tattoo before they left Cairo. Using only the clues below, determine the design each archaeologist chose for his or her tattoo, where on each person's body he or she had it done, and how much each tattoo cost.

1. Of Ryan and the person who paid $145 for the tattoo, one chose the sphinx design and the other had the tattoo done on his or her right ankle.
2. The person who had his or her shoulder tattooed didn't spend the least of all five and didn't choose the sphinx design.
3. The one who got the ankh symbol tattoo didn't spend $90 for it.
4. Neither Angelique (who didn't get the Nefertiti tattoo) nor the one who tattooed his or her forearm chose the ankh symbol.
5. Of Angelique and the one who spent the most money on the tattoo, one had the tattoo done on the shoulder and the other chose to have the tattoo done on his or her forearm.
6. Linda's tattoo cost more than the Nefertiti design, which cost more than the scarab beetle tattoo.
7. Between Tristan and the one who chose the sphinx design, one paid $90 and the other had his or her calf tattooed.

	Angelique	Erik	Linda	Ryan	Tristan	Ankle	Bicep	Calf	Forearm	Shoulder	Ankh	Eye of Horus	Nefertiti	Scarab Beetle	Sphinx
$65															
$90															
$112															
$145															
$260															
Ankh															
Eye of Horus															
Nefertiti															
Scarab Beetle															
Sphinx															
Ankle															
Bicep															
Calf															
Forearm															
Shoulder															

Prices	Customers	Placements	Tattoos
$65			
$90			
$112			
$145			
$260			

SOLVE RATE
15.0%

AVERAGE TIME
28 min, 21 sec

BEST TIME
8 min, 37 sec by linda27

The Pediatric Ward

Flu season is in full force now, and the hospital's pediatric ward already has five sick patients who are staying overnight for round-the-clock nurse monitoring. Each of the five children has a different nurse and a different room number, and during the last round of examinations, each was recorded with a different temperature. Using only the clues below, determine the room number and nurse assigned to each patient, and the patient's temperature taken during the last examination.

1. Neither Alec (who didn't have nurse Janet) nor the patient in room 1901 had nurse Brooklyn.
2. Ashley's temperature (taken by her nurse Katerina) was higher than the temperature recorded for the patient who had nurse Janet.
3. Between Avery and the patient with the 101.9 temperature, one had nurse Wilma and the other was in room 1215.
4. Of Ayla and the patient who had nurse Wilma, one had the 101.5 temperature and the other was in room 1679.
5. Nurse Janet's patient had a higher temperature than nurse Thelma's patient.
6. Between Alec and the patient with the 102.1 temperature, one was in room 1901 and the other was in room 2225.
7. The patient in room 2225 didn't have the lowest temperature and wasn't assigned to nurse Wilma.
8. The patient with the 101.5 temperature didn't have nurse Brooklyn.

Temperatures	Children	Room Numbers	Nurses
101.3			
101.5			
101.7			
101.9			
102.1			

Hiccup Cures

Angelica and four of her friends each had an attack of the hiccups during the previous week. Each attack lasted a different amount of time, and each person used a different folk remedy to successfully cure himself or herself. Using only the clues below, determine how long each attack lasted, where it occurred, and what remedy finally worked for each person.

1. The five friends were Gabriella, the one who had a hiccup attack in the pool, the one whose hiccups lasted for the shortest amount of time, the one who had a hiccup attack (which lasted only half as long as Ellie's) at school, and the one who stopped the hiccups just by holding his or her breath.
2. Of Angelica and the one who had the hiccups at the playground, one was cured just by holding his or her breath and the other had the longest hiccup attack of all five friends.
3. Between the person who had a hiccup attack start while in a car and the one whose attack lasted half an hour, one was cured by drinking water and the other by a good scare.
4. The person who hyperventilated to get rid of the hiccups didn't have an attack that lasted exactly one hour.
5. The one who had the hiccups at school had a longer attack than the one who had an attack at home (which lasted longer than 15 minutes).
6. Ellie's hiccup attack was twice as long as Alissa's.
7. Abraham didn't cure his hiccups by drinking water.

		Abraham	Alissa	Angelica	Ellie	Gabriella	Be Frightened	Drink Water	Eat Sugar	Hold Breath	Hyperventilate	Car	Home	Playground	Pool	School
Durations	15 minutes															
	30 minutes															
	1 hour															
	2 hours															
	4 hours															
Locations	Car															
	Home															
	Playground															
	Pool															
	School															
Cures	Be Frightened															
	Drink Water															
	Eat Sugar															
	Hold Breath															
	Hyperventilate															

SOLVE RATE
13.5%

AVERAGE TIME
19 min, 46 sec

BEST TIME
7 min, 2 sec by riffraff

Durations	People	Cures	Locations
15 minutes			
30 minutes			
1 hour			
2 hours			
4 hours			

At the DMV

There are few experiences in life that are duller than waiting in line at the DMV! Five people each arrived at roughly the same time and received a ticket number. Each was at the DMV for a different reason. Using only the clues below, determine each person's ticket number, the reason for his visit to the DMV, and what he did to pass the time while he waited.

1. The five people are Rowan (who didn't listen to music while he waited), the one who spent his time on the telephone, the one who needed to change his address, ticket #238, and ticket #240 (who also didn't listen to music).

2. The person who needed to retake his driver's exam had a lower ticket number than the person who spent his time reading a book.

3. Piper's ticket number was lower than Nehemiah's.

4. Of the person who had ticket #241 (who didn't read a magazine while he waited) and the one who spent most of his time on the telephone, one was Rocco and the other was there to renew his driver's license.

5. Of Marshall and the person who was there to retake his driver's exam, one brought a book to read and the other had ticket #240.

6. The driver who had to retake his exam had a ticket number that came right after the one belonging to the driver who had lost the title to his car and needed a replacement.

		Marshall	Nehemiah	Piper	Rocco	Rowan	Chg. Address	Custom Plates	Lost Title	Renew License	Retake Exam	Book	Magazine	Music	Sleep	Telephone
Numbers	#238															
	#239															
	#240															
	#241															
	#242															
Diversions	Book															
	Magazine															
	Music															
	Sleep															
	Telephone															
Reasons	Chg. Address															
	Custom Plates															
	Lost Title															
	Renew License															
	Retake Exam															

SOLVE RATE
12.5%

AVERAGE TIME
17 min, 9 sec

BEST TIME
5 min, 59 sec by lisaearls

Numbers	Drivers	Reasons	Diversions
#238			
#239			
#240			
#241			
#242			

Tempting Temp Work

Five applicants were lucky enough to find some temp-work through Pandora's Placement Service this week. Each of the five was assigned to a different business, for a different length of time. All five applicants passed their typing examinations, though each had a different words-per-minute (wpm) typing speed. Using only the clues below, find out which temps were placed at which businesses and for how long, and while you're at it, determine the typing speed for each!

1. Of the temp who went to Travel Etc. and the one who can type 56 wpm, one was Valentina and the other was given a three-week assignment (but doesn't type 62 wpm).

2. Between the applicant who boasts a 68 wpm typing speed (who didn't go to The Copy Stop) and the one who went to Cofeteria, one was Devon and the other received a fairly lengthy three month assignment.

3. Dorian can type faster than Asia (who isn't the slowest typist).

4. The one who went to Binder World can type six words-per-minute faster than the applicant who received the three-month long assignment.

5. The slowest typist unfortunately (but perhaps predictably) received the shortest assignment, which wasn't at Travel Etc.

6. Of Jackson and the applicant who was sent to Binder World, one can type at 68 wpm and the other received the one-month assignment.

		Applicants					Businesses					Employment				
		Asia	Devon	Dorian	Jackson	Valentina	Binder World	Coffeteria	Maxwell's	The Copy Stop	Travel Etc.	2 weeks	3 weeks	1 month	3 months	6 months
Typing Speed	50 wpm															
	56 wpm															
	62 wpm															
	68 wpm															
	74 wpm															
Employment	2 weeks															
	3 weeks															
	1 month															
	3 months															
	6 months															
Businesses	Binder World															
	Coffeteria															
	Maxwell's															
	The Copy Stop															
	Travel Etc.															

Typing Speed	Applicants	Businesses	Employment
50 wpm			
56 wpm			
62 wpm			
68 wpm			
74 wpm			

SOLVE RATE
11.7%

AVERAGE TIME
19 min

BEST TIME
2 min, 41 sec by Kazemizu

Career Day

As part of the school's Career Day activities, five students in Mrs. Leonardi's class had to give a 10-minute presentation about a profession that interested them. Each student chose a different profession, and each of the presentations was of a different length (only one actually finished in exactly 10 minutes, per teacher's orders). Using only the clues below, determine the profession chosen by each student, the length of each student's presentation, and the order in which the presentations were given in front of the class.

1. The student who went fourth gave a presentation that lasted either 10 or 11 minutes.

2. Of the student who wants to be an architect and Johan (who doesn't want to be a publisher), one gave the shortest presentation and the other went first.

3. Meredith's presentation lasted a minute longer than the last presentation given on Career Day.

4. Nathaniel didn't go first, and he never wanted to be a cowboy.

5. Bennett's presentation didn't last exactly 11 minutes.

6. Between the student who went third (who gave a shorter presentation than the one who wants to be a cowboy) and the one who wants to be a truck driver, one gave the 12-minute presentation and the other was Meredith (whose presentation lasted one minute longer than Johan's).

7. The student who went first gave a presentation that was one minute longer than the talk that was given fourth.

	Students					Professions					Orders				
	Bennett	Bryan	Johan	Meredith	Nathaniel	Architect	Biologist	Truck Driver	Cowboy	Publisher	First	Second	Third	Fourth	Fifth
9 minutes															
10 minutes															
11 minutes															
12 minutes															
13 minutes															
First															
Second															
Third															
Fourth															
Fifth															
Architect															
Biologist															
Truck Driver															
Cowboy															
Publisher															

Lengths	Students	Professions	Orders
9 minutes			
10 minutes			
11 minutes			
12 minutes			
13 minutes			

SOLVE RATE
11.3%

AVERAGE TIME
23 min, 37 sec

BEST TIME
4 min, 54 sec by jevin2008

Ticket Sales

James was getting the hang of running the ticket counter in the city's theater district, but a power outage wiped out his scheduling software. He now has to rely on hand-scribbled notes about which shows play when and where, and how many seats are still available for each. Using only the clues below, help James match each show to its theater and performance day, and figure out how many open seats are still available for each play.

1. *Old Siam* doesn't have the most open seats available and doesn't show on Wednesday. Wednesday's show has two fewer open seats compared to *Music Ally.*
2. Of *Aunt Agony* and Saturday's show, one has four open seats available and the other plays at the Gibson Theater.
3. Sunday's show (which isn't at the Roxie Theater) has the most open seats available of all five shows.
4. The Gibson Theater shows its performances either on Thursdays or Saturdays.
5. Of *Komedie Kiev* and the show performing at the Burdette Theater, one shows on Friday and the other is completely sold out—not a single ticket available.
6. The Porter Theater never has performances on Thursdays.
7. *Aunt Agony* isn't playing at either the Roxie or Burdette Theaters.

		Show Days					Titles					Theaters				
		Wednesday	Thursday	Friday	Saturday	Sunday	Aunt Agony	Komedie Kiev	Music Ally	Old Siam	Two Towers	Burdette	Gibson	Grand	Roxie	Porter
Open Seats	0															
	2															
	4															
	6															
	8															
Theaters	Burdette															
	Gibson															
	Grand															
	Roxie															
	Porter															
Titles	Aunt Agony															
	Komedie Kiev															
	Music Ally															
	Old Siam															
	Two Towers															

Open Seats	Show Days	Titles	Theaters
0			
2			
4			
6			
8			

SOLVE RATE
11.3%

AVERAGE TIME
38 min, 17 sec

BEST TIME
12 min, 21 sec by khead

Around the World in 80 Meals ...

Brian and four of his friends have started a small ethnic eating group, where every week one of them treats the rest to a nice dinner featuring a different, exotic cuisine, somewhere in one of the city's five main districts. The group decided to splurge this week, eating out every single night during the workweek. Using only the clues below, determine which friend paid the bill for each of the five nights, where the group went, and what cuisine the friends ate.

1. The five friends were the one who treated the group to dinner in Belmont, the one who took everyone out for Armenian food, the friend who paid for the Thai meal, Heather, and the one who footed the bill for Tuesday's dinner.
2. Of the friend who took the group to a downtown restaurant and the one who paid for Tuesday's meal, one is Kira and the other treated for the Ethiopian meal.
3. The dinner in the warehouse district was held sometime before the one in Highland Hills.
4. Kira treated the group the day before they went to the warehouse district.
5. Neither the Armenian restaurant nor the location for Thursday's meal (which wasn't paid for by Amelia) was in Highland Hills.
6. The group went to the Bolivian restaurant the day after they tried the Cambodian restaurant.
7. Between Heather and Emilio (who didn't take the group out to SoHo), one took the group out for Thai food and the other paid for Wednesday's meal.

SOLVE RATE 10.7%

AVERAGE TIME 25 min, 56 sec

BEST TIME 10 min, 8 sec by avecsoleil

It's All About the Ratings ...

With the economy worsening, the bigwigs at Global Mega Media have decided to review five of their more recent television station acquisitions to determine if any should be canceled as a cost-cutting measure. They've assembled a report on each television station, including each station's most recent ratings numbers (meaning the number of viewers) and an overview of the top-rated show on each channel. Using only the clues below, determine the viewership and channel number associated with each television station and the top-rated show currently running on each.

1. *Soap Suds* (which doesn't have the most viewers) doesn't air on BNRG, which has one million fewer viewers than the channel that airs *Powertrips*.
2. Channel #22 has fewer viewers than the channel that airs *Top Chow*, which has fewer viewers than TWL.
3. TWL, which isn't carried on channel #56, boasts the most viewers of all five channels.
4. Between PCR and the channel that airs *Moneygab*, one has three million viewers and the other is on channel #22.
5. Of channel #15 and the station that airs *Ponyville*, one is KWTM and the other has the smallest viewership of all five channels.
6. *Moneygab* doesn't air on either channel #15 or channel #56.
7. CVT isn't carried on channel #62.

	BNRG	CVT	KWTM	PCR	TWL	Moneygab	Ponyville	Powertrips	Soap Suds	Top Chow	15	22	43	56	62
1 million															
2 million															
3 million															
4 million															
5 million															
15															
22															
43															
56															
62															
Moneygab															
Ponyville															
Powertrips															
Soap Suds															
Top Chow															

SOLVE RATE
9.3%

AVERAGE TIME
41 min, 12 sec

BEST TIME
5 min, 23 sec by Laura

Viewers	Channel Names	Top Shows	Channel Numbers
1 million			
2 million			
3 million			
4 million			
5 million			

Appendix
Answers to Puzzles

1 Passport Pandemonium

April 4	Melany	Lawyer	Czech
June 27	Liliana	Architect	Bulgarian
July 8	Ayden	Doctor	Swedish
October 26	Brodie	Engineer	American
December 6	Perla	Politician	Serbian

2 Conspicous Consumption

2:00 pm	Micheal	Oysters	Newspaper
2:30 pm	Zoey	Hot Dogs	Radio
3:00 pm	Carter	Watermelons	Website
3:30 pm	Tristan	Chicken Wings	Magazine
4:00 pm	Savanna	Blueberry Pies	Television

3 If You Truly Love a Butterfly

$49,000	Simon	Third	Hesperiidae
$91,000	Pavel	Fifth	Nymphalidae
$179,000	James	Fourth	Riodinidae
$185,000	Michael	Second	Papilionidae
$188,000	Harold	First	Pieridae

4 Burning the Midnight Bean

$29,000	Esther	Bugishu	Dr. Hunter
$47,000	Donald	Harrar	Dr. Gwynne
$109,000	Brian	Colombian	Dr. Farling
$203,000	Francine	Peaberry	Dr. Irving
$244,000	Colin	Toraja Kalossi	Dr. Earthington

5 Recipe Disaster

25 minutes	Bean Casserole	350 degrees	Serves 2
30 minutes	Mac & Cheese	325 degrees	Serves 8
35 minutes	Roast Potatoes	365 degrees	Serves 12
40 minutes	Baked Ham	340 degrees	Serves 4
45 minutes	Candied Yams	375 degrees	Serves 6

6 Aerial Acrobatics

7400 feet	Jenya	15	Orange
7800 feet	Zachary	129	Silver
8200 feet	Gregory	3	Black
8600 feet	Diana	22	Purple
9000 feet	Frank	56	Red

7 American Centenarians

109 years	Lorenzo	Maryland	Exercise
110 years	Max	Virginia	Tea
111 years	Jasmine	Kentucky	Almonds
112 years	Daisy	Oklahoma	Laughter
113 years	Daniella	Nevada	Children

8 What's Their Sign?

First	Emily	Libra	Violet
Second	Jason	Cancer	Cyan
Third	Kevin	Capricorn	Gray
Fourth	Danny	Aquarius	Crimson
Fifth	Brook	Sagittarius	Blue

9 Walkie Talkies

150 feet	Rachael	Wanda	7
175 feet	Cody	Georgia	11
200 feet	Peter	Patsy	4
225 feet	Santiago	David	12
250 feet	Madison	Angie	8

10 Elemental

146	Dr. Havley	Relavisium	France
147	Dr. Wesley	Volutomium	England
148	Dr. Jackson	Poshtunium	Belgium
149	Dr. Ayden	Hurdonium	Russia
150	Dr. Fabian	Javelonium	Sweden

11 Catching the Wind

156 MPH	Mount Vista	September	1951
160 MPH	Rhoden Pass	November	1944
164 MPH	Parr's Peak	July	1925
168 MPH	Cap Canyon	January	1972
172 MPH	Gully Gorge	March	1988

12 Higher Education

2001	Giovanni	Mackinaw U.	Linguistics
2002	Jack	Tarleton Col.	Engineering
2003	Kelsey	Linton State	French Lit
2004	Uriel	U. of Wales	Anthropology
2005	Luna	E.S.C.	Biology

13 Supreme Court Precedents

1982	Worthington	Rosado	7-2
1985	Tinsley	Swain	5-4
1988	Benedict	Chamberlain	8-1
1991	Eckert	Hastings	6-3
1994	Sorenson	McGrath	9-0

14 Local Papers

25,000	Courier	$0.40	Friday
50,000	Daily Record	$0.50	Thursday
100,000	Norton News	$0.35	Wednesday
200,000	Silbo Times	$0.75	Monday
400,000	Observer	$0.25	Tuesday

15 Speed Trap

Monday	Owen	Off. Lipton	44 MPH
Tuesday	Savannah	Off. Vilray	56 MPH
Wednesday	Lesly	Off. Kipco	51 MPH
Thursday	Graham	Off. Freeh	49 MPH
Friday	Cynthia	Off. Payton	46 MPH

16 Favorite Sons

Monday	Northglenn	Lawrence	Jazz Singer
Tuesday	Cortez	Howard	Philanthropist
Wednesday	Evans	Randolph	Botanist
Thursday	Lafayette	Desha	Astronaut
Friday	Parker	Carroll	Olympian

17 The Film Festival

1:50	Bill	Comedy	First
2:00	Clara	Drama	Second
2:10	Linus	Musical	Third
2:20	Aaron	Documentary	Fifth
2:30	Miley	Action	Fourth

18 Shipwreck Diving

1845	Jonathan	Fortitude	South Africa
1846	Matthew	Guerrero	Vietnam
1847	Mya	Ibineza	Indonesia
1848	Philip	Hermione	Peru
1849	Madeline	Juvenal	Georgia

19 Moving Men

8:00 am	Braxton	Frank	Steve
10:30 am	Frasier	George	Paul
1:00 pm	Roger	Carlos	Michael
3:30 pm	Templeton	Herb	Jackson
6:00 pm	Smith	Bill	Landon

20 Solar Eclipses

2012	August	0.92	2 min 33 sec
2013	January	0.78	2 min 10 sec
2014	December	0.97	4 min 52 sec
2015	July	0.85	5 min 26 sec
2016	May	1.01	1 min 45 sec

21 Broken Bones

1992	Ankle	Base Jumping	8 weeks
1996	Femur	Cycling	10 weeks
1999	Rib	Skiing	5 weeks
2000	Wrist	Rock Climbing	6 weeks
2004	Collarbone	Skydiving	4 weeks

22 Roller Coasters

312 feet	Daniel	Reverse Ride	The Chiller
329 feet	Jessie	Vertical Drop	The Monster
345 feet	Lola	Inverted Seats	The Gremlin
370 feet	Melany	Dark Tunnel	The Maniac
391 feet	Delilah	Double Loop	The Thriller

23 And the Award Goes To ...

First	Camille	Thompson	Engineering
Second	Katherine	Marks	Biology
Third	Talia	Clarke	Mathematics
Fourth	Hector	Ackerman	Theology
Fifth	Victor	McGuire	Philosophy

24 Relocation Time

May	Jason	Betabytes	Miami
June	Hector	Compuweb	Seattle
July	Sara	Interslice	San Francisco
August	Vanessa	Selera	Chicago
September	Alina	Nanoware	New York City

25 Gas Guzzlers

22 MPG	Caiden	2007	Hatchback
25 MPG	Grayson	2008	Convertible
28 MPG	Brody	2004	Sedan
31 MPG	Andrea	2006	Minivan
34 MPG	Patrick	2005	Coupe

26 Merit Badges

10	Paul	Camp Grizzly	Lifesaving
11	Cartman	Camp Boulder	Orienteering
12	Andre	Camp Bravo	Sailing
13	Gregory	Camp Cedar	Climbing
14	Brian	Camp Tinder	Canoeing

27 Breakfast Rituals

5:45 am	Alana	Mocha Latte	Pink Frosted
6:00 am	Griffin	Black Coffee	Boston Cream
6:15 am	Zander	Decaf Coffee	Apple Fritter
6:30 am	Tatum	Café Latte	Bear Claw
6:45 am	James	Cappuccino	Jelly Filled

28 Classes and Classmates

Second	Savannah	History	145
Third	Leilani	Woodshop	415
Fourth	Andrew	Drama	221
Fifth	Allison	English	102
Sixth	Morgan	Home Ec.	406

29 Robot Warriors

AAAA	Zachary	Four	Crusher
AAA	Aden	Two	Mangler
AA	Jackie	Three	Destroyer
C	Giselle	Six	Trasher
D	Stephen	Five	Wrecker

30 Fudge Sale

$2.05	Mitchell	Peanut Butter	Walnuts
$2.20	Bradford	Chocolate	Raisins
$2.35	Moses	Vanilla	Macadamias
$2.50	Amari	Maple	Cranberries
$2.65	Devon	Marbled	Pecans

31 The Piano Quintet

First	Noe	Piano	Goldmark
Second	Philip	First Violin	Boccherini
Third	Walter	Viola	Elgar
Fourth	Amari	Cello	Shostakovich
Fifth	Michael	Second Violin	Saint Saëns

32 Purposeful Puzzlers

3	Jonah	Sudokus	6 months
5	Amir	Drop Quotes	2 years
7	Emilia	Logic Puzzles	3 months
9	Kaiden	Cryptograms	5 years
11	Cynthia	Acrostics	1 year

33 The Best-Sellers List

#1	Denise	Fuller	Valley of Hurt
#2	Lyla	Foster	Westwd. Winds
#3	Jenna	England	Palimpsests
#4	Kelly	Booker	A Man Like Him
#5	Rodney	Mcclure	How We Walk

34 The Model U.N.

11	Amaya	Libyan	Mrs. Baer
12	Emily	Nepalese	Mr. Manzella
13	John	Dominican	Mrs. D'Amico
14	Kaden	Belgian	Mr. Dykstra
15	Christopher	Chinese	Mrs. Schwartz

35 Domino Day

4,300,000	Grady	Setters	Third
4,450,000	Ivan	Topplers	Second
4,600,000	Hope	Kinetics	First
4,750,000	Ayden	Dominotes	Fourth
4,900,000	Chance	Fall Guys	Fifth

36 Shades of White

3 hours	Amaya	Seashell	Bedroom
3.5 hours	Nelson	Linen	Kitchen
4 hours	Adriana	Wicker	Office
4.5 hours	Lillie	Ivory	Bathroom
5 hours	Antonio	Antique White	Living Room

37 Plate Problems

Monday	Brad	DIV-996	Sports Car
Tuesday	Karina	JTR-500	Station Wagon
Wednesday	Lacey	MRM-019	Minivan
Thursday	Landon	MNU-665	Sedan
Friday	Josephine	SUV-332	Pickup

38 A Spoonful of Sugar Helps the Medicine Go Down

First	Meghan	Lime	Chicken Pox
Second	Naomi	Pineapple	Mumps
Third	Jennifer	Grape	Measles
Fourth	Brittany	Cherry	Flu
Fifth	Alice	Orange	Common Cold

39 Better Than Birdies ...

66	Heidi	#10	497 yards
67	Tracy	#16	520 yards
68	Jasmine	#5	411 yards
69	Sarah	#12	342 yards
70	Allison	#1	132 yards

40 Record Lows

-2	Crawford	March	1889
-6	Kossuth	December	1908
-10	Audubon	January	1978
-14	Jasper	February	1960
-18	Guthrie	November	1933

41 Pickle People

24	Victor	Half-Sour	Booth #3
30	Kylee	Bread & Butter	Booth #4
36	Camila	Dill	Booth #5
42	Talia	Gherkin	Booth #2
48	Hector	Sweet	Booth #1

42 Diamonds Are a Girl's Best Friend

2.2 carats	Jay	Canada	$2,400
2.5 carats	Walt	South Africa	$5,250
2.8 carats	Ian	Botswana	$4,090
3.1 carats	Grayson	Australia	$3,675
3.4 carats	Abe	Russia	$2,950

43 Catch of the Day ...

First	Katelyn	Chenin Blanc	Clams
Second	Sarah	Pinot Grigio	Tuna
Third	Bruce	Viognier	Oysters
Fourth	Mariana	Chardonnay	Mussels
Fifth	Valeria	Riesling	Swordfish

44 Change of Diet

35	Leila	Vitamin E	Broccoli
38	Kayden	Vitamin A	Soy Milk
41	Briana	Vitamin C	Wheat Grass
44	Lauryn	Vitamin D	Apples
47	Julianna	Vitamin K	Almonds

45 Unsafe Safes

3:15	Nancy	33-44-41	Diamond
4:54	Allison	25-11-55	Gold Bar
6:01	Khalil	45-50-19	Paintings
6:09	Cameron	14-52-35	Necklace
8:26	Lauryn	12-22-14	Old Books

46 Concert Night

Beethoven	Mrs. Celeste	7th grade	Fifth
Grieg	Mr. Aden	8th grade	First
Lizst	Mr. Marvins	9th grade	Second
Mozart	Mrs. Irving	10th grade	Fourth
Schubert	Mrs. Asia	6th grade	Third

47 Chess Champions

2004	Caro-Kann	Cesar	9:44
2005	English Opening	Victor	13:19
2006	Evans Gambit	Dallas	20:09
2007	Dutch Defense	Avery	15:22
2008	French Defense	Ruben	8:23

48 Power Plants

575 MW	Calexico	1990	Natural Gas
650 MW	Gustine	1981	Coal
725 MW	Kentfield	1979	Nuclear
800 MW	Escalon	1972	Wind
875 MW	Larkspur	1983	Water

49 Buyer's Market

$145,000	Jardens	Wesley Rd.	High Ceilings
$199,000	Martinsons	Eustis Way	Jacuzzi
$239,000	Carsons	Felton Dr.	Wood Floors
$255,000	Kemps	Minter Blvd.	Sun Room
$285,000	Kings	Baker Ct.	Skylights

50 The Only Thing We Have to Fear …

Monday	Holly	Glossophobic	Third
Tuesday	Morgan	Arachnophobic	Fourth
Wednesday	Dean	Claustrophic	Ninth
Thursday	Kristopher	Coulrophobic	Eighth
Friday	Julio	Agoraphobic	Sixth

51 It's All About Thyme!

5 minutes	Addison	Mint	Pavel Place
10 minutes	Georgia	Thyme	Cedar Court
15 minutes	Sidney	Cilantro	Lorry Lane
20 minutes	Beau	Basil	Winsome Way
25 minutes	Mallory	Parsley	Deadwood Dr.

52 Near-Earth Asteroids

1.5 miles	8DOQ01P	Rogers	December
3 miles	IB80PLZ	Tibbits	November
6 miles	LP4G9MO	Millicent	August
12 miles	SS51MWE	Wallingford	March
24 miles	MQUYT3Z	Halberstrom	April

53 For the Birds …

18	Hailey	Blue Jay	Potato Skins
19	Felipe	Heron	Onion Rings
20	Allesandra	Condor	Chili Fries
21	Phoenix	Oriole	Soup of the Day
22	Cadence	Vulture	Buffalo Wings

54 Pool Heaters

79°F	Cyrus	Amanus 250	18,000 gal.
81°F	Levi	Aquatron	25,000 gal.
83°F	Pablo	Chlorfree II	13,000 gal.
85°F	Sawyer	Buford X62	15,000 gal.
87°F	Grant	Cozy Comfort	10,000 gal.

55 Dress Shoes

8	Daven	Wingtip	White
9	Philip	Monk	Chestnut
10	Everett	Derby	Burgundy
11	Albert	Loafer	Black
12	Gustavo	Oxford	Dark Brown

56 Poker Hands

King High	Jack	$46	Coin
Two Eights	Luna	$15	Hat
Pair of Nines	Kelsey	$24	Sunglasses
Three Fours	Giovanni	$178	Ring
Four Aces	Uriel	$39	Rabbit's Foot

57 Balancing the Checkbook

406	Ernest Cowell	$250.00	Decorator
407	Bill Johnson	$105.56	Plumber
408	Fanny Taylor	$62.16	Baker
409	Carol Rowe	$72.98	Singer
410	Derrick Pile	$56.40	Landscaper

58 Mountaineers

21,250 feet	Katherine	California	Mt Dharma
21,750 feet	Lilly	Wyoming	Mt Timsickle
22,250 feet	Daynara	Alabama	Mt Alaska
22,750 feet	Cali	New Hampshire	Mt Miniver
23,250 feet	Cory	Michigan	Mt Coffin

59 Comic Books

Dinodramas	Jamie	1972	$65
Lia Luxor	Kendra	1963	$25
Li'l Legends	Ralph	1983	$49
Magnet Man	Catherine	1945	$99
Terror Eyes	Esther	1978	$79

60 Bowling Night

92	Felipe	13 lb.	Pink
105	Mariana	12 lb.	Blue
124	Gary	14 lb.	Black
163	Mitchell	10 lb.	Green
202	Wendy	15 lb.	Silver

61 Tallest Trees

273 feet	Aldrich	Bald Cypress	Kulpsville
279 feet	Lillith	Coast Redwood	Monessen
285 feet	Mellifont	Sequoia	Donora
291 feet	San Pejedro	Douglas Fir	Exeter
297 feet	Hannah	Sitka Spruce	Catasauqua

62 Comedy Night

8:00 pm	Jonas	St. Louis	Politics
8:30 pm	Nolan	Omaha	Parenting
9:00 pm	Juan	New York	Office Work
9:30 pm	Harmony	Chicago	Relationships
10:00 pm	Daniel	Tacoma	Food

63 Eco-Friendly Employees

8:34 am	Ariel	4th floor	10-Speed Bike
8:40 am	Joe	5th floor	Segway
8:46 am	Nathanael	3rd floor	Mountain Bike
8:52 am	Sasha	1st floor	Scooter
8:58 am	Dulce	2nd floor	Skateboard

64 For the Dogs …

May 17	Marmot	Border Collie	Speak
August 7	Theo	Dachshund	Sit
September 5	Diva	Chihuahua	Stay
September 22	Sadie	Maltese	Roll Over
November 17	Kenzie	Pomeranian	Come

65 Some Heavy Lifting …

162 lb.	Titus	Norway	Coach Kinski
164 lb.	Lee	Finland	Coach Ervatz
166 lb.	Magnus	Denmark	Coach Herzog
168 lb.	Pavel	Sweden	Coach Padoll
170 lb.	Jakku	Iceland	Coach Mitka

66 At the Salon

First	Anna	Brown	Vonda
Second	Brianna	Red	Tiffany
Third	Callie	Blonde	Sharon
Fourth	Patty	Silver	Helga
Fifth	Gloria	Black	Jackie

67 High IQs

156	Skyler	45	Artist
160	Andy	23	Writer
164	Bryan	57	Professor
168	Esther	38	Physicist
172	Ramon	31	Astronomer

68 Driest Deserts

1.1 inches	Tenexalub	Mali	300,000 sq mi
1.2 inches	Darukapa	China	609,000 sq mi
1.5 inches	Li-Licapite	Eritrea	445,000 sq mi
1.7 inches	Fumarote	Peru	756,000 sq mi
2.3 inches	Pocamo	Mexico	883,000 sq mi

69 Light Testers

25 W	Mason	192 hours	Ceiling Fan
40 W	Priscilla	253 hours	Track Light
60 W	Roman	160 hours	Desk Lamp
75 W	Russell	124 hours	Outdoor Lamp
100 W	Nicholas	139 hours	Wall Sconce

70 Rainy Days

18 inches	Astera	November 13	1914
19 inches	Haylow	March 9	1933
20 inches	Blue Hills	July 30	1959
21 inches	Tallyhon	February 21	1988
22 inches	Quillayute	October 2	1972

71 Two Tickets to Paradise

March 19	Bethany	Aruba	George
March 20	Johanna	Barbuda	Hubert
March 21	Mia	Martinique	Emeril
March 22	Nayeli	Grenada	Franklin
March 23	Bryanna	Saint Kitts	Dexter

72 Dance Lessons

Monday	Taylor	Mambo	7:00 pm
Tuesday	Kelvin	Cha-Cha	7:30 pm
Wednesday	Kaitlyn	Waltz	8:00 pm
Thursday	Ricky	Rumba	8:30 pm
Friday	Janiya	Foxtrot	6:30 pm

73 New Species

1968	Drewsilia	Bee	Suriname
1969	Horacinia	Rodent	Paraguay
1970	Calvinicus	Turtle	Guyana
1971	Randolphia	Frog	Uruguay
1972	Elijahphicus	Monkey	Bolivia

74 Lumberjack Games

First	Cameron	Logroll	#98
Second	Victor	Single Buck	#154
Third	Howard	Speed Climb	#90
Fourth	Sydney	Hot Saw	#36
Fifth	Kyle	Block Chop	#121

75 Musical Tryouts

First	Sebastian	Guitar	Bulgaria
Second	Taylor	Viola	Ukraine
Third	Kayleigh	French Horn	Romania
Fourth	Giovanni	Cello	Poland
Fifth	Brennan	Piano	Moldova

76 Skyscraper Dreams

3015 feet	DeSouza	122 stories	China
3060 feet	Cuniford	119 stories	Japan
3105 feet	Eisenberg	124 stories	India
3150 feet	Bellachoz	114 stories	United States
3195 feet	Ainsworth	116 stories	Malaysia

77 Bike-a-Thon

28 miles	Isaiah	$375	Actron ZX
31 miles	Layla	$425	Rollins II
34 miles	Bailey	$250	Trak T450
37 miles	Dana	$320	Cobra X50
40 miles	Jason	$295	Zelok 5

78 Lost in Translation

First	Collin	Oskian	Mountain
Second	Alyssa	Siclamian	Spear
Third	Seth	Liburnian	Mother
Fourth	Riley	Gestapian	Horse
Fifth	Jordan	Raythean	Sun

79 One Romantic Night

6:00 pm	Brad	Titanium	Emerald
6:30 pm	Dirk	Platinum	Diamond
7:00 pm	Chet	White Gold	Amethyst
8:00 pm	Adam	Yellow Gold	Sapphire
8:30 pm	Eli	Silver	Ruby

80 The Numismatist

1789	Dutch	Fine	$85
1815	French	Very Fine	$160
1836	Italian	Good	$90
1858	Spanish	Poor	$125
1862	English	Fair	$239

81 Mesa Peoples

240-360 AD	Kevin	Pachape	25,000
360-480 AD	Jason	Cochupta	50,000
480-600 AD	Cassandra	Kipaquatl	75,000
600-720 AD	Lionel	Minapiato	15,000
720-840 AD	Christopher	Tucakopi	5,000

82 Early Flights

6:05 am	Sydney	Cedar Rapids	392
6:15 am	Johnny	Lincoln	102
6:25 am	Iris	Cranston	555
6:35 am	Collin	Baltimore	345
6:45 am	Tarlton	Boise	229

83 Mythology Papers

First	Hannah	86	Lycurgus
Second	Josiah	89	Endymion
Third	Noah	83	Antigone
Fourth	Johnny	92	Eurydice
Fifth	George	98	Agamemnon

84 Put That on a Record and Sell It …

Monday	Jorge	Sad to See You	Panoply
Tuesday	Hayden	A Single Kiss	Streetwise
Wednesday	Angela	Happy Times	Titustown
Thursday	Ian	One More Time	Leonite
Friday	Gary	Summer Blues	Ballyhoo

85 Chili Peppers

25,000 SHU	Griffix	Mexico	February
50,000 SHU	Tarawa	Panama	April
100,000 SHU	Riki-kuku	Thailand	July
200,000 SHU	Capacine	India	October
400,000 SHU	Devil's Hand	Honduras	September

86 Broadband Users

1 Mbps	Jasper	Fiber-Optic	MP3s
2 Mbps	Sidney	Satellite	Video Chat
4 Mbps	Kevin	DSL	Movies
8 Mbps	Riley	Power Line	Home Business
16 Mbps	Ellie	Cable	Gaming

87 Dinner Dilemmas

Monday	Rachel	Chianti	Mangoes
Tuesday	Allen	Chardonnay	Seafood
Wednesday	Brooklyn	Pinot Noir	Gluten
Thursday	Ernesto	Burgundy	Dairy
Friday	Skylar	Bordeaux	Peanuts

88 The Most Important Meal …

Monday	Javon	Pancakes	Mineral Water
Tuesday	Liana	Oatmeal	Coffee
Wednesday	Karina	Cereal	Ceylon Tea
Thursday	Rodrigo	Waffles	Tomato Juice
Friday	Timothy	Bacon and Eggs	Orange Juice

89 Peace Corps

1991-1993	Samuel	Tanzania	Education
1993-1995	Arianna	Honduras	Medicine
1995-1997	Luis	Indonesia	Agriculture
1997-1999	Veronica	Cambodia	Water Issues
1999-2001	Ezekiel	Armenia	Environment

90 Anuakian Kings

1542-1511 BC	Darigalus	Goat	Four
1511-1495 BC	Phylarisea	Dolphin	Three
1495-1491 BC	Cayophalum	Eagle	Seven
1491-1448 BC	Abidonas	Bull	Twelve
1448-1432 BC	Minoacam	Dog	Nine

91 Scholarships

$5,000	Kyra	Menifee	Engineering
$10,000	Mitchell	Weslaco	Anthropology
$15,000	Chase	Beale	Medicine
$20,000	Abigail	Hemet	Law
$25,000	Tate	East Alton	Architecture

92 Orchid Fever

$140	Myles	Pigeon Orchid	Tuesday
$160	Kenzie	Calypso Orchid	Wednesday
$180	Alicia	Cooktown Orchid	Friday
$200	Laura	Fly Orchid	Monday
$220	Callie	Tiger Orchid	Saturday

93 Disastrous Presentations

Monday	April	Volcanoes	B+
Tuesday	Jack	Hurricanes	A
Wednesday	Ricky	Wildfires	A-
Thursday	Eduardo	Earthquakes	B-
Friday	Keith	Tornados	B

94 A Rough Day at the Phone Company

Monday	Jackie	Brewer	867-5309
Tuesday	Amelia	Marston	281-0911
Wednesday	Trey	Tillman	368-9614
Thursday	Maurice	Venter	589-2812
Friday	David	Appleton	502-9182

95 Horse Stables

#1	Taylor	Morgan	Flash
#2	Meredith	Appaloosa	Magdalena
#3	Georgia	Arabian	Patches
#4	Omar	Clydesdale	Dario
#5	Keira	Thoroughbred	Angel

96 Home Run Leaders

14	Walter	Kings	.418
15	Jason	Giants	.439
16	Roger	Outlaws	.400
17	Dante	Grizzlies	.407
18	Carlos	Warriors	.419

97 Buy Low, Sell High

$0.75	Scott	HOPN	Manufacturing
$1.00	Derrick	AMBR	Pharmaceutical
$1.25	Brett	CFWT	Technology
$1.50	Leslie	GGML	Financial
$1.75	Connor	TLVU	Energy

98 Pen Names

2002	Nina Knowles	Lamentations	Matt Jenkins
2003	Leslie Lane	Persian Days	Zach Friese
2004	Chase Kent	Agamemnon	Guy Coraline
2005	Jay Walden	Bay of Tears	Paul Ponts
2006	Kyle Clark	Ended Dreams	Bev Willard

99 A Mile in Their Shoes ...

3:59	Gloria	Wahoos	Silver
4:03	Ramon	Marlins	Green
4:08	Jay	Blue Hens	Blue
4:11	Esmeralda	Hurricanes	Black
4:24	Maddox	Spartans	Red

100 Deep Sea Fishing

30 lb.	Yesenia	Sailfish	1:10 pm
45 lb.	Mason	Amberjack	3:35 pm
60 lb.	Gabriela	Barracuda	3:59 pm
75 lb.	Nancy	Marlin	10:48 am
90 lb.	Grace	Tuna	9:30 am

101 Leaps and Bounds

2.35 meters	Francis	8.1 meters	4.5 meters
2.33 meters	John	8.5 meters	5.0 meters
2.29 meters	Hadley	8.8 meters	5.2 meters
2.25 meters	Alex	8.6 meters	5.4 meters
2.21 meters	Hugh	8.2 meters	4.9 meters

102 Genome Sequencing

600,000	Jose	Nanorudium	June 2012
1,200,000	Karla	Mycothelium	May 2012
2,400,000	Ruben	Ventrilium	April 2012
4,800,000	Amir	Carsonelium	July 2014
9,600,000	Brian	Protoforelum	March 2013

103 The Town Hall Meeting

7:00 pm	Nate	Madison St.	Construction
7:15 pm	Priscilla	Paul Circle	Street Lights
7:30 pm	Masha	Campus Drive	Potholes
7:45 pm	Lincoln	Bluff Avenue	Neighbors
8:00 pm	Josephine	Oak Ridge Rd.	Dogs Barking

104 The Bridge Era

1932	Thurgood	13,861 yards	Jackson
1933	Milford Pass	10,254 yards	Nillith
1934	Ingleside	11,490 yards	Valentine
1935	Ridgewood	13,733 yards	Iampiah
1936	Liberty	16,028 yards	Frederick

105 Folk Songs

2:35	Brittany	"Playtime"	First
3:10	Jacob	"Winter Wind"	Fourth
3:21	Neville	"Never Again"	Second
3:27	Quinton	"Callous Soul"	Third
3:56	Genesis	"Moontide"	Fifth

106 Auto Insurance

$565	Reese	$1,000	Pickup
$590	Jeffrey	$250	Sedan
$615	Guadalupe	$500	SUV
$640	Makenna	$750	Coupe
$665	Herbert	$1,500	Convertible

107 Speedboats

First	Jordan	302 MPH	Great Western
Second	Jules	271 MPH	Sea Giant
Third	Hayden	283 MPH	Odyssey
Fourth	Ashton	279 MPH	Bravery
Fifth	Hanson	285 MPH	Viking

108 Census Numbers

18,728	Ali	Tyrone	11,021
19,001	Titus	Conyers	11,513
19,222	Addison	Eastman	12,440
19,310	Emma	Hinesville	12,019
20,197	Destiny	Alpharetta	11,984

109 Coast Guard Calls

54.5°	Captain Pride	-168.2°	11:43 pm
55.5°	Bayford Skol	-166.0°	11:20 pm
56.5°	Tied for Life	-164.7°	10:08 pm
57.5°	Jessie's Girl	-163.1°	10:52 pm
58.5°	Heaven Sent	-165.3°	10:59 pm

110 Ceramics Class

Monday	Caroline	Vase	Green
Tuesday	Isabelle	Ashtray	Blue
Wednesday	Jalen	Bowl	Purple
Thursday	Kaitlynn	Flower Pot	White
Friday	Brenda	Coffee Mug	Orange

111 Having a Whale of a Time

June	Rowan	Birthing	Pilot Whales
July	Madelynn	Dive Depth	Right Whales
August	Dennis	Range	Humpback Whales
September	Rachael	Songs	Sperm Whales
October	Jasper	Diet	Blue Whales

112 Everything Went Swimmingly ...

First	Cali	3	Denmark
Second	Megan	7	Italy
Third	Natalie	4	United States
Fourth	Kaitlyn	1	Sweden
Fifth	Parker	6	Canada

113 The Sweet Taste of Success

$25	Morgan	Lemon Bars	Table 3
$30	Jayson	Apple Pie	Table 4
$35	Brenda	Brownies	Table 5
$40	Linda	Carrot Cake	Table 2
$45	Gary	Pecan Sandies	Table 1

114 Cross-Country Kitsch

$5.00	Nicholas	Ball of Twine	Texas
$9.00	Michaela	Aluminum Cow	Pennsylvania
$13.00	Hannah	Penny House	Ohio
$17.00	Jenna	Wax Museum	Oklahoma
$21.00	Andrew	Mystery Hole	Indiana

115 Clever Inventions

9,412,210	Dane	Mousetrap	1
9,450,183	Luna	Pool Cover	11
9,599,672	Jesse	Door Hinge	3
9,608,495	Mekhi	Lawn Mower	16
9,671,336	Davis	Engine Coolant	8

116 Car Shopping

$39,000	Wendtfar	28 MPG	Keyless Entry
$45,000	Marcuzza	19 MPG	MP3 Player
$51,000	Finestra	22 MPG	Nav. System
$57,000	Poltron	25 MPG	Heated Seats
$63,000	Goromati	30 MPG	Convertible

117 Almost as Good as the Real Thing ...

$25	Elly	Skirt	Hugh Bosch
$30	Rochelle	Pantsuit	Guy Vanchy
$35	Estelle	Blouse	Georgia Mann
$40	Alyssa	Dress	Effendi
$45	Marcy	Purse	Gupshie

118 The Petting Zoo

First	Camille	Llamas	Five
Second	Christopher	Sheep	Thirteen
Third	Angelo	Goats	Ten
Fourth	Ally	Calves	Eight
Fifth	Adriana	Rabbits	Six

119 Gold Fever

0.02 ounces	Sadie	6 days	Balder's Bend
0.03 ounces	Angel	5 days	Captain Creek
0.05 ounces	Francesca	7 days	Vindal Pass
0.08 ounces	Emanuel	4 days	Middle River
0.12 ounces	Maximilian	3 days	Seneca Stream

120 Hardwood Floors

Monday	Leilani	Pine	Bedroom
Tuesday	Athena	Mahogany	Living Room
Wednesday	Anthony	Oak	First Floor
Thursday	Chad	Cherry	Whole House
Friday	Stephanie	Maple	Dining Room

121 Philatelists

$525	Talon	1931	8¢
$600	Kimberly	1912	11¢
$675	Jackie	1923	12¢
$750	Reece	1927	5¢
$825	Kadence	1934	3¢

122 Antarctic Adventure

265 days	Daugherty	Kansas	7
275 days	Timberton	Louisiana	9
285 days	Parker	Wisconsin	4
295 days	Blankley	South Carolina	6
305 days	Jackson	Oregon	12

123 Talk, Talk, Talk

450	Linda	Violet	Hands-Free
500	Rebekah	White	Camera
550	Kaden	Blue	Smart Phone
600	Jaylen	Silver	MP3 Player
650	Talia	Pink	Flip-Phone

124 New Stars

6 parsecs	Roy	Phylarian	5.0
12 parsecs	Keaton	Beta Colaris	8.1
24 parsecs	Blake	Dendricle II	9.4
48 parsecs	Pierce	Minitarius	2.5
96 parsecs	Esmerelda	Zinfadron	1.2

125 Checking Accounts

Balloons	Julius	Farmar	Student
Clowns	Emma	Lipton	Retirement
Dogs	Spencer	Garston	Super-Saver
Horses	Braden	Pollis	Premium
Sunset	Carter	Neville	Economy

126 Keeping Up with the Joneses ...

4156	Kamryn	Indigo	Victorian House
4157	Jason	Pink	Ranch House
4158	Theodore	Violet	Bungalow
4159	Roberto	White	Country House
4160	Laura	Tan	Duplex

127 The Barbershop

First	Darren	Bowl Cut	Brown
Second	Trevor	Caesar Cut	Gray
Third	Matthew	Mohawk	Black
Fourth	Alan	Flat-Top	Blond
Fifth	Jay	Crew Cut	Red

128 Wacky Water Bills

$135	Max	May	#134
$143	Owen	July	#302
$151	Lillian	April	#280
$159	Kassandra	March	#255
$167	Eliza	June	#192

129 Incunabula

1494	Horwitz	Infortiatum	$5,600
1495	Solomon	Missale Romanum	$14,950
1496	Lilliford	Polycronicon	$4,250
1497	Payton	Chronicon	$3,500
1498	Mellon	Aquila Volante	$9,800

130 Stormy Seas

Category 1	Darla	September 15	3 days
Category 2	Charlotte	August 29	1 day
Category 3	Eustis	September 28	6 days
Category 4	Angie	October 6	5 days
Category 5	Becka	October 17	2 days

131 Teachers' Pets

2nd grade	Mrs. Graves	Room 209	Ant Farm
3rd grade	Mr. Tarkle	Room 222	Frog
4th grade	Mr. Carson	Room 115	Snake
5th grade	Mrs. Ashley	Room 102	Spider
6th grade	Mrs. Harmon	Room 118	Mouse

132 Waterfalls

475 meters	Kassandra	Ejibou	1995
482 meters	Ryland	Tambaroon	2007
489 meters	Julamongry	Comarongo	2005
496 meters	Diamond Drop	Brahmatan	2002
503 meters	Clarafin	Miraclee	1998

133 Good Fences Take Good Laborers ...

$600	Tom Lane	6 days	Four
$800	Jim Beall	3 days	Five
$1,000	Bob Roth	4 days	Six
$1,200	Mike Green	5 days	Three
$1,400	Ed Jones	7 days	Two

134 A Five-Alarm Catastrophe

First	Griffin	Dimples	Topper Way
Second	Felix	Princess	Racine Street
Third	Jackie	Mittens	Hyde Lane
Fourth	Louis	Cardamom	Brook Street
Fifth	Wesley	Whiskers	Cape Court

135 Lawyers

2005	Zion	Malpractice	Ohio
2006	Selena	Tax	Wisconsin
2007	Damian	Bankruptcy	Florida
2008	Kaylin	Criminal	Tennessee
2009	Leilani	Immigration	California

136 In Walt's Wallet

$2,500	Mordett	19.5%	02/2013
$3,500	Crident	9.5%	12/2014
$4,500	Fidelis	12.9%	09/2012
$5,500	Primocarte	4.9%	04/2015
$6,500	Deltron	2.9%	06/2013

137 Providing Some Illumination

$35.00	Kelvin	Aisle Six	Halogen
$37.50	Clara	Aisle Three	LED
$40.00	James	Aisle One	Mercury-Vapor
$42.50	Jenna	Aisle Seven	Sodium-Vapor
$45.00	Caleb	Aisle Four	Neon

138 Island Cruise

June 8	8:30 am	Isanti	Zip Line
June 11	10:45 am	Puyallup	Volcano
June 14	12:00 pm	Ephrata	Snorkeling
June 17	6:00 pm	Watonga	Horseback
June 20	2:30 pm	Barnhart	Rainforest

139 Serving Their Country

1989	Jocelyn	Marines	New Jersey
1993	Melissa	Navy	Alaska
1997	Natasha	Army	California
2001	Brooklyn	Air Force	Texas
2005	Beau	Coast Guard	Alabama

140 Fruits of Their Labor ...

Monday	Paige	Kiwis	$120
Tuesday	Mary	Apricots	$89
Wednesday	Dante	Pineapples	$37
Thursday	Heidi	Watermelons	$55
Friday	Anahi	Limes	$24

141 Time for a Test ...

72	Trevor	Mrs. Koralis	English
76	Kayla	Mr. Ackerman	Geometry
81	Gage	Mr. Mockel	Physics
89	London	Mr. Reinsford	Chemistry
96	Isaiah	Mrs. Rocek	Biology

142 Track and Field

5 months	Braydon	49	Javelin
6 months	Landon	54	Pole Vault
7 months	Joshua	80	400m Race
8 months	Layla	26	100m Hurdle
9 months	Karla	12	Long Jump

143 The Dart Toss

15	Melody	20	Camera
20	Stella	25	Rubber Ball
25	James	5	Stuffed Bear
30	Kendra	15	Cowboy Hat
35	Nivena	10	Water Pistol

144 Extreme Gardening

3 weeks	Angelines	Pink	7.0
4 weeks	Farabelles	Orange	5.9
5 weeks	Gelundias	Yellow	5.2
6 weeks	Aprilias	White	6.4
7 weeks	Estrellias	Red	5.5

145 The Halloween Weigh-In

7:00 pm	Angelina	Zombie	2.6 pounds
7:15 pm	Cameron	Witch	1.1 pounds
7:30 pm	Aden	Werewolf	1.5 pounds
7:45 pm	Julissa	Vampire	1.9 pounds
8:00 pm	Adrianna	Mummy	2.3 pounds

146 Free-Diving

92 meters	Josephine	3:13	England
95 meters	Priscilla	3:15	Germany
98 meters	Mackenna	3:18	Denmark
101 meters	Natasha	3:10	Canada
104 meters	Myra	3:02	France

147 It's Knot as Easy as It Looks

First	Avery	Group E	Bowline
Second	Sam	Group B	Half-Hitch
Third	Ashton	Group C	Sheet
Fourth	Norbert	Group D	Sheep Shank
Fifth	Dustin	Group A	Halyard

148 The Meteorite Hunters ...

1:30 pm	Anya	South	Two
1:45 pm	Dustin	West	Three
2:00 pm	John	Southeast	Twelve
2:15 pm	Brenda	East	Six
2:30 pm	Ken	Southwest	None

149 On Line at the Music Store

First	Xander	Country	$9.99
Second	Brenna	Blues	$12.99
Third	Ricardo	Classical	$10.49
Fourth	Marc	Jazz	$13.49
Fifth	Valentina	Hip Hop	$13.99

150 The Science Fair

Monday	Braden	Magnetism	Wyoming
Tuesday	Carson	Earthquakes	Connecticut
Wednesday	Allison	Volcanoes	Michigan
Thursday	Nicole	Electricity	South Carolina
Friday	Francisco	Cloud Formation	Kentucky

151 Greener Grass

1/2 acre	Dakota	Friday	Zoysia
1 acre	Tyler	Tuesday	Red Fescue
2 acres	Jamie	Saturday	Bluegrass
2.5 acres	Cadence	Sunday	Bermuda
4 acres	Reid	Thursday	Ryegrass

152 Best Ball

215 yards	Tate	1 Iron	Irvington
230 yards	Lebron	Driver	Pinseeker
245 yards	Abel	3 Wood	Triple Play
260 yards	Matthew	5 Wood	Greenford
275 yards	Chevy	2 Iron	Fairwood

153 Prom Night

7:58 pm	Kevin	Felicity	Black
8:00 pm	Nicholas	Alice	Navy Blue
8:02 pm	Maxwell	Cathy	Silver
8:04 pm	Franklin	Jennifer	Red
8:06 pm	Stephen	Denise	Purple

154 Busy Day at Court

9:00 am	Judge Emmis	Bank Robbery	12
10:25 am	Kelso	Car Theft	32
1:15 pm	Judge Powers	Forgery	19
3:40 pm	Judge Mackey	Reck. Driving	24

155 Radio Winners

89.3	Andrew	WKPC	100th caller
94.6	Jennifer	WRFT	21st caller
99.1	Roman	WSPR	49th caller
101.1	Amber	WTLD	11th caller
104.5	Dorian	WOLD	3rd caller

156 Deli Delight

145	Arthur	Corned Beef	Sourdough
146	Michael	Salami	Rye
147	Casey	Pastrami	Pumpernickel
148	Abigail	Roast Beef	White
149	Mario	Liverwurst	Wheat

157 Earth Tremors

2.3	Saravello	25 seconds	3:25 am
2.6	Yosalinda	10 seconds	5:04 am
2.8	Amaya Hills	23 seconds	4:59 am
3.1	Leonardi	4 seconds	6:42 am
3.6	Chrisville	17 seconds	9:03 am

158 Pizza Pandemonium

6:06 pm	Dakota	Onions	Sicilian
6:07 pm	Scott	Pepperoni	Wheat Crust
6:08 pm	Gregory	Sausage	Hand Tossed
6:09 pm	Paola	Mushrooms	Deep Dish
6:10 pm	Liam	Green Peppers	Thin Crust

159 We All Scream for Ice Cream

$2.49	Connor	Sprinkles	Chocolate
$2.59	Joanna	Cherries	Coffee
$2.69	Javier	Hot Fudge	Strawberry
$2.79	Carly	Whipped Cream	Pistachio
$2.89	Kimberly	Peanuts	Mint

160 Credit Cards

475	Philip	Evening Trust	Sailboat
550	Rafael	Minute Card	Van Gogh
625	Makayla	Tenth Bank	Puppy
700	Sarai	Purple Card	Snowman
775	Cole	Bank of Lima	Flowers

161 Positive Cash Flow

$2,000	Rodney	Mr. Perkins	Accounting
$4,000	Carmen	Mr. Baldwin	Human Resources
$6,000	Pierce	Mrs. Fowler	Operations
$8,000	Irma	Mrs. Carr	Reception
$10,000	Orlando	Mr. Lawson	Sales

162 Rocket Man

August	Celera III	New Mexico	Television
September	Seltron V	Florida	Radio
October	Ares II	Arizona	Secret Gov't
November	Triton II	Texas	GPS
December	Vesta I	California	Telescope

163 Gold Medalists

Figure Skating	Stephen	Fourth	United States
Luge	Zachary	Second	Denmark
Ski Jump	Terry	Third	Finland
Snowboarding	Clayton	Fifth	Canada
Speed Skating	Nicholas	First	Sweden

164 Cookies for a Cause

Monday	Kailey	Black and White	Environment
Tuesday	Janiyah	Gingerbread	Homeless
Wednesday	Brenda	Almond	School
Thursday	Caitlyn	Peanut Butter	Elderly
Friday	Ariel	Chocolate Chip	Orphanage

165 Christmas Gifts

11	Xavier	Astroboy	Blue & White
12	Brian	Robot Wars	Red & White
13	Matthew	Mega Rally	Red & Green
14	Russell	Demon Guild	Gold & Silver
15	Uri	Stalactia	Blue & Gold

166 Maternity Ward

May 3	Janiyah	8 lb. 6 oz.	Bellamy
May 4	Miguel	7 lb. 9 oz.	Francone
May 5	Kristopher	7 lb. 11 oz.	Thomas
May 6	Cesar	8 lb. 7 oz.	Hilbern
May 7	Steven	8 lb. 2 oz.	Giatris

167 On the Lecture Circuit ...

August	Serenity	Jackson Pollock	Austin
September	Matthew	Gustav Klimt	San Francisco
October	Emily	Paul Cezanne	New York
November	Keegan	Claude Monet	Miami
December	Makenna	Pablo Picasso	Chicago

168 Quiz Show

150 points	Estrella	Biologist	Montana
175 points	Kaitlyn	Engineer	Virginia
200 points	Chandler	Teacher	Delaware
225 points	Tatum	Musician	South Dakota
250 points	Brendan	Artist	Alabama

169 New Holidays

July 16	Waitress Day	Rep. Simms	Nevada
July 19	Mechanic Day	Rep. Novak	Arkansas
July 22	Mailman Day	Rep. Webber	Florida
July 25	Mayor Day	Rep. Ritter	New Jersey
July 28	Janitor Day	Rep. McCabe	Virginia

170 Shipping Rates

12 ounces	90296	6" × 10" × 8"	$6.05
16 ounces	56253	4" × 6" × 6"	$6.57
20 ounces	30218	6" × 6" × 6"	$7.13
24 ounces	81125	6" × 8" × 6"	$5.68
28 ounces	44592	8" × 12" × 8"	$5.29

171 Healthy Eating

5 points	Saniya	Almonds	10 weeks
9 points	Perla	Oatmeal	12 weeks
13 points	Madison	Tuna	6 weeks
17 points	Quinton	Salmon	14 weeks
21 points	Clayton	Walnuts	8 weeks

172 WWI Airshow

First	Sennford	Fokker Dr.I	Sweden
Second	Parisien	Nieuport 28	Denmark
Third	Davids	Sopwith Camel	United States
Fourth	Grayson	Spad S.VII	Germany
Fifth	Littleton	Albatros D.II	New Zealand

173 Maid Services

Monday	Summer	1:00 pm	Cantrell
Tuesday	Leo	10:00 am	Williams
Wednesday	April	4:30 pm	Lane
Thursday	Audrey	8:00 am	Holland
Friday	Charlie	2:30 pm	Downs

174 Athletic Amphibians

First	Kaitlyn	Roger Ribbit	Lane Four
Second	Erik	Green Gus	Lane One
Third	Catherine	Leaping Larry	Lane Two
Fourth	Sydney	Froggy Fred	Lane Three
Fifth	Braxton	Hopping Hank	Lane Five

175 If You're Going to San Francisco ...

$125	Brayden	SOMA	Free Parking
$150	Gage	Noe Valley	Free Wi-Fi
$175	Brielle	North Beach	Shuttle Bus
$200	Alondra	Telegraph Hill	Kitchenette
$225	Noel	Potrero Hill	Gym and Spa

176 Land for Sale

25 acres	Mark Medine	$1.5 million	Leander
50 acres	Kyle Kip	$1.2 million	Roxboro
100 acres	Lilly Lyre	$1.6 million	Conover
200 acres	Jack Jones	$1.4 million	Hidalgo
400 acres	Chad Colt	$1.8 million	Orrville

177 Fill 'Er Up!

$1.98/gal.	Alessandra	#4	9 gallons
$2.04/gal.	Madalyn	#1	10 gallons
$2.10/gal.	Raegan	#2	15 gallons
$2.16/gal.	Dennis	#5	12 gallons
$2.22/gal.	Ella	#3	5 gallons

178 Dieters Delight

8 pounds	Maxine	Raw Foods	3 months
11 pounds	Nicholas	Vegan	6 weeks
14 pounds	Katelyn	Juicing	6 months
17 pounds	Francisco	Portioning	5 months
20 pounds	Spencer	Low Carb	2 months

179 Concert Week

Monday	Cindy Fall	8:30 pm	$39
Tuesday	Belle Curves	7:15 pm	$45
Wednesday	Instinct	8:00 pm	$25
Thursday	Orange Rain	7:00 pm	$65
Friday	Terminus	7:45 pm	$30

180 The People Have Spoken

182	Ulbright	Green	Judge
42,918	Richards	Democrat	Teacher
59,222	Cowling	Republican	State Senator
326,717	Dalton	Constitution	Mayor
450,013	Jackson	Libertarian	Lawyer

181 The SATs

1920	Lindsay	800	Edina High
1940	Ava	730	Byram High
1960	Samara	690	Moberly High
1980	Rowan	780	Anoka High
2000	Davis	750	Sikeston High

182 Clam Diggers of Ochiauoato

Monday	Marvin	8:49 am	-2.33 feet
Tuesday	Pablo	9:34 am	-2.40 feet
Wednesday	Dennis	6:30 am	-2.30 feet
Thursday	Charley	8:03 am	-2.32 feet
Friday	Walter	7:17 am	-2.37 feet

183 Tapas Crawl

First	Roberto	Los Diamantes	Croquetas
Second	Marley	Ermita	Pork Stew
Third	Pierce	La Flauta	Bacalao
Fourth	Rose	Café Elvira	Roast Ham
Fifth	Nayeli	Bar Sevilla	Empanadas

184 The Sky's the Limit

Monday	Nathaniel	Mars	Gravity
Tuesday	Mateo	Jupiter	Asteroid
Wednesday	Skyler	Mercury	Orbit
Thursday	Felix	Saturn	Magnetic Field
Friday	Karen	Venus	Composition

185 Message in a Bottle

3 months	Roman	Portugal	Jean
5 months	Phillip	France	Beatrice
7 months	Natano	Spain	Carole
9 months	Rila	Morocco	Tennery
11 months	Marisol	Brazil	Valence

186 To the Rescue ...

50 miles	Melany	Wood Stork	East
100 miles	Cash	Brown Pelican	North
150 miles	Hudson	Snowy Egret	Northeast
200 miles	Francesca	Roseate Tern	Southwest
250 miles	Lucas	White Ibis	West

187 Exploring the Explorers

Cabot	Sophie	Peter	Web Video
Columbus	Zoe	Denton	Costumes
Drake	Talia	Marcy	Diorama
Magellan	Clayton	Templeton	Antique Coin
Verrazzano	Nehemiah	Aliyah	Old Maps

188 Computer Club

25 GB	Janelle	3.0 GHz	Scanner
50 GB	Kayleigh	1.6 GHz	Webcam
100 GB	Cesar	2.2 GHz	DVD Burner
200 GB	Julian	2.5 GHz	18" Monitor
400 GB	Madison	2.0 GHz	Matching Bag

189 Skee Ball Tournament

110	Chase	Lane 3	Pencil Case
140	Kaitlyn	Lane 9	Toy Horse
150	Delaney	Lane 6	Water Gun
260	Jenny	Lane 1	Eraser
350	Ronald	Lane 4	Comb

190 Conference Calls

Monday	Lukale Inc.	#6558345	9:30 am
Tuesday	Mateo Ltd.	#4450190	10:45 am
Wednesday	Zilcro Ind.	#1827181	4:45 pm
Thursday	Ellcom Plus	#9790533	3:30 pm
Friday	Ferico Fin.	#5367917	2:15 pm

191 Musical Prodigies

11	Isabella	Vermont	Piano
12	Kevin	Washington	Clarinet
13	Dan	Alabama	Viola
14	Bailey	Oklahoma	Piccolo
15	Kiley	Georgia	French Horn

192 Egyptian Tattoos

$65	Tristan	Calf	Ankh
$90	Ryan	Bicep	Sphinx
$112	Angelique	Shoulder	Scarab Beetle
$145	Erik	Ankle	Nefertiti
$260	Linda	Forearm	Eye of Horus

193 The Pediatric Ward

101.3	Ayla	1679	Brooklyn
101.5	Avery	1556	Wilma
101.7	Alec	2225	Thelma
101.9	Anderson	1215	Janet
102.1	Ashley	1901	Katerina

194 Hiccup Cures

15 minutes	Abraham	Be Frightened	Car
30 minutes	Gabriella	Drink Water	Home
1 hour	Alissa	Eat Sugar	School
2 hours	Ellie	Hold Breath	Playground
4 hours	Angelica	Hyperventilate	Pool

195 At the DMV

#238	Piper	Custom Plates	Music
#239	Rocco	Lost Title	Telephone
#240	Nehemiah	Retake Exam	Magazine
#241	Rowan	Renew License	Sleep
#242	Marshall	Chg. Address	Book

196 Tempting Temp Work

50 wpm	Devon	Coffeteria	2 weeks
56 wpm	Asia	The Copy Stop	3 weeks
62 wpm	Valentina	Travel Etc.	6 months
68 wpm	Jackson	Maxwell's	3 months
74 wpm	Dorian	Binder World	1 month

197 Career Day

9 minutes	Johan	Biologist	Fifth
10 minutes	Meredith	Truck Driver	Fourth
11 minutes	Bryan	Architect	First
12 minutes	Nathaniel	Publisher	Third
13 minutes	Bennett	Cowboy	Second

198 Ticket Sales

0	Saturday	Komedie Kiev	Gibson
2	Friday	Old Siam	Burdette
4	Thursday	Aunt Agony	Grand
6	Wednesday	Two Towers	Roxie
8	Sunday	Music Ally	Porter

199 Around the World in 80 Meals ...

Monday	Kira	Downtown	Armenian
Tuesday	Amelia	Warehouse	Ethiopian
Wednesday	Heather	SoHo	Cambodian
Thursday	Brian	Belmont	Bolivian
Friday	Emilio	Highland Hills	Thai

200 It's All About the Ratings ...

1 million	PCR	Ponyville	22
2 million	KWTM	Soap Suds	15
3 million	CVT	Moneygab	43
4 million	BNRG	Top Chow	56
5 million	TWL	Powertrips	62